STUDIES IN GDR CULTURE AND SOCIETY 14/15

Changing Identities in East Germany

Selected Papers from the Nineteenth and Twentieth New Hampshire Symposia

Edited by
Margy Gerber and Roger Woods

UNIVERSITY
PRESS OF
AMERICA

Lanham • New York • London

Copyright © 1996 by
University Press of America,® Inc.
4720 Boston Way
Lanham, Maryland 20706

3 Henrietta Street
London, WC2E 8LU England

Co-published by arrangement with the
International Symposium of the German Democratic Republic

Library of Congress Cataloging-in-Publication Data

New Hampshire Symposium on the German Democratic Republic
(19th : 1993 : World Fellowship Center)
Changing identities in East Germany : selected papers from the
nineteenth and twentieth New Hampshire Symposia / edited by Margy
Gerber and Roger Woods.
p.   cm. -- (Studies in GDR culture and society ; 14/15) English and
German.
Rev. papers from the symposia held in June 1993 and in June 1994 at
the World Fellowship Center near Conway, N.H.
Includes bibliographical references.
1. Germany (East)--Political culture--Congresses. 2. National
characteristics, East German-Congresses. 3. Germany (East)--
Intellectual life--Congresses. 4. Germany--History--Unification,
1990--Congresses. I. Gerber, Margy. II. Woods, Roger. III. New
Hampshire Symposium on the German Democratic Republic (20th :
1994 : World Fellowship Center) IV. Title. V. Series.
DD290.29.N49   1993   943.08--dc20   96-14661 CIP

ISBN 0-7618-0322-X (cloth: alk. ppr.)

☉™The paper used in this publication meets the minimum
requirements of American National Standard for information
Sciences—Permanence of Paper for Printed Library Materials,
ANSI Z39.48—1984

This volume is dedicated to the memory of Hartmut Zimmermann.

Table of Contents

Acknowledgments

The editors wish to thank Hamish Reid of Nottingham University and the other experts on East German culture and society whom they consulted in the preparation of this volume.

They also extend their thanks to Campus Verlag (Frankfurt am Main) for granting permission to publish a revised and translated version of Virginia Penrose's article, which originally appeared in the collection *Demokratie oder Androkratie? Theorie und Praxis demokratischer Herrschaft in der feministischen Diskussion* (1994); to Psychosozial-Verlag (Gießen) for permission to print an English version of Annette Simon's text, which first appeared in her book *Versuch, mir und anderen die ostdeutsche Moral zu erklären* (1995); and to Janus Press (Berlin) for permission to publish a revised and translated version of Jan Faktor's article, which was included in *Die Leute trinken zu viel* (1995).

The editors gratefully acknowledge the financial support of the Goethe-Institut Boston, the German Marshall Fund of the United States, the Deutsche Forschungsgemeinschaft, the British Academy, and the various universities which enabled the German affairs specialists whose work is collected here to attend the 19th and 20th New Hampshire Symposia.

Introduction

This double volume comprises selected revised papers delivered at the Nineteenth and Twentieth New Hampshire Symposia on East Germany, which were held at the World Fellowship Center near Conway, NH in June 1993 and June 1994. The topics of the two conferences were "The GDR Revisited: A Reevaluation of the German Democratic Republic in the Context of the Present" and "Issues of Integration – Issues of Segregation: Progress and Obstacles on the Way to Real Unity in the New German States." Despite the varying objectives of the symposia – one looked back, the other surveyed the present and looked to the future – a common theme manifested itself at the conferences and represents a "red thread" which links the papers collected here: past and present East German identity.

In some of the articles, identity is the main topic; in others, it is tangential. Taken as a whole, however, the articles form a mosaic illustrating the many ties between past and present: the continuing influence of GDR values and practices – of past social, political, and economic circumstances – on East German identity today. Any attempt to understand post-unification East German society must be based on in-depth understanding of GDR society, the complexity and ambivalence of which have become more clear as a result of recent research. GDR life patterns also figure as a negative foil for new identities: transitions from old to new East German identities involve the renouncing – or forfeiting – of values and practices fixed by the old system. New identity is also dependent on attaining personal and collective clarity about the GDR past, including individual and group roles and responsibility.

Three of the seventeen articles in this double volume describe and analyze aspects of the GDR's dissident or counter culture. Jan Faktor, who moved to East Berlin from his native Prague in the

1970s, contrasts East Berlin left-wing intellectuals with comparable groups in other East bloc countries, explaining why non-conformist GDR intellectuals maintained their faith in the possibility of creating a more just social order long after such hope had been lost elsewhere in the East. French Germanist Jacques Poumet analyzes the underground journals which appeared as autonomous voices of dissent in the Leipzig sub-culture in the years just prior to the *Wende*. And the East Berlin musicologist Peter Wicke describes the (unsuccessful) official efforts to control rock music throughout the four decades of the GDR.

Other articles deal with the necessity of looking back at the GDR past and discuss first attempts to do so. After presenting the various public forums which have been established for judging the GDR past, Roger Woods opts for *Aufarbeitung* at the level of the individual as a means of gaining a more subtle understanding of how people lived their lives in the GDR. He places trust in the ability of writers and other intellectuals to assist in the process, pointing to the fictional biographies of Olaf Georg Klein as one example. Günter Erbe and Christiane Zehl Romero discuss the reflections of East German writers (Christa Wolf, Christoph Hein, among others) on their role in East German society and their very different efforts to define a new role for themselves as writers in post-unification Germany. In a close reading of Volker Braun's apocalyptic play *Böhmen am Meer*, Theodore Fiedler analyzes Braun's "delegitimizing critique of both socialism and capitalism" and concludes that Braun, disillusioned with the socialist utopia and calling reason itself into question, finds solace in the "Katastrophengang der Geschichte."

In two further studies involving the GDR past, the Halle Germanist Ulrich Meyszies asks how GDR literature can be studied in an adequate fashion and argues for viewing it as a complex system comprising the many cultural, social, political, and economic factors which influenced its production, distribution, and reception; and historian David Hackett, in his investigation of monuments as contributors to a country's political culture, discusses the GDR's instrumentalization of Buchenwald as a means of forging a sense of national identity.

The remaining articles deal directly with the transition from old to new identities. The East Berlin psychotherapist Annette Simon describes her image of the West, the beginnings of which date back to her early childhood, and the influence it had on her experience of German unification and her adjustment to Western society. The American political scientist Virginia Penrose demonstrates that the social and political structures of GDR society shaped and continue to affect East German politicians' understanding of democracy and political processes. While their West German colleagues accept majority rule, interpersonal competition, and striving for power as legitimate aspects of politics, East German politicians favor political consensus, collectivism, and cooperation, social norms of GDR society which were internalized into personal values. Lothar Probst's discussion of the Round Table model, which was widely used in the GDR in the transitional period before unification, confirms Penrose's findings on East German interest in collective decision making and consensus-building political discussion.

In his composite sketch of the Heilmann family, the Leipzig cultural sociologist Michael Hofmann illustrates the effects of post-unification structural change on East German marital relations, in particular in the common "mixed" marriages of women employed in the service sector and skilled industrial workers. The Berlin cultural sociologist Thomas Koch analyzes the new group awareness and self-confidence – the sense of East German identity – that is rapidly becoming a political phenomenon in the East. Evidence of an East German identity is also provided by the newspaper preferences of the East Germans, which the British Germanist John Sandford shows to be overwhelmingly East German, both in regard to origin as well as content and style.

Finding parallels between the psychological adjustment required of the East German population and Elisabeth Kübler-Ross's model of the five stages of dying, Germanist Nancy Lauckner discusses the treatment of problems of integration, including the loss of identity, in recent East German literature. And, as historian Horst Freyhofer shows, identity is also a major issue for the Sorb community of East Germany, which has no special minority rights under the Basic Law. The legal equality of individuals, guaranteed by the Basic Law, proves to be a practical disadvantage for the Sorb minority, for equality by itself means assimilation. It is a question of ethnic and political identity, which in the case of the Sorbs are not the same.

Some of the articles surmise about the future integration of the two German states. As Thomas Koch points out, the heightened group awareness of the East Germans, the noted development of a sense of separate East German identity, can in the long run be a positive factor in the integration process.

Margy Gerber

The Special Position of Young, Left-wing GDR Intellectuals in the Former Eastern Bloc

Jan Faktor

Many left-wingers in the GDR admired the leading intellectuals in the Czech opposition and regarded them as models. There was Havel, of course, and then Uhl and Dubcek, Pelikán and Mlynár. Sometimes I really found it painful, because I knew that this admiration could often only be due to false hopes or a lack of information. Important differences were overlooked, for example, the fact that most Czech intellectuals after the shock of 1968 could only really be characterized as "bourgeois"; at any rate, certainly not unequivocally as on the left, although they tended to be viewed implicitly in this way. Peter Uhl was of course quite rightly admired in the GDR for his courage. But unfortunately people did not realize that, politically, he was a peripheral figure and that he was not taken very seriously in Prague on account of his dogmatism. But that is another story.

For me as a Czech, living from the mid-1970s half of the time, then from 1978 all the time, in East Berlin, and with left-wing friends in the GDR, their ways were not so hard to grasp. In conversation with them I always found myself imagining how absurd many of their views would sound in Prague. And I was forced to come up with some kind of quick response.

In the GDR many hopes lived on even though they were more or less dead everywhere else in the Eastern bloc. They lived on not just in the minds of the older generation of left-wingers, but also in the minds of the young on the left. But one thing struck me immediately even at the time: the particular GDR way of looking at things was not just distorted in some minor way; it could not be explained merely by the fact that it had been "too long" since any tanks had

1

rolled in against would-be reformers. This GDR view was notice-
ably different. Most of those I came to know did not have that look I
noticed so often in the eyes of damaged and disillusioned people in
other Eastern European countries. My East Berlin friends had an
unquestioning faith which was unmistakable and unique to them.
But this faith did not have its origins in any naive virtue, it was not a
sign that the education system or official propaganda had been
successful. There could be no doubt about that. I knew the people
too well. Some had been thrown out of their institutes and were
working in factories. Many had made a conscious decision not to
have a career. So their faith had nothing to do with conformism; on
the other hand, I gradually came to realize that it was not exclusively
a home-grown philosophy either. This faith came, like the music, or
the parkas, or the sticky tape that really was sticky, like "Kenn-
zeichen D" and "Weltspiegel," and so many other things, from the
West. One of its roots ran from left-wing discussions in the West,
from the extra-parliamentary opposition, and from communist or
other (e.g., anarchist) groups. This faith drew some of its strength
from the Western Left's anger at its not very maternal system, and
from an awareness of the wider problems facing the world as a
whole. But it also drew strength from the fact that those people one
knew personally in the West were also unable to influence events
and that they were also unhappy. Often these were very close
friends from former times. And this faith was further fed by a never-
ending stream of neo-Marxist, or left-wing, alternative political
writings smuggled into the GDR. All this could then be thoroughly
processed at the theoretical level and reinforced by drawing on a
wide range of sources.

Yet it was not primarily information pure and simple that made
up this "infiltration of ideas." In the process of my own "assimilation" I was able to observe that not facts were crucial, but rather
those things gathered from one's own authentic experience in the
West. They may have taken the form of television interviews which
were eagerly digested, or of one's own discussions with friends
visiting from the West. And this had absolutely nothing to do with
dry theories. It was not difficult to sense that Western intellectuals
gave their accounts with absolute sincerity, that their views were
genuinely held. East Germans could experience at first hand that
these views were just as bitter as their own. And these views could
not be swept aside; they were authentic.

Hence, the faith of the GDR Left did not just grow in a vacuum
as some kind of illusion. It also grew on the basis of hard information; the Left over there was real and alive (how realistic it was, is

another matter entirely). This had particular consequences for the "East": it could easily cause people to develop a particular form of blindness; and this is what actually happened. The (imperialist) part of reality which one wanted to do battle with, and which went a long way towards justifying one's own theories and counter-visions, was situated beyond the border. And, funnily enough, in addition to the authenticity of the Western Left, illusions were imported about matters that one was actually much nearer to oneself.

Nevertheless, all this Eastern and Western experience that I was able to gain either indirectly in the GDR or directly helped me enormously. And I am extremely grateful for it, even though, given my views, I could never quite feel at ease in these circles. The enthusiasm for pretty humorless theorizing, the semi-conspiratorial to conspiratorial meeting in groups which shared the hope of a more just social order were just too alien for me. (As a result I later went to the other – stubbornly apolitical – extreme.)

Fortunately, the GDR Left overcame some of its distance from reality and became somewhat less preoccupied with theory in the 1980s. There were ever more other ways of being politically active; not just at the level of culture, but also in environmental and human rights groups. It is above all through this work that the GDR Left took a step nearer to reality. Ideology took a back seat, and the intellectual opposition switched over from "theory" to "practice." Only a few of the intellectuals I got to know in the 1970s clung to their left-wing dogma in the 1980s.

Many take great pleasure in reproaching those GDR intellectuals who did not become dissidents in line with some particular – e.g., Czech or Polish – set of criteria or other. It was suggested (especially after the *Wende*) that they should all have the decency to develop a bad conscience – because organized opposition was inadequate or came too late ("there was nothing like 'Charta 77'. . . .") or because they did not have the courage to risk this or that, etc. They were accused in a roundabout manner of cowardice, inconsistency, opportunism, of fearing that they might lose their privileges. Amid these accusations the large mass of people who had no privileges to lose was forgotten. Also, those doing the accusing ignored the fact that, in the GDR, a "sphere subject to a broad range of ideological influences" from the West, it was simply impossible to cross certain ideological bridges.

There were quite obvious reasons for GDR intellectuals not developing as they should have. This had obvious consequences: it remains an unfortunate fact that there was not enough distance between the non-conformist GDR intellectuals I am primarily concerned with here and the official ideology, even if one acknowledges that the Western influence was partly to blame. And this was one further reason for being reluctant to attack the state. It is easy to be critical about this situation, of course, if one wishes to be, but one should not throw in inappropriate recommendations, which would anyway be coming too late, nor should one indulge in stereotypical criticism of all concerned (including those who were most certainly not opportunists).

Another point: GDR society never experienced the brutal disruptions and breaks which the CSSR underwent from 1969 onwards, where tens of thousands of intellectuals were eventually thrown out of their jobs, regardless of the losses to the system this involved. Once this had happened, they no longer had so much to lose. For Czech dissidents, working in the opposition was the only way they could remain active, and it was a way of keeping intellectually fit. As for "Charta 77," I would ask that one more thing not be forgotten: it was not a mass movement. And for the average Czech citizen it always provided a convenient alibi.

I have learnt to respect the views of the GDR Left. I always found these views alien, but they were also understandable and acceptable. And I have also learnt to see their special nature as the result of that unique phenomenon in Europe – the division of Germany.

Large-scale and – as far as potential opposition was concerned – almost uninterrupted migration in the direction of the Federal Republic was one further factor which determined the special position of the GDR in the Eastern bloc. This resulted in losses not just from all branches of the intellectual elite; it also had a major impact on the sociological structure of the GDR intelligentsia and the particular form of opposition which emerged from it. The departure of those intellectuals who could not come to terms with the GDR, either because they were bourgeois intellectuals (or right-wing, or anarchists, or whatever else), coupled with the arrival of Western intellectuals who looked upon the GDR as their state, caused a shift to the left in the intellectual spectrum of the GDR. Hence, it was natural that those who eventually came to criticize "actually existing socialism" should come initially from the left and that they were once responsible for helping to maintain the official system. It was logical, too, that the Right in the GDR was an insignificant force – it had either quit the country or, with good reason, it had fallen silent. It was not until the 1980s that right-wing youth broke through the barrier of fear, and the breakthrough took a brutal and anti-intellectual form.

In the GDR of the 1980s, large-scale opposition did not manage to establish itself for a variety of reasons. Also, GDR citizens were not badly off in material terms (or else GDR poverty did not seem so bad compared with the poverty in the Third World), and therefore did not find the reality of their own country so objectionable. In addition, the intellectual horizons of those who might have provided a more broadly based consensus or support for opposition was "extra-mural" – the "people" spent their evenings watching television programs produced in the nearby West and came to their own, often quite different, conclusions. Long before the *Wende* there sat in GDR parlors – as if manufactured in test tubes – not only apolitical, well-behaved citizens of the Federal Republic, but also hard-line nationalists and the next generation of Young Socialists, and so on.

I do not wish to comment on the sudden failure of the citizens' movements as citizens' movements; it is not my place to comment. Nor do I wish to blame anyone for the way things turned out. If anything, I would only blame those who try to explain the failure by looking for the reasons everywhere except on their own doorstep. For a long time they helped to prepare the ground for the West German deluge after the *Wende* through their attitudes, the attitudes of the Left.

Getting it wrong is inevitable when nations live together. Beyond the GDR's eastern border – in the land of the Czechs – people got it wrong in a different way. For many Czechs, GDR citizens were all the same: inflexible, naive, loyal to the state, and – not just in ideological terms – somewhat stupid. That is the way people make their judgments from a distance about those they do not know. And that is because most people only knew the well-behaved, boring, and respectably dressed petty bourgeois families who flooded into the Republic in the summer. The not entirely un-justified dislike of GDR citizens also helped divert attention away from one's own good behavior, petty bourgeois ways, and willing-ness to conform. Czechs knew little or nothing at all about the left-wingers, those who rejected authority, the drop-outs, or the opposi-tion taking shape under the wing of the Church; they knew nothing at all about the growth of the various opposition groups, either. Or else, they did not particularly believe the information coming out of the GDR. And they remained blind to the fact that it was simply in entirely different political circumstances – but for all that, quite purposefully and, by different standards, consistently – that opposi-tion was growing and sometimes assuming forms which were unthinkable in the CSSR of the time. For all these reasons, the surprise of fall 1989 that came out of the "East in the West," of all countries, was that much greater.

Translated by Roger Woods

Underground Journals in and around Leipzig in the 1980s

Jacques Poumet

Starting in the 1980s a special kind of independent journal came into existence in the GDR. The journals were produced by hand, combined graphics and text, had a very modest circulation (fewer than 100 copies), and were passed on virtually from hand to hand rather than being distributed through official channels. There were more than thirty such independent magazines.

The designations given to this type of journal vary – original-graphic, samizdat, subcultural, alternative. The purpose, however, was always the same: to create a basis for the publication of uncensored texts and to promote the development of an "other" public sphere in the GDR.

After Biermann's expatriation and the subsequent emigration of prominent GDR authors, an entire generation experienced societal and cultural paralysis. Well-known authors sometimes succeeded in getting critical, or oppositional, texts past the censor, but most young authors did not stand a chance, and many felt condemned to internal exile or silence. An existential factor was thus the catalyst for the creation of all these journals. The goal was to break out of isolation, overcome resignation, and establish communication between authors and artists who had no access to the regular public sphere.

The first journals were founded in Berlin and Dresden in 1982: *Entwerter oder* (Berlin) and *Und* (Dresden). In the following years the focus shifted to Berlin and by the end of the 1980s it was above all the Berlin journals that garnered the attention of outside – and

7

sometimes also local – observers.[1] However, provincial intellectual centers played a role in this movement as well: Dresden with the aforementioned *Und* (later *Und so weiter*); Jena and Weimar with *Dämmerung* and *Reizwolf*; Halle with the short-lived *Galeere*; and Leipzig with five titles, *Anschlag*, *Glasnot*, *Zweite Person*, *Sno'Boy*, and *Messitsch*, which shall be my topic here.

Anschlag started appearing in 1984 (two years after the first Berlin and Dresden journals). Three years later (1987) three more magazines were suddenly founded: *Zweite Person*, *Glasnot*, and *Messitsch*. At the end of 1988 *Sno'Boy* published its first issue, 0. The founding of these five journals can serve as an indication of the increased need and interest in this variant of literary journalistic communication at the end of the 1980s.

Anschlag published a total of ten issues (two issues per year). In the beginning the texts were typed; later issues were computer-produced. The journal was richly illustrated with original graphics and photos. The early numbers had twenty-five copies; starting with *Anschlag V*, fifty.

---

[1] See *Mikado oder der Kaiser ist nackt. Selbstverlegte Literatur in der DDR*, ed. Uwe Kolbe, Lothar Trolle, Bernd Wagner (Darmstadt: Luchterhand, 1988); *Sprache und Antwort. Stimmen und Texte einer anderen Literatur aus der DDR*, ed. Egmont Hesse (Frankfurt am Main: Fischer, 1988); *Abriß der Ariadnefabrik*, ed. Andreas Koziol and Rainer Schedlinski (Berlin: Druckhaus Galrev,1990); *Vogel oder Käfig sein - aus unabhängigen Zeitschriften der DDR*, ed. Klaus Michael and Thomas Wohlfahrt (Berlin: Druckhaus Galrev, 1991). This latter anthology contains sixteen contributions from Leipzig journals, above all, texts by well-known authors (Gert Neumann, Barbara Köhler, Elke Erb, Bernd Igel), which do not reflect the multiplicity of the Leipzig journals. See also: Antonia Grunenberg and Wolfgang Schlott, "Alles ist erlaubt - zur 'anderen Kultur' in der DDR und in der Sowjetunion, am Beispiel der Kulturmetropolen Ost-Berlin, Dresden und Moskau," in *Veränderungen in Gesellschaft und politischem System der DDR*. Edition Deutschland Archiv (Cologne: Wissenschaft und Politik, 1988); Thomas Günther, "Die subkulturellen Zeitschriften in der DDR und ihre kulturgeschichtliche Bedeutung," in *Aus Politik und Zeitgeschichte. Beilage zur Wochenzeitung Das Parlament*, B 20/92, 8 May 1992, pp. 27-36; Klaus Michael, "Papierboote. Selbstverlegte Literaturzeitschriften in der DDR," in *Jenseits der Staatskultur. Traditionen autonomer Kunst in der DDR*, ed. Gabriele Muschter and Rüdiger Thomas (Munich: Hanser, 1992), pp. 62-82; Klaus Michael, "Feindbild Literatur. Die Biermann-Affäre, Staatssicherheit und die Herausbildung einer literarischen Alternativkultur in der DDR," *Aus Politik und Zeitgeschichte. Beilage zur Wochenzeitung Das Parlament*, B 22-23/93, 28 May 1993, pp. 23-31; and Klaus Michael, "Samisdat-Literatur in der DDR und der Einfluß der Staatssicherheit," *Deutschland Archiv*, 26, No. 11 (1993), pp. 1255-66.

Glasnot ran to eight issues. The texts were typed; here too one finds graphics, drawings, and black and white photos interspersed between the texts. With *Sno'Boy* (five issues total) the publishing technique was the same. The editions had fifty copies.

Zweite Person, which was produced by silkscreening, reached a total of five issues, with ninety copies each. This journal contained few illustrations – in 1989 none at all.

Messitsch is the only journal that was duplicated on photographic paper. Before the *Wende* seven issues appeared – with arbitrary numbering (Number 7 appeared in 1988, Number 3 in 1989). Its production method permitted printings of varying size (twenty copies at first; later seventy). Unlike the other journals, *Messitsch* is illustrated with cartoons.

Anschlag X was in press in October 1989. Contentwise it is thus a pre-*Wende* publication. Due to the events of October 1989 *Sno'Boy IV* could not appear until November of that year. However the preparation of the number predates these events, with the exception of a short afterword that comments on an article written before the mass demonstrations. On the other hand, *Glasnot VIII*, which went to press on December 22, 1989, is definitely a *Wende*-issue and contains among other things pamphlets from October.

Zweite Person, *Glasnot*, and *Anschlag* ceased publication after the *Wende*. *Messitsch* lived on a bit longer under the title *Krise im Aufbruch*. *Sno'Boy*, the youngest of the journals, continued as *Connewitzer Kreuzer*. With the same publisher (Peter Hinke) and in connection with Connewitzer Verlagsbuchhandlung (also founded by Hinke), it appeared monthly from September 1990 to April 1991 as the *Kulturbeilage* of the Leipzig newspaper *DAZ* (*Die Andere Zeitung*). When the newspaper folded in the spring of 1991, the magazine went it alone as *Kreuzer* and quickly mutated to become the cultural magazine of the city of Leipzig. In this radically altered form the *Sno'Boy* successor has survived until now.

As was the case with similar magazines in other cities, the titles of the journals signaled in a clear, sometimes provocative way the intention and claim of the editors. *Anschlag* connoted "Anschlag aufs Gehabte";[2] *Glasnot* referred with clear-as-glass clarity to the "New Thinking" in the Soviet Union; *Zweite Person* and *Messitsch* emphasized the goal of communication and dialogue.

---

[2] Wolfgang Hilbig in a letter to the editor, *Anschlag II* (1984). The underground magazines do not have numbered pages; the contributions were typed separately by the individual authors and then combined to form the issue.

That these journals are Leipzig products is clear from the origins of the authors and artists (*Glasnot* was edited in Leipzig and Naumburg, but the majority of the authors are from Leipzig), the special attention given to the art scene in Leipzig, and the many Leipzig themes. Symbolic meaning is assigned to the demolition of the Universitätskirche in May 1968. *Anschlag I* concludes with a well-known picture of the blasting of the church: an attack (*Anschlag*) on the cultural history of the city and on the identity of its citizens. *Sno'Boy I* contains a report about the events of this time which serves as a sort of manifesto. For the twentieth anniversary of the demolition, *Zweite Person* put together a documentation which examines the political reasons for the church's destruction.[3] Apart from this spectacular event the authors looked upon their city with a mixture of affection and repugnance: "Leipzig, du ding" is the title of a poem in which the poet ascertains with horror that one has to look at this "Chimäre / aus dreck und gestank" – the city of Leipzig – as a part of oneself.[4]

Despite their many similarities the five journals have different orientations: *Glasnot* carries the subtitle "Meinungen-Literatur-Bilder" and addresses political topics with particular frequency. That the Naumburg faction of the editorial staff was associated with the theological seminary in Naumburg is obvious: Christian viewpoints are articulated as such. Criticism of the forms of work in socialist society represents another main focus (*Glasnot VII* is devoted to this issue).

Anschlag, which has the longest history, went through a clear development: the first four numbers (1984-86) are above all poetry issues; the subsequent issues contain an increasing number of political contributions. By the end of the 1980s a discussion forum had evolved out of the earlier reservoir of unpublished poetic and prose works: two thirds of the contents of *Anschlag VIII* (1987) are devoted to overtly political topics. Time and again *Anschlag* set itself apart with its especially imaginative covers: *Anschlag IV* is bound in a map of Leipzig (also an assertion of identity); *Anschlag VIII*, in computer punch cards; *Anschlag IX*, in a recyclable egg carton with the regulation stamp: "Vorsicht, nicht verbrennen."

Zweite Person conceived of itself as a "Zeitschrift für geistigen Austausch" and, while not totally excluding political themes, dealt predominantly with literature; contributing to the "intellectual ex-

---

[3] *Zweite Person*, No. 2, 1988.
[4] Henry W., "Leipzig, du Ding," *Sno'Boy 0* (1988).

change" are, for example, texts from Marcel Duchamp, Francis Ponge, Joseph Beuys, and Jacques Lacan. *Sno'Boy* presents itself as "gesunden Gegensatz zu den einseitigen, trivialen und pseudo-intellektuellen Publikationen der 'independent' (OFF) - Szene unseres Landes."[5] Leipzig themes are very strongly represented. *Messitsch* is devoted mainly to the underground music scene.

In spite of the modest size of their editions, these publications are very important signs of the times. An indication of this is the early interest of official collectors. The Sächsische Landesbibliothek started acquiring the issues published in Dresden and other cities in 1985 – after September 1987 at the special request of the Stasi;[6] and the Deutsche Bücherei in Leipzig (National Library of the GDR) systematically collected *Anschlag* and *Glasnot*, starting in 1987.[7] Viewing and borrowing the magazines was limited, however. In the Federal Republic the Schiller National Museum in Marbach acquired incomplete volumes of *Anschlag* and *Zweite Person* during this same period.

These independent magazines provide insight into the process of fermentation which led to the events of October 1989. They lay bare the sore spots of the collective consciousness and articulate the questions and doubts of the broader population circles.

Between Opposition and Resistance

The editors and authors of these magazines proceeded from a basic position that condemns censorship and denounces the criminalization of dissidents. The creation of their own independent, if limited, forum was used – among other things – to propagate the texts of banned authors, a prominent spot being given to the Leipzig writer Gert Neumann. Texts of well-known opponents of "actually existing" socialism from neighboring countries (Vaclav Havel, Adam Michnik, Alexander Solzhenitsyn) were circulated in this manner, as well as excerpts from the works of banned theorists (Trotsky, Bakunin, Marcuse).

There was some limited communication between the journals: in *Anschlag* a co-editor of *Glasnot* repeatedly expresses his intentions of leaving the country, and Sascha Anderson's reaction to the

---

[5] "Wortvor," *Sno'Boy 0*.

[6] See Klaus Michael, "Samisdat-Literatur," p. 1264.

[7] The actual collection of the Deutsche Bücherei is probably more extensive than this.

Rimbaud essay of Volker Braun,[8] who criticized the new tones of
the young literature, was reprinted in the Berlin journal *Schaden* as
well as *Anschlag*.[9] As a rule, however, the jump to a broader public
was hard to realize in these circumstances. Significantly, the first
article in *Anschlag VI* is dedicated to an exhibition of all previously
published original-graphic journals in the Berlin Samariterkirche: an
indication of how unusual it was to venture out beyond the local
circle.[10]

In an article about the "literary opposition" in Warsaw during the
German occupation, a connection is made between the publishing
activity of the original-graphic magazines and the resistance concept.
Between 1939 and 1945 a handful of writers wrote and distributed
an illegal, typewritten literary journal in Warsaw. The reader in the
GDR is tacitly encouraged to draw a comparison between that
journal and the one he is holding in his hands. The conclusion that
is drawn from this episode from the Second World War is easily
applicable: "Diese ganze Angelegenheit mag als Beweis dafür
gelten, daß es für die totalitären Regimes sehr schwer ist, mit dem
Wort zu kämpfen, und daß das Wort schneller und wirkungsvoller
über die Grenzen dringt, als es die Menschen draußen beurteilen
können."[11]

The magazines' editors repeatedly point out that this or that text
included in the issue was read in a church facility or presented at a
church seminar. In this connection, too, one can see how much
social and political criticism was articulated in the protected space of
the Church and how important the religious enclave was for the
development of critical or oppositional groups. However, this fact
does not preclude criticism of the role of the Church. After 1987
these magazines question the function of the Church in the overall
strategy of the state. *Glasnot* is concerned about the normalizing role
of the Church, whose official representatives endeavor to cool
heated emotions. The words of a woman minister who, commenting
on the protest action during the Rosa Luxemburg demonstration in
January 1988, spoke of "fehlender Spiritualität und Mangel an

---

[8] Volker Braun, "Rimbaud. Ein Psalm der Aktualität," *Sinn und Form*, 37, No.
5 (1985), pp. 978-98.
[9] Sascha Anderson, "Fixierung einer Metapher," *Schaden 8* (1985) and *Anschlag
V* (1986).
[10] The exhibition "Wort und Werk" was held in June 1986.
[11] Czeslaw Milosz, "G.G.," *Zweite Person*, No. 3, 1989.

Zentriertheit" evoke dismay.[12] And two years before the *Wende Anschlag* asserted that the Church was helping stabilize relations in the GDR: that it was partially defusing the critical potential for the state and contributing when necessary to the disciplining of the "Eigeninitiativler."[13] This explains why this otherwise nonreligious magazine makes room for the internal criticism of the hierarchy of the Church, publishing for example the leaflet "Absage an Praxis und Prinzip der Abgrenzung" (1987).[14]

The magazines were especially persevering in their dismantling of the official representation of the value and reality of work. The hypocrisy of official discourse could be exposed particularly well here. Unbearable working conditions are repeatedly described – both with clinical objectivity and rebellious pathos. The text "Begegnungsfern" portrays a worn-out pensioner: "Du hattest gearbeitet, warst der pathogenen Umgebung mit ihren geistigen Schwätzern verfallen. Während sie ihren Begriff von Arbeit predigten, ließen sie dich allmählich verkommen."[15] Excerpts from *Rotter und weiter* by Thomas Brasch, published in *Zweite Person*, refute the prescribed clichés about the beauty of work. Brasch expresses his hatred of those writers who went along with this official view from the comfort of their desk chairs. He counters them with the depiction of crippled workers and the widespread reluctance to work.[16]

"Die Zeit ist angebrochen"

All of these journals reflect the rise of the "New Thinking" in the Soviet Union and the changes taking place in Poland and Hungary. Contrary to the official stance, which dismissed it all as "Tapetenwechsel," these journals are very much influenced by *glasnost* and *perestroika*, and devote considerable space to Gorbachev's politics (two thirds of *Anschlag III*, for example). With direct quotations ("Wir brauchen die Demokratie wie die Luft zum Atmen") or in parable form they express the conviction that the time for major

---

[12] Günter Bock, "Splitter im Kopf," *Glasnot V* (1988).

[13] Karim Saab, "Lieber Hans-Friedel Fischer," *Anschlag VII* (1987).

[14] In *Anschlag VIII* (1987).

[15] Torsten Ziesche, "Begegnungsfern," *Glasnot I* (1987).

[16] Thomas Brasch, "Rotter und weiter," *Zweite Person*, No. 2, 1989. See also: Reiner Flügge, "Für Fürst und Freiheit - Rede des Apollon vom Dach des großen Schauspielhauses," *Zweite Person*, No. 1, 1989.

changes is also come in the GDR.[17]

The name of the journal *Glasnot* speaks volumes. A poem by Michael Klein about Stalin published there renders the feeling of suffocation which was a salient characteristic of the mood in intellectual circles immediately prior to the fall of 1989.

> Gespräch mit Stalin
>
> Wir leben noch in deinem Schatten
> und riechen
> den Rauch
> von den Scheiterhaufen deiner Inquisition
> doch die Kugeln der Mörder
> machen uns nicht mehr betroffen
> da sie uns nicht mehr treffen
> heute köpft man ohne Beil
> die Hinrichtung macht nur Mund-tot
> vergessen sind nicht Mandelstams Verse
> aber seine Leiden
> zu sehr haben wir uns
> an deine namenslose Gegenwart gewöhnt
>
> wir sterben noch in deinem Schatten
> wenn wir nicht endlich
> in die Sonne treten.[18]

The reappraising of Stalinism that was banned from public discussion is a constant topic in these journals. It is occasionally furthered by articles reprinted from the *Moskauer Nachrichten* on the economic reforms in the USSR, which are regarded as an alternative to both the centralized socialist economy and the market economy of the West.[19] The "dritte Weg" is apparently still an option. This type of discussion was possible only in journals that refused to be dictated to, such as these. A documentation of the banning of the journal *Sorbischer Student*, the newsletter of the Sorb students in the GDR, can serve as an illustration. In October 1988 this journal published an article on the dissension of the

---

[17] Hans-Jürgen Fischbeck, "Zeugnis der Betroffenheit," *Zweite Person*, No. 1, 1988; Heidemarie Härtl, "AWWAKUM," *Anschlag VI* (1986) – "Die Zeit ist angebrochen . . . ."

[18] Michael Klein, "Gespräch mit Stalin," *Glasnot VII* (1989).

[19] Cf., for example, "Offener Brief an Michael Gorbatschow," *Zweite Person*, No. 2, 1989.

population living near Chernobyl. It also reported on the freedom of the press in Poland, about Stalin's purges, and about the losses the USSR incurred during the war in Afghanistan. The counterreaction was not long in coming; the journal was banned in December. The documentation of the banning, which was published in *Zweite Person*, concludes with the open letter of a Sorb studying in Leipzig who signs his name and points out parallels between the banning of the Sorb journal and the banning of the Soviet monthly *Sputnik*, which occurred at the same time.[20]

The rigid attitude of the GDR is perceived as unbearable in view of the radical change taking place in the East. The journals targeted both the paralysis of the state and the paralysis of broad sections of the population. A hypnosis demonstration in a large movie theater in Leipzig three months before the fall demonstrations had symbolic character for the author of the report in *Sno'Boy*. A row of hypnotized volunteers marched in step on the stage, while another member of the audience, likewise hypnotized by the will of the master, beat time: a humiliating spectacle, according to the commentator, in which the picture of an oppressed and weak-willed people could be seen.[21] The feeling of isolation felt by many of those who advocated protest is frequently reflected, as, for example, in the following poem by Andreas Klich:

ZEUGNIS

DAS VOLK DER DDR
WIRD IN DIE
NÄCHSTE KLASSENSTUFE
DES SOZIALISMUS
VERSETZT :

BETRAGEN	:	SEHR GUT
ORDNUNG	:	GUT
FLEISS	:	BEFRIEDIGEND
MITARBEIT	:	GENÜGEND.[22]

The Ministry of State Security is not a central theme in any of the journals. Only occasionally are incidents reported in which the

---

[20] Hans-Friedrich Fischer, "Glasnost – sorbische Studenten und die Domowina," *Zweite Person*, No. 3, 1989. The documentation of the ban is in the same issue.
[21] M. Uschko, "Demonstration des scheinbar Unmöglichen," *Sno'Boy 4 (1989)*.
[22] Andreas Klich, "Zeugnis," *Glasnot VI (1988)*.

Stasi clearly had a hand. It happened to Lutz Rathenow, for example, that his publisher, after having been shown a file by the "Security Forces," was no longer willing to accept his poems. Lutz Rathenow concludes: "Auf zwei Gebieten hat es die DDR zur Weltspitze gebracht: im Spitzensport und im Geheimdienst."[23]

More disquieting is the story of an encounter in front of the Stasi building in Leipzig. One evening the author sees an old friend who in earlier years had belonged to the same nonconformist poetry circle coming out of Stasi headquarters. The Stasi had taken harsh measures against this "Verschwörergruppe" at the time. Now the old friend has gone over to the other side, in this instance, however, in a non-conspiratorial way.[24]

Many authors were of course aware that the Stasi was often present, and there is no lack of irony about this "reassuring" security.[25] However, the extent of the infiltration of unofficial collaborators far exceeded what anyone imagined at the time. For example, *Glasnot* frequently printed poems by Knud Wollenberger, who, as was later learned, had been spying on his wife, the civil rights campaigner Vera Wollenberger, since 1982. The danger of overinterpretation notwithstanding, his texts deserve to be read again in light of this new knowledge.[26]

In these journals there is frequent criticism of the mocking of democracy by the authorities, including, for example, the decision to demolish the Universitätskirche. In May 1968 – without public discussion – the City Council approved a project for the remodeling of Karl-Marx-Platz which involved the pulling down of the church, which had withstood the bomb attacks of 1943. A wave of protest and public petitions inundated the courthouse. The Theology Department of the University was blamed for the protest; it supposedly had incited public opinion against the city fathers. The

---

[23] Lutz Rathenow, "An einen Verlagsleiter," *Zweite Person*, No. 3, 1989.

[24] Holger Jackisch, "Turmgesellschaft," *Sno'Boy* 2 (1989).

[25] As, for example, in a poem by Heidemarie Härtl in *Anschlag VIII* (1987) in which a group of protesters witness the discreet entrance of the Stasi into their pub:

> Folgerichtig erschien die Geheimdienststreife
> in den bekannten Uniformen:
> Offizier Lederjacke, Soldat Anorak.
> Schon ging es uns allen etwas besser.

[26] See Hajo Steinert, "Die Szene mit der Stasi," *Die Zeit*, 29 November 1991.

protest movement threatened to take on countrywide proportions. In order to stifle it, the church was blown up only eight days after the Council's decision. In spite of the sealing off of the city center, many people came to witness the operation in silent protest.

The razing of the Universitätskirche is cited as an example of the command system and the complacency of the socialist leaders in power. The commentator in *Sno'Boy* acknowledges that such a thing would no longer occur, since historical monuments are now seen in a different light. He points out, however, that the present decay of the city also reflects the lack of regard for public opinion, the same disregard that twenty years earlier led to the destruction of an edifice which was a part of Leipzig's identity.[27]

The Pain of Confinement

The torturing thought of being shut in recurs in these journals and is expressed in a wide variety of ways. It is a sore spot in the collective consciousness that can be activated even tacitly. Any word or image that even remotely connotes walls or barriers functions as an emotive word that roots about in the wound. Reference to the etymology of the word "paradise" (from the Persian "pairidaeza," meaning "city wall" or "bulwark") is reason to read a story about the Garden of Eden as a parable of the GDR.[28]

In 1985 *Anschlag* used a quote from Voltaire as the motto for its third issue:

> In manchen Ländern hat man angestrebt, daß es einem Bürger nicht gestattet ist, die Gegend, in der er zufällig geboren ist, zu verlassen. Der Sinn dieses Gesetzes liegt auf der Hand: "Dieses Land ist so schlecht, und wird so schlecht regiert, daß wir jedem verbieten, es zu verlassen, weil es sonst die ganze Bevölkerung verlassen würde." Ihr tätet besser daran, all euren Untertanen Lust zu machen, bei euch zu bleiben, und den Fremden, zu euch zu kommen.[29]

The 1989 issue of *Anschlag* is bound in the sort of double mesh sold commercially as painter's mesh (for scraping off paint). When the reader opens the issue, he opens up the grating and finds himself

---

[27] Peter Hinke, "Freie Bemerkungen nicht nur zum Thema Universitätskirche," *Sno'Boy 1* (1989).

[28] Michal Scholze, "Das Paradies auf Erden," *Anschlag VI* (1986).

[29] Quoted from the article "Gleichheit" in *Philosophisches Wörterbuch* (Leipzig: Ph. Reclam Jr., 1984).

"behind bars." And the bars have a sticker: "Made in GDR."

The frustration about the closed borders is expressed repeatedly and openly. An encounter with foreign students is a painful reminder of the author's own confinement.[30] The pain can be found in an internalized form in the sexual fantasies of a homosexual man from Leipzig: "[Er] träumt sich als Grenzpfahl, stacheldrahtumwickelt, stoßend, unheilbare Wunden reißend, über die noch lange viel gesprochen wird." This text was written within the context of a gay encounter group in which everyone was asked to write about his "shadow," that is, "über jene Seiten von sich selbst, die er nicht mag, oder mit denen er Probleme hat."[31]

The question of emigration arises for many authors. The debate over motivation and justification for leaving started in 1984. The frustrations of daily life and the wish to avoid military service figure as reasons for the younger generation; for the older people in this social milieu, these factors are outweighed by the feeling that life is no longer bearable without "freie Artikulation des Geistes" and that the country has no future.[32] As a rule, leaving the country is seen as a last resort that one can fall back on when all other possibilities are exhausted.[33] Not least of all, the journals themselves felt the effect of the problem. One *Anschlag* editor and one *Glasnot* editor left for the West, and many an occasional contributor as well.[34]

When an Irish play about emigration from Ireland is performed in Leipzig (Brian Friel: *Ich komme, Philadelphia*), the review in *Sno'Boy* stresses the turmoil of the man who is leaving.[35] The conflict of staying or leaving is expressed in countless poems. Here are examples by Karim Saab, Uwe Romanski, and Michal Scholze:

> Für O.
> (An die Schwalben im Sommer)
>
> . . . Ich
> stehe unten
> und

---

[30] Heidemarie Härtl, "Theaterfestival," *Zweite Person*, No. 1, 1988.

[31] Michael Sollorz, "Eine Verwandlung," *Sno'Boy 3* (1989).

[32] Torsten Ziesche, "Und ich lebe . . . im Mai," *Anschlag IV* (1985).

[33] Cf. Torsten Ziesche, ". . . Mustern," and Andreas Reimann, "Beispiel untypischen Lebens," both in *Anschlag III* (1985); Gert Neumann, "Brief in das Gefängnis," *Anschlag II* (1984).

[34] For example, Karim Saab, Torsten Ziesche, and Silvia Morawetz.

[35] J.J., "Philadelphia, ich komme," *Sno'Boy 0* (1988).

möcht fragen
wollt ihr nicht
statt
gespalt'ner schwänze
meinen januskopf
haben
so
könnt' ich
in tollkühnem flug
kopf und kragen
für
ein klares gesicht
wagen [36]

An meines Landes Leut'

. . . bleib doch
wer will
und geh
wer kann

wohin auch immer
in sich selbst
vielleicht . . . [37]

Zwei Vögel

Ich bin
zwei Vögel

der eine will nach dem Süden
der andere will bleiben

im Frühjahr sehen sie sich
vielleicht wieder

fast unwahrscheinlich
zu verschieden sind sie

---

[36] Karim Saab, "Für O.," *Anschlag II* (1984).
[37] Uwe Romanski, "An meines Landes Leut'," *Sno'Boy 2* (1989).

zwei Vögel
bin ich [38]

Being split in two is one of the recurring metaphors that lends itself to expressing an existential feeling characterized by a sense of suffocation, vague or acute fear, and the experiencing of a hostile environment. Metaphors of the desert and disease recur as well. The desert connotes emptiness, isolation, ice, and cold. A "Deutscher Winter" has established itself permanently; one can survive only in a "Versteck," and the cold paralyzes all movement.[39]

Nocturnal Leipzig functions as a metaphor of the inner and external wasteland:

> In dieser Stadt gibt es Brücken, auf denen ich mich über das Fließende hinwegsetze. Brücken, die an kein anderes Ufer führen; von Möwen verschriene Bögen, unter denen Echo meinen Schritt belauert. Kettenbrücken über morastigen Rinngräben . . . über dieser Stadt gibt es in bestimmten Stunden ein paar Sterne . . . Irrlichter auf dem Weg ins Bewohnbare.[40]

In this description the senseless is accompanied by the diseased. The city of Leipzig is outwardly sick and decaying, and this sight produces delusions of fearsome monsters: "nervöse Monster ohne Fell und Knochen, die Panik ausatmen . . . eine Armee mutierter Krebszellen hocken sie da in Moder und Kohledreck." Not only are the physical surroundings sick; the entire society is sick and pathogenic.

"Symptome einer Nacht" is the name of a poem in which the country is dominated by lepers, cripples, and epileptics. Consequently, those people are shot who do not kiss leprous growths, do not dislocate their hips, or who practice neurology. The epilogue reads: "Pflanze ich mir einen Aussatz ein, und wenn, welchen? / Wie gekonnt hinke ich?"[41] Sarcasm can be a means of coping with this feeling of malaise, but pessimism and the impression of general paralysis and lack of prospects often dominate.[42]

---

[38] Michal Scholze, "Zwei Vögel," *Zweite Person*, No. 1, 1989.

[39] Andreas Klich, "Deutscher Winter" and "Versteck," *Glasnot VI* (1988). Cf. Torsten Ziesche, *Glasnot IV* (1988).

[40] Christian Heckel, "Flügel schlagen," *Zweite Person*, No. 1, 1989.

[41] Axel Helbig, "Symptome einer Nacht," *Anschlag VIII* (1987).

[42] For example, M. Scholze, "Das Paradies auf Erden," *Anschlag VI* (1986). The following lines from Karim Saab's poem "Skizze 35/1984" (*Anschlag II*,

Decay and Environment

In the clashes of October 1989, the decay of the city plays an important role in Leipzig. The indignation at the decrepitude of the building stock was vented in these days and contributed not insignificantly to the discrediting of really existing socialism. The original-graphic journals anticipated this debate long before the *Wende*. The theme was there for all to see, so to speak: *Anschlag IX* (1988) contains the page-sized photo of a dilapidated apartment building in Leipzig on the door of which the residents had fastened a protest placard: "Diese verwahrloste Bude wird von der GWL verwaltet. 9 Arbeiterfamilien wohnen hier unter menschenunwürdigen Verhältnissen." With numerous photos *Sno'Boy* also documents the wretched condition of many streets and houses in Leipzig.[43] And for *Zweite Person* Leipzig now has a new type of ruins, the "Verwaltungsruine," a consequence of the laissez-faire attitude and indifference of the authorities. These ruins are thus products and proof of a "innere Verwahrlosung und Achtlosigkeit des Menschen als Einzelner wie als Träger gesellschaftlicher Verantwortung oder Inhaber von Staatsgewalt."[44] The problem thus becomes the focal point of the debate about socialism's prospects or lack of prospects.

The carefully covered-up environmental problems are persistently treated in these journals. The documenting of generally known conditions is already tantamount to protest against the official silence about these problems. Devastated brown coal landscapes and scum-covered "rivers" no longer deserving of the name illustrate the journals. "Der Elbe bei Dresden sieht man den Atlantik nicht an," writes Barbara Köhler in *Anschlag VII*.[45] Issue IV of the same jour-

---

1984) are an example of the use of sarcasm as a defense mechanism:

Ausreiseanträge werden ohne Begründung genehmigt -	WILLKÜR.
Selbstschußzäune gelten als Volkseigentum -	ERRUNGENSCHAFT.
Eichhörnchen sind selten geworden -	RUHE.
Am nächsten Morgen soll das Abendprogramm wiederholt werden –	HOFFNUNG

[43] *Sno'Boy 3* and *4* (1989).
[44] Bernd Igel, "Ansätze – aus dem Tagebuch," *Zweite Person*, No. 1, 1989.
[45] Barbara Köhler, "Papierboot," *Anschlag VII* (1987).

nal plays a caper with a photo of Goethe's statue at the Naschmarkt in Leipzig showing Goethe adorned with a gas mask (the caption: "Mein Leipzig lob' ich mir"). At this time the officially circulated satirical magazine *Eulenspiegel* could treat the theme of air pollution only with delicacy or in passing. The arrogance of power is striking in the record of a petition (*Eingabe*) discussion with the mayor of Leipzig in regard to informing the population about the emission levels: "So schlecht ist die Luft in Leipzig gar nicht," Mayor Seidel has the audacity to claim.[46]

In the late 1980s, after Chernobyl, there are numerous reports about ecological disasters, and, in addition to factual reports, a comprehensive debate about ecology develops which includes reflections about "gentle" energy sources, about the connection between ecology and democracy, and the perverted relationship between man and nature.[47] The mounting horror at the destruction of the environment is manifest in the following parody on a poem of Goethe:

> Über allen Gipfeln ist Ruß
>
> Am Gickelhahn spürest du
> kaum einen Wald
>
> Die Vögelein schweigen, schweigen, schweigen, schweigen.
>
> Huste nur, huste, husten musste, balde
> schweigest du auch.[48]

The original-graphic journals of the 1980s in the GDR articulate both a feeling of the times which was prevalent in the society as a whole in various forms, and the special claims of certain groups and circles (civil rights activists, environmentalists, artists' circles). In the run-up to October 1989 these journals expressed the growing uneasiness of the intelligentsia and broader circles of the population at the isolation of the country and the accumulation of insolvable problems; this can be seen in the increasing amount of space devoted to the political debate. The events at the end of 1988 and the beginning of 1989 (banning of *Sputnik*, rigging of local elections,

---

[46] Torsten Drogi, *Glasnot I* (1987).

[47] For example: T. Abriss, "Der Lauer-Report," *Sno'Boy 2* (1989); Dirk Schümann, "Von der Wirtschaftsplanung zur Planwirtschaft," *Anschlag X* (1989); Bernd Igel, "Ansätze," *Zweite Person*, No. 1, 1989.

[48] Armagedeon Patina, "Über allen Gipfeln ist Ruß," *Glasnot II* (1987).

official condoning of the repression in China) strengthened the feeling that the cordoning off of the GDR and the sealing in of the majority of its population were anachronistic. Various aspects of the syndrome which Hans-Joachim Maaz would describe in greater detail after the *Wende* are examined, for example, school life, the experience of prescribed untruths, and the imbuing of the system-preserving "socialist consciousness."[49]

The literary-artistic section of the samizdat journals is informed by the resolute rejection of established literature and established kinds of publication. Published GDR literature almost never appears in these magazines. The writers are instead completely engrossed in their personal struggle for autonomy and in their efforts to develop their own language.

One cannot help but notice the large percentage of autobiographically colored texts. On the other hand, experiments with language and "avantgarde" artistic means are present only to a modest degree. Critics speak out against attaching so much importance to matters of form[50] or reprimand young authors who take the bull by the horns "bis hin zur hundertprozentigen Unzugänglichkeit."[51] The Leipzig "Szene" is clearly more reserved in regard to language experimentation than the Berlin Prenzlauer Berg.

As one would expect, special attention is given to the unofficial art scene in Leipzig, especially the gallery EIGEN+ART. This underground gallery, which was founded in a *Hinterhof* in 1985, had become the crystallization point of unofficial artistic life of the city. *Anschlag* devoted a special issue to it.[52]

All the varying opinions on the quality of the texts notwithstanding, Barbara Köhler's metaphor of a "paper boat" is just as applicable to the literary as to the non-literary sections of these magazines:

---

[49] For example, Knud Wollenberger, "Sie waren nicht einmal schlecht," *Glasnot V* (1988); Torsten Ziesche, ". . . Mustern," *Anschlag III* (1985); Andreas Reimann, "Beispiel untypischen Lebens," *Anschlag III* (1985).

[50] Peter Poltrie, "Wer will schon Erklärungen," *Anschlag VI* (1986).

[51] Adolf Endler, "Fakt-Notizen zu einem phantasmagorischen Unterhaltungstatsachenroman," *Anschlag IX* (1988).

[52] *Anschlag* Sonderheft Eigen+Art im Gespräch (1988). Cf. articles by Dirk Schümann, Else Gabriel, Judy Lybke, Olaf Nicolai on the performance "ALLEZ! ARREST!" in the gallery EIGEN+ART, in *Anschlag X* (1989), and a short description of the gallery in *Sno'Boy 4* (1989). See also *Zelleninnendruck*, ed. Egmont Hesse and Christoph Tannert. Exhibit Catalogue (Leipzig, 1990); and Judy Lybke, "ALLEZ! ARREST!" in *Niemandsland*, No. 8, 1989, pp. 116-21.

PAPIERBOOT . . . Papier voller Irrfahrten und Abenteuer, wenn das Land uns verlassen hat und die Hoffnung uns fahren läßt, Papier auf dem wir zu uns kommen, auf dem wir untergehen, unsere Barke unser gebrechlicher Grund. Sachsen am Meer – AHOI.[53]

Translated by Margy Gerber

---

[53] Barbara Köhler, "Papierboot," *Anschlag VII* (1987).

Pop Music in the GDR between Conformity and Resistance

Peter Wicke

A look at the checkered and contradictory history of pop music in the political and social context of the GDR requires a few preliminary remarks.

Popularity and linkage with the cultural interests and needs of young people are an inherent aspect of this music. However, popularity can be neither prescribed nor forced, and therefore it would be wrong to assume that the administrative undertakings which I shall sketch below necessarily say something about the music itself. The cultural processes themselves were anything but an empty imitation of the cliché-ridden declarations of the SED leadership.

Secondly, pop and rock music – these are the only kinds of music I shall be dealing with here – exist in a complex interrelationship of local, national, and global cultural contexts. Anglo-American productions and trends, which were accessible via the Western media, were always dominant in the GDR, as elsewhere; GDR music played a role, but it was limited.

Musicians were dependent in ways which transcended their particular circumstances: they were dependent on their young audiences who took their lead from international trends; they were dependent on the technology with which international aesthetic standards were set and which was available only within the realm of the media; and

25

they were again dependent on the media because, without success in the media, public acceptance at the local level was seldom possible, and even then only to a very limited degree. In the case of the GDR these dependencies, which are inherent to the trade, meant a complicated and risky balancing act between the demands of the young for cultural and, to some extent, political self-determination, and the control and instrumentalization of pop music which the SED apparatus sought to achieve. One cannot get a hold on this complex situation with convenient terms like "conformist" and "alternative," "*staatsnah*" and "*staatsfern.*"

And one last preliminary remark: young people – the "Kampfreserve" of the Party, to use one of its militant expressions – were far too important for the SED leadership to entrust their music to the cultural authorities. The political reins were held instead by the Departments of Security, Youth, and Agitation in the Central Committee. Thus it was not a homogeneous political-bureaucratic apparatus that reigned over cultural affairs, but rather a tangle of administrative agencies, official channels, and commissions, with differing, often even contradictory premises, not infrequently engaged in petty warfare with each other, and united at best by their general incompetence.

It is necessary to go somewhat back in time and reconstruct events at the most significant junctures. The first principles for dealing with pop music in the GDR were laid down as early as the 1950s. The Union of Composers and Musicologists of the GDR took up the issue at its constituent meeting in April 1951, laying claim to the right to speak for popular music. That even well-known composers and musicologists put forth the thesis that the time had finally come to turn entertainment into art can be attributed to tradition and to the *Zeitgeist*. But that this was followed by a ruthless actionism which used every political argument, no matter how simplistic, against anyone and anything that went against the aesthetic paradigms of the *Gralshüter* of music, at a time when the SED apparatus itself had yet to show any interest in such questions, remains inexcusable. Polemic statements like the following, which is in reference to a work of Afro-American bebop, produced a militant rhetoric which had little to do with art, but which was all too gladly seized upon in later years: "That is a sort of music that represents chaos, that is chaos, that is not only the preparation for war but war itself. That is the attempt to smuggle war into the minds of people."[1]

---

[1] Georg Knepler, "Musik, ein Instrument der Kriegsvorbereitung," in *Musik und*

The unholy alliance of aesthetic antipathy and political verdict which can be seen here in the making dogged popular forms of music until 1989. The interest of the Mielke ministry in punk rock, to which it in 1984 attributed "characteristics of degeneracy and asociality,"[2] is just one more example. The greater the aesthetic antipathy, the higher the estimate of the subversive effects of pop music, even when in the end, as was the case with punk rock, the gigantic spying apparatus could make out only 900 fans in the entire country.[3]

The actions of the Union of Composers and Musicologists, which in 1952 asserted its leadership role in the making of cultural policy by establishing the "Arbeitsgruppe Tanzmusik," led to the issuance of two regulations, which, although peripheral at the time, became highly significant later on. The "Anordnung über die Befugnis zur Ausübung von Unterhaltungs- und Tanzmusik," dated March 27, 1953, stipulated in its first paragraph that "persons who regularly or irregularly play dance or entertainment music in pubs and restaurants or at other events of any kind . . . [must] be professional musicians."[4] This licensing process was made more flexible with the passage of a second directive on January 14, 1957,[5] which permitted amateur musicians to perform dance and entertainment music under certain conditions; the granting of this permission was left up to "Zulassungskommissionen," which extended the famous "Musikerpappe," the formal prerequisite for playing in public places. Originally most likely nothing more than a bureaucratic-administrative regulation introduced for financial and tax purposes and with the additional goal of raising artistic standards by coupling the music profession with professional training, it became a rigidly applied instrument of repression in the 1960s.

The second regulation from this time which became highly significant in later years was the ruling on repertoire quotas, the

---

Gesellschaft, No. 2, 1951, p. 25. Translations of this and subsequent quotations are by Margy Gerber.

[2] Cf. Walter Süß, "Was wußte die Stasi über die Neonazis in der DDR?" *Die Zeit*, 30 April 1993, p. 40.

[3] Ibid.

[4] "Anordnung über die Befugnis zur Ausübung von Unterhaltungs- und Tanz-musik, vom 27. März 1953," in *Zentralblatt DDR, Ausgabe B*, Berlin 1953 (No. 11), p. 137.

[5] "Anordnung Nr. 2 über die Befugnis zur Ausübung von Tanz- und Unterhal-ungsmusik, vom 14. Januar 1957," in *Zentralblatt DDR, Ausgabe B*, Berlin 1957 (No. 4), p. 62.

"Anordnung über die Programmgestaltung bei der Unterhaltungs-
und Tanzmusik" of January 2, 1958.[6] In and of itself a protective
device known in other countries as well, it limited the share of
foreign music to a maximum of 40 percent, not including music
from the East bloc countries. This so-called 60/40 regulation likewise became a widely used instrument of repression; deviation from
the rule, which was very common in everyday practice, served as
justification for banning musicians in individual cases. The regulation was also used to rescind the licenses of disc jockeys whose
events had been classified as gatherings of what Mielke called
"feindlich-negative Kräfte." At the same time, however, the regulation did not keep the SED ideologues from directing the youth
station Jugendradio DT64 gradually to increase the ratio of Western
music from 40 percent to over 80 percent.[7]

   This political pragmatism was manifest in the SED's dealings
with popular music in the 1960s and became the salient characteristic of the Party's politics in this area. Everything in the way of
guidelines, instructions, criteria, and orientations that had been
prescribed for popular music, especially under the aegis of the
Union of Composers and Musicologists, was all cast aside in
September 1963 when the Politburo issued a communiqué on youth
politics entitled "Der Jugend Vertrauen und Verantwortung." It
launched an amazing liberalization – and at the same time justified
the Party's claim of competency in all matters dealing with the
development of popular music – with the sentence: "The Socialist
Unity Party of Germany has nothing in common with all those who
distrust our young people."[8] The Union lost its so hastily assumed
leadership role in this area and never regained it.

   This youth communiqué of the SED, with which Ulbricht obviously hoped to win the support of the young generation after the
building of the Wall – he presumed, most likely realistically, that the
older generations would never get over its having been built – paved
the way for the Beatles to move onto the socialist turntables of VEB

---

[6] "Anordnung über die Programmgestaltung bei der Unterhaltungs- und Tanzmusik, 2.1.1958," in *Zentralblatt DDR, Ausgabe B*, Berlin 1958 (No. 1), p. 5.
[7] In-house communication of Arthur Becker, President of the State Radio Committee (Staatliches Rundfunkkomitee) to the management of DT64, a copy of
which is in my possession.
[8] "Der Jugend Vertrauen und Verantwortung – Kommuniqué des Politbüros des
Zentralkomitees der SED zu Problemen der Jugend in der DDR," in *Der Jugend
Vertrauen und Verantwortung beim umfassenden Aufbau des Sozialismus.*
Schriftenreihe des Staatrates der DDR, No. 5, 1963, p. 16.

Deutsche Schallplatten, gave considerable leeway to the many GDR beat groups which formed in the Beatles' wake, and freed even the radio waves from the strait jacket Lipsi, a form of socialist dance music which, having first seen the light of day at the Lauchhammer dance music conference of the Union of Composers and Musicologists in 1959, knotted the legs of even the most skilled dancers. The number of beat groups quickly rose to match that found in other countries. Most of their music was instrumental, which minimized the potential for conflict with the state. The FDJ took the lead and organized competitions for "guitar groups," as GDR beat groups were officially called.

That Ulbricht's course very soon encountered resistance in some quarters of the Politburo was undoubtedly not solely due to the new tones in his youth policy. However this was the issue used to air and settle the smouldering conflict. Documents found in the SED Archive show that it was Honecker who, in his capacity as security chief, personally directed the events that followed.[9] At first glance, it seems bizarre to think of popular music as a weapon in the power struggle between factions of the SED leadership. However the documents preclude a different conclusion, as is also the case in regard to a series of similar moves against Honecker himself in the 1970s, which I shall touch on briefly below.

In the spring of 1965 the security forces under Honecker's direction stepped up their surveillance of young musicians and their fans. Every beer glass that was broken on the dance floor was zealously registered; meticulous lists were submitted each month to the Politburo. Squad cars of the Volkspolizei, notorious as "Gammlertaxen" ("drop-out taxis"), picked up young people by the dozen at the slightest sign of non-conformity – long hair, bell-bottom trousers, wild dancing – and took them to the station "to check their papers."

In the fall of 1965 "guitar groups" were totally banned in Leipzig, which was the stronghold of the East German beat movement at the time; the authorities cited the "Anordnung über die Befugnis zur Ausübung von Unterhaltungs- und Tanzmusik." When – on October 31, 1965 – some 2500 young people tried to vent their anger in a cautious demonstration, they ran straight into the arms of the readied security forces, who quickly and ruthlessly suppressed the demonstation.

These events were of far-reaching significance for the develop-

---

[9] See Michael Rauhut, "Beat in der DDR 1964 bis 1972. Politische Koordinaten und alltägliche Dimensionen." Dissertation, Humboldt University, Berlin, 1993.

ment of pop music in the GDR; provoking anger in young people by means of arbitrary actions against their music became one of the standard tactics used in the waging of various proxy wars. Time and time again, on the local as well as the national level, political differences were aired by contending that the harmfulness of a given course could be seen in the supposed negative effects it was having on the young generation and therefore on public order and the security of the country. Canceling a rock concert for some unconvincing reason was a way of producing proof of these negative effects. In 1975-76 a similar campaign against Honecker's liberalization course, headed by the first secretary of the SED's regional organization in Berlin, caused many musicians, including some of the most popular, to leave the country.

In 1965 the events led to a radical change of course which first found expression at the infamous 11th Plenum of the Central Committee in December 1965. The fact that Honecker, who was in charge of security, gave the report of the Politburo at this meeting, which was devoted to culture and ideology, was of vast symbolic significance. From then on, it was the security forces who determined what was aesthetically acceptable. For a long time to come, even after rock music was supported on a broad basis, "hard rhythms" were considered subversive. In the 1970s blues came under attack because blues' fans were classified as "feindlich negativ." New wave, punk, and breakdance shared this fate. Mielke's apparatus had determined that long hair was an expression of a "hostilely negative attitude," with the result that up to the mid-1970s rock musicians had to conceal their manes under hair nets when they performed on television.

However, official disapproval could also have the opposite effect. At the end of the 1960s the potential for conflict in the beat and youth sectors was considered so great that once again a change of course was deemed necessary. This was because, despite the repressive measures, which were considerably augmented after the 11th Plenum, there was no stopping the young generation's enthusiasm for beat music. Every group that was banned was simply formed again, some even four or five times, with the same members. At the end of 1969 the Central Committee's Department of Agitation seized the initiative and launched a concerted action involving producers, authors, composers, and musicians associated with GDR radio, which under the motto "Aktion Rhythmus" was to produce "jugendgemäße Tanzmusik." This represented a de facto recognition of beat and rock music. The conditions were that the texts be sung in German and long hair be hidden from view at official public performances.

If it cannot be prevented, maybe at least it can be exploited – this undoubtedly was the plan of the initiators. Dance music, as it continued to be called in the Party apparatus, was now seen as a means of satisfying the (newly recognized) cultural needs of young people; at the same time, it was supposed to contribute to the "development of socialist personalities" and to the propagation of "socialist ideas and values." A final attempt to define what this was supposed to mean was undertaken at a conference on dance music sponsored by the Ministry of Culture in November 1972; the result was an abstract formulation about the "basis of the socialist societal order," on which everything else, in order to be tolerated, was somehow supposed to rest. After this, no further attempts were made to lend cultural-political legitimation to this pragmatism.

Flanked by the operation "Jugendtanzmusik" of the FDJ's Central Council, which was responsible for the amateur sphere, a system of bureaucratic management of all pop music developments in the GDR came into being and remained in place, more or less unchanged, until the demise of the GDR. In all administrative sectors from the national level down to the counties and cities – in the youth organization, in the labor union, in the departments of culture of the state organs – commissions, working groups, and special ad hoc committees were created which were responsible for the musical concerns of the young generation. Several national working groups were formed to coordinate activities: the Arbeitsgruppe Tanzmusik of the Ministry of Culture; the Arbeitsgruppe Tanzmusik of the Union of Composers and Musicologists; the central Arbeitsgruppe Tanzmusik of the Zentralhaus für Kulturarbeit; the Arbeitsgruppe Jugendtanzmusik of the Zentralrat of the FDJ; the Arbeitsgruppe Tanzmusik of the national presidium of the FDGB (Federation of Labor Unions), the steering committee of the operation "Rhythmus" of the State Radio Committee. They mostly coordinated each other. The same structure was reproduced on the district and county levels.

To coordinate all these coordinators – the formulation is not at all excessive: it is taken from the guidelines of the committees – the Komitee für Unterhaltungskunst beim Ministerium für Kultur was founded in 1973. In 1977, it was restructured and turned into a separate agency which took on union-like characteristics and was responsible for all popular art forms. The apparatus became incarnate in exhibitions, competitions, and workshop weeks on the county, district, and national levels. It sponsored, developed, hindered, arranged, censored, permitted, regimented, directed, and

estimated; occasionally there were missives from the lofty heights of
the Politburo on matters of security, youth policy, and political
agitation, or Margot Honecker's Ministry of Education interfered,
likewise laying claim to its responsibility for the musical concerns of
the young generation. The GDR's deficiency economy did its part to
make musicians dependent on the mushrooming bureaucracy for the
myriad aspects of their existence: from the allocation of gas and
vehicles, to permission to print posters and the provision of paper
for printing the posters, to telephone service, and even to the solving of housing problems, not to mention travel.

Still, the hackneyed rhetoric of bureaucratic discourse that prevailed in official channels should not obscure the fact that the
constantly invoked unity of the SED, its uniformity of action, was
pure fiction. What one authority tolerated or even encouraged could
be prevented or even openly boycotted by another. For example,
recordings made on the AMIGA label of VEB Deutsche Schallplatte
with the permission of the Minister of Culture might be banned for
broadcast by the Central Committee's Department of Agitation even
before they were released. Abstruse nonsense like hair length or hair
color could lead to embittered trench warfare or petty arbitrariness,
or the constantly repeated charge of jeopardizing public order and
security. The coordination mania which produced ever more commissions, working groups, and executive committees is a testimony
to their diminished control.

The picture would be far from complete, however, if one took
the bureaucratic-administrative system which I have sketched to be
the cultural reality of the GDR. Despite all the regimentation, young
people in the GDR were not passive inhabitants of a cultural prison
– the unhindered presence of the West German media kept this from
happening. Instead – both as musicians and as fans – they played an
active role characterized by cultural and, to a lesser degree, even
political self-assertion. This was also the case among some of the
employees in the burgeoning administration and official channels, in
the media and the bureaucracy. Not all kept to the official line; some
persistently endeavored to liberalize the system.

Thus even in the 1960s the massive repressive measures against
beat music did not really change the course of things. Young people
developed strategies for asserting themselves and used them against
the apparatus boldly and effectively. One of the most effective
strategies was pro forma conforming in order to avoid repressive
measures. Generations of musicians developed dummy socialist
repertoires in order to obtain the necessary permission to perform.
The young fans likewise discovered more and more ways of indulg-

ing their passion for music, often playing cat-and-mouse games with the authorities and skillfully taking advantage of the latters' bureaucratic denseness.

A flexible, informal communications system made it possible to change the location of events on short notice when a confrontation with the authorities seemed imminent. Everyone who was part of the scene knew what was scheduled, and for when and with whom, without public notice. Moreover, the network of clubs, culture centers, and open-air performance facilities had become uncontrollable for all practical purposes. The authorities kept close tabs on the main cultural facilities: the centrally directed culture centers, the county culture centers, and the FDJ youth clubs, which, although run by the FDJ, were state facilities. Most performances took place far from these infrastructural hubs and involved a wide assortment of supervisory organizations – the Gesellschaft für Deutsch-Sowjetische Freundschaft, the Kulturbund, the labor union, even industrial plants. Furthermore, being assigned to an organization as far as finances were concerned did not necessarily mean that this organization was politically responsible for the content of the performance. This opened up a wide range of possibilities, and generally solutions could be found. When there was no alternative, those involved in the *Szene* took recourse to the protected space of the churches – to hold blues masses in the 1970s, punk concerts in the 1980s – and then resurfaced somewhere in the unsurveyable cultural infrastructure, usually in the provinces. The line between the official and subcultural form of these processes was blurred in every respect.

One of the self-assertion strategies was to take advantage of conflicts between the various authorities and exploit their Achilles' heels. In the second half of the 1960s, for example, beat groups often performed in village pubs on the periphery of the cities or in rural areas, because the authorities here, in contrast to the urban areas, were simply not up to reacting. The development of youth culture and rock music in the GDR was marked by an unfailing instinct for weaknesses in the Party apparatus. Bogus claims of residence in Berlin as a way of exploiting the loopholes in the crisscross of central and local competences can serve as an illustration, as can the evolving tacit agreement between bands and their fans to undermine official attempts to instrumentalize musical events by maintaining the appearance of conformity, which included accepting the measured-out official support and the necessary compromises, and within these constraints jointly producing a cultural reality that was totally different from the one intended. It often happened that the moralizing tenor of GDR rock recordings was literally played away or danced away during live performances, simply drowned out in the unleashed sensuousness of the music. At any rate, evading censorship by means of metaphorical or figurative language in the song texts or their musical implementation – song texts had to be submitted in written form for approval, while their realization in music was not subject to censorship – was an essential skill for musicians.

Another example of the cultural self-assertion strategies of young people was the gradual metamorphosis of public locales – often right before the eyes of the cultural authorities – into national *Szenetreffs* for group cultures such as blues, heavy metal, punk, new wave, hip-hop – in the southern part of the GDR even country and western in original cowboy outfits. The cultural infrastructure was suffused with an informal infrastructure which skillfully evaded the authorities, especially since tip-offs about imminent surveillance or trouble as a rule came from well-wishers within the state apparatus itself or resulted from their own interest in not attracting the attention of the central authorities.

Thus in the course of time a sort of stalemate evolved which was furthered by a high degree of incompetence on the part of the cultural authorities. Ideological blinders left them unable to recognize the cultural processes at work among young people. Just to understand the developments described above required a subtlety of which the authorities were not capable. Whatever understanding there was came from outside the GDR, not from the analysis of the cultural situation at home. When in 1984 the Mielke ministry began to take notice of punk music, it was not reacting to developments in the GDR – there were no signs of punk music at that time – but instead to an article on this form of youth culture in the Federal Republic which had appeared shortly before in *Der Spiegel*. The influences were ridiculously slight, but the apparatus had one more category for determining "negative" developments. This notwithstanding, up to 1989 Party functionaries who still had not learned to pronounce the word properly made public speeches in which they denounced "Western punk," not noticing that punk existed under their very noses, since they had not the slightest idea what they were talking about.

The ideology-oriented concept of art with which the authorities operated thus worked to the disadvantage of its originators. Their cultural management was oblivious to the processes in progress, just as their fixation on the ideological purity of the textual messages prevented their noticing that their control over the means of cultural production was slipping away. The network of private recording studios which slowly came into existence supplied not only the media – in 1988 80 percent of new productions came from private studios – but also an "alternative" audience, which had its own network for distributing music cassettes. The unwieldy regulatory apparatus was oriented toward ideology and security; for developments of this kind there were no rules or structures of responsibility. Economic constraints limited the authorities' scope of action as well.

Towards the end the situation manifested all the characteristics of the grotesque. Under the direction of the Department of Agitation of the Central Committee, the media mounted an ideological crusade, using the very same Western music that they wanted to exorcise from the "hearts and brains" of the young generation. The FDJ spent precious hard currency to have international stars such as Bob Dylan, Joe Cocker, and Bruce Springsteen perform the very music it had once gone to great lengths to prevent being heard. The cultural authorities were non-plussed because the young generation of musicians paid no attention to their regulations – and did not need to, since they could produce their music in private studios. None of this mattered much to East German youth. By this time they had already largely taken their leave of the GDR, even though this leave-taking did not become reality until the summer of 1989.

Translated by Margy Gerber

"Nuancen und Zwischentöne" versus "muskelprotzende Prosa": Autobiography and the Project of Explaining "How it Was" in the GDR

Roger Woods

In the context of reassessing the GDR this article examines some of the critical responses to collective, public, official attempts at judging the GDR as a whole and the role individuals played in the GDR. It also examines some of the ways in which critical intellectuals, often writers, are reflecting not just on their own past but on that of their fellow citizens and even on that of invented characters. Can such reflection on individuals have some collective, public purpose which might in turn inform or serve as a backdrop to official judgments? This and similar questions are being examined by prominent critical intellectuals from the days of the GDR such as Stefan Heym, and by other, less prominent, critical intellectuals who grew up in the GDR and entered the public arena after unification. Still others come from insider reformer circles which existed under the old regime. West German political scientists and cultural historians are also participating in the debate, sometimes (but by no means always) as the adversaries. The discussion is bound up with the question of what new role East German intellectuals might assume in the united Germany, and, more generally, with the question of how East Germany might find a distinctive voice which transcends nostalgia and bitterness.

Since German unification there have been many attempts at reassessing the GDR – from the revival of totalitarianism theory as a model to often unconvincing accounts of what might be rescued from the GDR as some kind of East German contribution to German identity.[1] Early reassessments often explicitly or implicitly separated out the population into *Täter* and *Opfer*, yet it soon became clear that this model did not do justice to a more complex reality. Empirical research into milieus in East Germany undermines any simplistic notion of a monolithic GDR in which people either supported or opposed the system. Political culture in the GDR was clearly complex, and this research confirmed the need for an understanding which transcends the framework within which public judgments are currently being made.[2]

An appreciation of this complex reality expressed itself as uncertainty and unease in public debate: in March 1992 members of the Bundestag established the Enquete-Kommission des Bundestages zur Aufarbeitung der Geschichte und der Folgen der SED-Diktatur under the chairmanship of Rainer Eppelmann (CDU). The commission was made up of 16 MPs and 11 experts, and it was established not least because it was felt that legal procedures were an inadequate means of repairing the damage done to individuals in the GDR. Disappointment over the limitations of the legal system in dealing with the GDR – where, for example, some key figures of the old order could be charged with no more than misuse of funds – are summed up in the words: "Man hat Gerechtigkeit erwartet und den Rechtsstaat bekommen."[3]

---

[1] See my chapters "Civil Society, Critical Intellectuals, and Public Opinion in the New *Bundesländer*," in *Studies in GDR Culture and Society 11/12: The End of the GDR and the Problems of Integration*, ed. Margy Gerber and Roger Woods (Lanham/New York/London: University Press of America, 1993), pp. 53-70; and "The East German Contribution to German Identity," in *Studies in GDR Culture and Society 13: Understanding the Past – Managing the Future*, ed. Margy Gerber and Roger Woods (Lanham/New York/London: University Press of America, 1994), pp. 25-38.

[2] See Thomas Meyer, "Gleichzeitiges und Ungleichzeitiges in der politischen Kultur in Ost- und Westdeutschland," in *Deutsche Ansichten. Die Republik im Übergang*, ed. Michael Müller and Wolfgang Thierse (Bonn: Dietz, 1992), pp. 25-40.

[3] Dirk Hansen in "Debatte des Deutschen Bundestages am 23. September 1993 über die Verlängerung strafrechtlicher Verjährungsfristen," *Das Parlament*, 40, 1 October 1993, pp. 6-7. (Hansen is an FDP member of the Bundestag.) See also Karl-Dietrich Bracher's criticism of the restricted interpretation of the concept of the *Rechtsstaat* when it comes to dealing with the East German past ("Auf dem Wege zu einer anderen Republik. Adalbert Reif im Gespräch mit dem Historiker Karl-Dietrich Bracher," *Universitas*, 48, No. 565 [July 1993], pp. 683-98).

No sooner had the Commission been established than prominent civil rights campaigners, church leaders, and politicians, including Friedrich Schorlemmer, Wolfgang Thierse, and Joachim Gauck, suggested a tribunal as a way of coming to terms with the past which would be independent of the courts and free from the restrictions imposed by legal procedures. The Tribunal zur Aufklärung der DDR-Vergangenheit would, its founders declared, attempt to establish standards of right and wrong, decency and dignity, standards which would then be applied in a subtle way which took account of the realities of life in the GDR.[4] In March 1992 Friedrich Schorlemmer said on the occasion of the establishment of the "Forum für Aufarbeitung und Erneuerung" in Leipzig that the forum should re-examine everyday life in the GDR and seek to explain why 95% of the population "allowed themselves to be organized."[5]

But this initiative was attacked by those who argued that a tribunal would be held in a political culture which subjects the past to a simplistic logic of friend and foe, good and evil, just and unjust, true and false.[6] A tribunal might degenerate into an inquisition. Instead, "offene und öffentliche Gespräche" were called for.[7] Dissatisfaction with the Bundestag Commission also led to the establishment of a so-called alternative Enquete-Kommission, chaired by Wolfgang Harich.[8]

---

[4] Joachim Gauck, Friedrich Schorlemmer, Wolfgang Thierse, Wolfgang Ullmann, Gerd and Ulrike Poppe, Marianne Birthler et al, "'Die Wiederherstellung von Wahrheit tut not.' Plädoyer für ein Tribunal zur Aufklärung der DDR-Vergangenheit," *Blätter für deutsche und internationale Politik*, No. 3, 1992, p. 380.

[5] Quoted by Rüdiger Thomas, "Aufklärung statt Abrechnung: Anmerkungen zum Umgang mit der DDR-Geschichte," in *Deutschland. Eine Nation - doppelte Geschichte*, ed. Werner Weidenfeld (Cologne: Wissenschaft und Politik, 1993), p. 268. My translation here and throughout.

[6] See, for example, Michael Brie, "Themen, Maßstäbe und Teilnahme – ein Tribunal zur DDR," in *Ein Volk am Pranger? Die Deutschen auf der Suche nach einer neuen politischen Kultur*, ed. Albrecht Schönherr (Berlin: Aufbau, 1992), p. 111.

[7] Albrecht Schönherr, "Geleitwort," in *Ein Volk am Pranger?*, p. 11.

[8] See Lothar Bisky, Peter-Michael Diestel, Klaus Grehn, and Wolfgang Harich, "Versöhnung statt Vergeltung?" *Neues Deutschland*, 2/3 October 1993, p. 9. Diestel (CDU) comments on the Bundestag Enquete-Kommission: "Es ist mir wichtig, es diesen Herrschaften der Enquete-Kommission nicht zu überlassen, unsere Geschichte endgültig zu bewerten."

The problems associated with an *Aufarbeitung* which deals with structures and groups prompted a call for *Aufarbeitung* at the level of the individual. Individuals faced the ethical dilemma of how to uphold their moral integrity while playing an active role in the GDR. Dietrich Böhler, Dean of the Faculty of Philosophy and Social Sciences at the Free University in Berlin, notes that, instead of attempting to understand the dilemma, the media judge individuals by a simplistic morality which condemns as complicity any compromise which East Germans may have made in order to have an effect in the public sphere.[9]

Günter Gaus points out that what is needed is not any simplistic account of how East Germans either resisted or succumbed to persecution. What is worth examining are the almost imperceptible ways in which people came to some kind of arrangement with the system and thus became responsible for its maintenance. There was no single point when compromise became complicity; there was rather a series of compromises from motives which were not always opportunistic. Gaus asks how this transition from compromise to complicity might be understood, and significantly he homes in on private reflection by individuals, "die ganz individuelle Selbstbesinnung."[10]

If attention gradually turned to the position of the individual, it was in an attempt to offer a more subtle understanding of how people lived their lives in the GDR. Judgments of entire groups, Rüdiger Thomas argues, are never likely to do full justice to a complex situation.[11] The idea of individuals examining themselves is seized upon by Stefan Heym when he highlights the imperfections of any system of justice one might use to tackle the problem of compensation for those who suffered at the hands of the GDR authorities. He comes down in favor of a private and individual confrontation with the past. Everyone must know when he or she behaved badly or in a cowardly manner, and the final reckoning should be a reckoning with one's conscience.[12]

---

[9] Dietrich Böhler, "Erinnern, Wiederholen, Durcharbeiten – in verantwortungsethischer und republikanischer Hinsicht," *Deutsche Zeitschrift für Philosophie*, 40, No. 3 (1992), pp. 305-11.

[10] Günter Gaus, "'Es ist an der Zeit, daß einer aufsteht und nein sagt,'" *Blätter für deutsche und internationale Politik*, No. 3, 1992, p. 294.

[11] See Thomas, "Aufklärung statt Abrechnung," p. 269.

[12] Stefan Heym, *Filz. Gedanken über das neueste Deutschland* (Munich: Bertelsmann, 1992), p. 106.

The (originally) East German philosopher Manfred Riedel argues that remembering must start with the individual, and he too advocates looking in upon oneself:

> Nicht die Gesellschaft ist verblendet, sondern der einzelne wird durch gesellschaftliche und historische Prozesse so konditioniert, daß er nichts sieht oder nichts sehen will. Das entschuldigt ihn nicht. Es geht mir gerade darum, daß ein Verständnis von Erinnerungsarbeit am Individuum ansetzen muß.[13]

Unlike Heym, however, he offers this individual approach not as purely private reflection. It clearly has a public role to play, for he sees writers as potential guides in this process, and he refers specifically to Christa Wolf's *Was bleibt* as the only work until that point to provide such guidance. Riedel favors a move away from consideration of the ways in which East German society indulged in collective self-deception, not least because he sees this as providing a let-out for the individual (p. 84). Reflection about individuals can be a public activity, and it is not necessarily an alternative to judgment.

Johannes Kuppe (Bundeszentrale für politische Bildung) also homes in on the public function of presenting GDR history in such a way that individuals will be able to see themselves as part of it. Kuppe sees this as a task for historians, but he also argues that West German historians are unfamiliar with East German history, and many East German historians are not in a position to take on the task after years of "Instrumentalisierung" by the SED. Moreover, Kuppe argues, any account of the past which is based only on professionalism is likely to be inadequate. What is needed in addition is a high degree of sensitivity and empathy.[14]

It may be that in the situation Böhler, Gaus, Heym, Riedel, and Kuppe describe, literature will turn out to be a particularly appropriate vehicle for probing the complex and ambiguous reality of living in the GDR. Tackling complex and ambiguous reality is clearly a function of literature in every society, and East German writers are being called upon to take on this task. In an important

---

[13] Nadine Hauer, Helga Königsdorf, Hans-Martin Lohmann, Manfred Riedel, and Friedrich Schorlemmer, "Schuld ist ein gesellschaftlicher Verblendungszusammenhang," in *Erinnern, Wiederholen, Durcharbeiten*, ed. Brigitte Rauschenbach (Berlin: Aufbau, 1992), p. 84.

[14] Johannes Kuppe, "Was bei der Aufarbeitung der Vergangenheit zu bedenken ist," *Deutschland Archiv*, 25, No. 9 (1992), pp. 978-81.

contribution to *Sinn und Form*, Hans-Peter Krüger takes up the idea of explaining as a project when he suggests that East German intellectuals must find a way of conveying in terms which can be widely understood how East Germans dealt with conflicting claims. He also takes up the point that existing legal and political mechanisms are inadequate for tackling East Germany's past. There are no "professionell geordnete Lösungsmuster," and intellectuals have to rise to the challenge of publicly seeking new frameworks ("Orientierungssuche").[15]

Are East German intellectuals showing any signs of providing the guidance and insights commentators claim they could offer? In her TV interview with Günter Gaus, reproduced in *neue deutsche literatur*,[16] Christa Wolf suggests that East Germans are no longer so eager to forget their past, and she refers to letters she has received from East Germans who were willing to reflect on it in a way which has nothing to do with GDR nostalgia. Instead, they are looking for a way of developing which does not involve casting aside their old identity. Wolf admits that these people are a tiny minority, yet their attitude gives her hope. She seems to connect this with a mission to explain when she points out that West Germans have little knowledge of how life was in the GDR and make no attempt to find out. Instead they resort to accusations of guilt, thus encouraging East Germans to deny their own past. In this "tribunal atmosphere" (p. 38) one cannot be honest with oneself.

Werner Creutziger takes up the point when he writes of the danger that West Germans will take advantage of East Germans' willingness to subject their past to critical scrutiny, with the East Germans being characterized as a "Volk von opportunistischen Duldern oder Komplizen eines Unrechtssystems."[17] The simplistic categories of public debate limit the opportunities for understanding, Creutziger argues, but he insists that there is intellectual and moral work to be done, and East Germans should not give in to the temptation to fall silent or allow themselves to be pushed into a nostalgia which would mark the end of any serious attempt to come to terms with their past.

---

[15] Hans-Peter Krüger, "Ohne Versöhnung handeln, nur nicht leben," *Sinn und Form*, 44, No. 1 (1992), p. 43.

[16] "Auf mir bestehen. Christa Wolf im Gespräch mit Günter Gaus," *neue deutsche literatur*, 41, No. 5 (1993), pp. 20-40.

[17] Werner Creutziger, "Verlockung zum Schweigen. Vom Umgang mit unserer Vergangenheit," *neue deutsche literatur*, 42, No. 1 (1994), p. 192.

The project of remembering and reassessing in a way which starts with the individual is reflected in many research projects currently underway on East Germany. It is striking just how many projects are based on reconstructing biography – "Biographie- und Lebenslaufforschung." For example, Dieter Geulen, Professor of Education at the Free University in Berlin, has reported recently on his empirical research among four generations of East Germans, in which he aims at a "verstehende Rekonstruktion der DDR-Sozialisation" which might help put an end to West German stereotypes of the "Ossi."[18] Some of the hearings of the Bundestag Commission of Inquiry also take the form of autobiographical accounts.[19]

Any project of self-examination is likely to be fraught with difficulties, quite apart from those which may come from a not infrequently hostile West German response. In the case of biographical research, the "life history interviews" conducted by Lutz Niethammer, Alexander von Plato, and Dorothee Wierling among 150 East Germans shortly before the *Wende* served to undermine the idea of a monolithic SED and provided a more subtle view of "what was possible in the SED."[20] Biographical and autobiographical distortion was still an obvious danger, however, in a society where interviewees had reason to fear that the authorities might gain access to the records of the interviews (p. 24). This limitation caused the interviewers to ask themselves whether their project had not been made redundant by the events of the fall of 1989, since after the collapse of the old order interviews could take place in a more open atmosphere. Yet after 1989, the interviewers rightly argued, the project took on a new significance: the original pressure to conform to social and political norms in the GDR was superseded by a new pressure to show one's critical distance from the state. In the circumstances of a united Germany, East Germans' memory would "never function in the same way again" (pp. 67-68).

This was confirmed in a report on follow-up interviews conducted with some of the same East Germans about their lives before

---

[18] Dieter Geulen, "Typische Sozialisationsverläufe in der DDR: Einige qualitative Befunde über vier Generationen," *Aus Politik und Zeitgeschichte. Beilage zur Wochenzeitung Das Parlament*, 25 June 1993, p. 37.

[19] See for example Rolf Schälike's account of his early years in "Anhörung der Enquete-Kommission," *Deutschland Archiv*, 26, No. 6 (1993), pp. 740-60.

[20] Lutz Niethammer, Alexander von Plato, and Dorothee Wierling, *Die volkseigene Erfahrung* (Berlin: Rowohlt, 1991), pp. 9, 17.

and after the *Wende*. Of the 150 people interviewed in 1987 only twenty were willing to give a further interview in 1990. Evaluating these twenty interviews, the report's author notes that the retelling of the past after the collapse of the old regime frequently indicated a reassessment of the degree of the interviewees' involvement with the East German system. Moreover, involvement often came to be justified in terms of some subversive purpose such as support for the disadvantaged or pursuit of essentially Christian policies.[21]

When it comes to the problems of using literature as a forum for self-examination, Manfred Jäger warns that nobody should be allowed to dispense with a thorough analysis of their own political position and to opt instead for an ambiguous, artistic treatment and an appeal to unfathomable human nature.[22] In the case of literary autobiography Günter de Bruyn points to the problems of remembering as he works on the sequel to *Zwischenbilanz*. The most disturbing thing about reading his Stasi files is, he declares, the realization that there were gaps in his memory, that he had suppressed or reinterpreted memories in order to portray himself in a more favorable light. He concludes that this is disastrous for anyone engaged in the writing of autobiography.[23]

It is against this background of potentially new distortions and suppressions taking the place of the old that Olaf Georg Klein has made a notable literary attempt to do what East German intellectuals are being urged to do – to explain what it meant to be born an East German citizen, to grow up in the GDR, and to interact with official structures. His book, *Plötzlich war alles ganz anders*, takes the form of a series of fictional autobiographies, or autobiographical sketches, and Klein makes full use of the literary form in his contribution to the public discussion about how to remember the GDR past.[24]

---

[21] Dorothee Wierling, "Gewendete Biographien?" in *Erinnern, Wiederholen, Durcharbeiten*, pp. 217-27.

[22] Manfred Jäger, "Auskünfte. Heiner Müller und Christa Wolf zu Stasi-Kontakten," *Deutschland Archiv*, 26, No. 2 (1993), p. 145.

[23] Katharina Festner and York-Gothart Mix, "Günter de Bruyn im Gespräch," *Deutschland Archiv*, 27, No. 5 (1994), pp. 508-16.

[24] Olaf Georg Klein, *Plötzlich war alles ganz anders. Deutsche Lebenswege im Umbruch* (Cologne: Kiepenheuer & Witsch, 1994). Two chapters of Klein's book appeared as "Nicht mehr Ost, noch nicht West" in *Sinn und Form*, 45, No. 6 (1993), pp. 962-87.

In its format the book takes the tradition of GDR documentary literature one experimental step further: the characters who tell their life stories are invented, yet they interact with real figures from the GDR. By inventing a wide range of characters, Klein is able to touch upon many of the key questions about how to assess the GDR. He tells of the vicar at odds with the regime, the artist who quit the GDR in 1984 after being pushed into opposition by a system which demanded regular demonstrations of loyalty. He also tells the story of a retired Stasi officer with responsibility for monitoring Church activity, of a journalist and SED member, and of a young unemployed worker.

Klein suggests that his work is partly aimed at his fellow East Germans when he explains that he seeks to enable people who were on one side of an experience to understand those who were on the other side of the same experience. But Klein is also addressing Western readers when he comments that those who have never known the situations he describes may come to appreciate the underlying contradictions and subtleties (p. 10). In this respect, Klein seems to latch onto a tradition of GDR literature, the appeal of which lay in its "probing of contradictory modes of being."[25] He declares:

> Es geht nicht um vordergründige Wertungen, sondern vielmehr um Nuancen und Zwischentöne . . . . Es kam mir darauf an, die Risse, die Sprünge und die Widersprüche in den Personen so darzustellen, daß ein allzu selbstgerechtes Urteil des Lesers abgemildert und er eher in die Richtung einer – auch – kritischen Selbstbefragung gelenkt wird.
>
> (pp. 9-10)

Yet, like others engaged in the project of using biography to understand the past, Klein is aware of the problems of recollection:

> Ist nicht jeder ein eigener "Kosmos", hat nicht jeder seine Wertungen und Interpretationen, stellt sich heute so dar und morgen anders, versucht er nicht, sich zu verstecken, ist er nicht einseitig und vergeßlich, und hat er nicht seine Erfahrungen und Erinnerungen entsprechend der jeweiligen Situation anders "eingefärbt"? (p. 11)

Although Klein promotes a subtle understanding of life in the GDR, he does not renounce the idea of judgment totally. His foreword moves from a rejection of simple categories to an exploration of the

---

[25] Krüger, "Ohne Versöhnung handeln, nur nicht leben," p. 47.

capacity of literature to describe the situation of the individual in a way that will soften judgment, but finally he moves back to the vocabulary of judgment, even of the courtroom:

> *Wer* diese fiktiven Personen nun "in Wirklichkeit" sind, muß der Leser selbst entscheiden, ähnlich einem Richter, der sich aus Indizien, der Anklage und der Verteidigung sein Bild macht, um dann nach verein-barten Prinzipien zu verurteilen oder loszusprechen, nicht ganz ohne einen Blick auf sich selbst. (p. 12)

The sketch entitled "Uns ist so viel verlorengegangen an wirk-lich schönem Leben . . ." is particularly noteworthy for the way it enters the broader debate on how to assess and judge the GDR. Presented in the form of a monologue in the first person, it tells of a woman who grew up in the GDR. Her father was a carpenter who studied after the war and became a lecturer, i.e., he was someone who benefited from the particular form of social mobility encour-aged in the early years of the GDR. It was obvious ("selbst-verständlich") that she would join the Party since she believed it was pursuing the honorable goal of a society free from exploitation (p. 38). Building the "antifaschistische Schutzwall" was "a logical step" to ward off economic collapse (p. 38). Of course ("natürlich") she joined the FDJ, like everyone else in her class (p. 40). She had no contact with anyone from the Church.

The woman started work as a kindergarten nurse. She describes the contacts the kindergarten had with a soldier. (It was standard practice in the GDR to establish such contacts in order to foster a positive attitude among young children towards the NVA.) Here the first hint of authorial criticism enters the telling of the life story. Klein employs simplistic language to suggest a lack of mature reflec-tion on the part of the woman, and he thus introduces a certain distance between himself and the narrator: "Die Kinder haben Bilder hingeschickt, und er [the soldier] hat uns geantwortet, mit einem sehr netten Brief" (p. 39). The *Schießbefehl* is described as "ein kompliziertes Thema" (p. 40). The woman was later recruited onto the Central Council of the FDJ: "Das fand ich eigentlich toll" (p. 43).

Her ability to explain is also limited when she states that the FDJ College she attended demanded absolute obedience, but rejects any idea of its being a totalitarian organization. She concludes: "Aber vielleicht kann man das nicht einschätzen, wenn man es nicht selber miterlebt hat" (p. 42). Here she reaches the same conclusion as Richard Schröder, the theologian and one-time leader of the SPD

Fraktion in the Volkskammer, who argues that Westerners did not experience the GDR past and are not in a position to judge: "Sie müssen sich von uns erzählen lassen, wie es war, und hier wenigstens mal zuhören, auch wenn es schwerfällt."[26] Yet, unlike Schröder, she concludes that those who did not experience the GDR cannot judge it because she is frustrated at not being able to convey how it was to her own satisfaction.

When she tries to explain why she did not want to accept a job as FDJ Secretary in a large enterprise, she uses official phrases to make her point about the effect it would have on her family life. She recalls her words to the SED Secretary: "Ich habe ein Kind. Dieses Kind braucht Geborgenheit. Die Familie ist die kleinste Zelle der Gesellschaft, und wenn die nicht funktioniert, funktioniert das andere auch nicht . . ." (p. 44).[27] The SED Secretary's response was to offer her a place for her child as a weekday boarder at a nursery. This response came as a profound shock to her, and as a result her political commitment started to waver, and this at a time when her work obliged her to represent the official line more and more explicitly: she presented cases and made recommendations on proposed marriages between GDR citizens and foreigners. Still, she explains that she actually looked forward to it because it involved dealing with people. She recommended approval for some marriages which did not meet the formal requirements, when, as she explains: ". . . rein menschlich gesehen mußte man sagen, das war eine echte Beziehung" (p. 50). One application she supported was turned down by the group, which had a Stasi officer as an observer, and the applicant threatened to kill himself. Her reaction was to spend an extra "fünf persönliche Minuten" with the man, "obwohl ich Mitarbeiterin im Staatsapparat war und das eigentlich nicht hätte machen dürfen. Aber ich habe meine Arbeit intuitiv so gesehen, daß ich für die Menschen da bin" (p. 51).

Her work was criticized by the Ministerium für Staatssicherheit, and she was moved to dealing with applications to leave the GDR. Here the work was harder, the applicants more aggressive. The result: "Jeden Tag bin ich mit einem inneren Druck zur Arbeit gegangen. Ich wurde immer unsicherer in meinen Äußerungen, war

---

[26] Quoted by Jürgen Habermas in "Die normativen Defizite der Vereinigung," in *Vergangenheit als Zukunft*, ed. Michael Haller (Zürich: pendo, 1990), pp. 66-67. Original statement in the *Frankfurter Allgemeine Zeitung*, 2 January 1990.

[27] The idea of being directed into a particular job is a recurrent finding in biographical research projects. See Dieter Geulen, "Typische Sozialisationsverläufe," p. 38.

überhaupt kein Mensch mehr. Auch in der Familie und für die Kinder war ich nicht mehr voll da" (pp. 53-54). She describes how the contradictions in her life became more acute, and thus reflects Krüger's argument that people existed on both sides of the equation of power and control in the GDR, and there developed "eine Kultur sich selbst widersprechender Individuen."[28]

As Klein's story progresses, the narrator's language becomes more sophisticated and reflective, and this illustrates how the form of fictional autobiography can chart an inner development and thus go some way towards answering Lutz Niethammer's concern that in a united Germany East Germans' memory would "never function in the same way again." The narrator comes to formulate ideas which are directly related to dissident calls for freedom to travel, heard while the GDR still existed. After the *Wende* she was ashamed that she supported the system, especially when privileges enjoyed by senior Party members came to light. She realizes that, although her response to proposed marriages was humane, it was disgraceful that the state interfered in family matters at all (pp. 55-56). On the other hand, when she reflects on her role in the official order she declares that her work was the product of the society she lived in. She is sad that she did this work, that she "had to do this work," as she puts it, but she feels that she did much to help people (p. 56).

The story is particularly important since it deals with many of the issues in the public discussion about remembering and judging the past: the inexperience and idealism of youth; the need to overcome the Nazi legacy; conformism; the willingness not to condemn a whole system on the basis of one's personal experience; the capacity for self-deception but also for self-criticism; the scope for humane action in an inhumane system; the stress of living with profound contradictions, of existing on both sides of the power equation.

It is equally important to remember just who is describing this life and the way he describes it. Klein's biography suggests that, unlike the central figure in his story, he did not do what was "a matter of course." Born in 1955 in Berlin, he grew up in the GDR. He refused military service, and he worked in the theatre, as a furnaceman, and as a medical orderly before going on to study theology and work at the Berlin-Brandenburg Evangelische Akademie.

Through his language Klein introduces critical distance. But as the main character's capacity for critical thought grows, the critical

---

[28] Krüger, "Ohne Versöhnung handeln, nur nicht leben," p. 46.

distance between the author and this character narrows. Yet there is no single message one can take from the story. The extra five minutes the main character was prepared to spend with a potential suicide victim come across as a grotesquely inadequate response. The idea that the central figure could look forward to her job since it involved working with people indicates so much self-deception about the nature of the work that the reader is repelled.

It may be that Klein raises more questions than he answers, and that his fictional life stories illustrate Manfred Jäger's point about literature being misused as an intentionally ambiguous medium. On the reception side, it may be that the subtleties of literary accounts of life in the GDR will always lose out to what Jürgen Habermas calls the "muskelprotzende Prosa" of political language in Germany today.[29] The project of explaining "how it was" in the GDR is gradually getting underway. Or rather, a vast range of projects with different approaches and different purposes. Empirical researchers, innovative politicians, critical intellectuals, and literary figures alike seem to be agreed on the need for such a project, if not on the need for a plurality of perspectives. If subtle explanation of what it meant to be a citizen of the GDR can make itself heard above a public discussion dominated by the simplistic categories of responsibility for or opposition to the old order in the GDR, it will be an important contribution to the kind of understanding which must precede judgment.

---

[29] Jürgen Habermas, "Die Lebenslüge der Bundesrepublik. Wir sind wieder 'normal' geworden," *Die Zeit*, 11 December 1992.

Die ostdeutschen Schriftsteller auf der Suche nach einem neuen Selbstverständnis

Günter Erbe

Hans Mayer gebraucht in seinem Buch *Wendezeiten. Über Deutsche und Deutschland* die Formeln "Leiden an Deutschland" und "unglückliches Bewußtsein," um die Situation des Schriftstellers in Deutschland zu beschreiben.[1] Den Topos "Leiden an Deutschland" entlehnt Mayer Thomas Mann, dessen Tagebuchblätter aus den Jahren 1933/34 unter diesem Titel veröffentlicht worden sind. Sie enthalten Beobachtungen und Kommentare des unter den Vorkommnissen in seinem Land leidenden Emigranten. Was sich als Befindlichkeit des ausgebürgerten, ins Exil verjagten Dichters darstellt, wird für Mayer zu einer Grunderfahrung des deutschen Schriftstellers mit der politischen Macht und den Verhältnissen in Deutschland. In der von Hegel stammenden Formel vom "unglücklichen Bewußtsein" reflektiert sich eine entzweigebrochene Wirklichkeit, der ungelöste Gegensatz zwischen humanem Denken und Fühlen und inhumaner gesellschaftlicher Praxis.

Mayer verwendet beide Formeln im Hinblick auf die deutsche Literatur nach 1945 in differenzierender Weise. In Westdeutschland sei durch die Restaurationspolitik die alte Konfrontation von Geist und Macht, von Literatur und Politik wiederhergestellt worden. Im Unterschied dazu sei die DDR von Beginn an ein Staat der Schrift-

---

[1] Hans Mayer, *Wendezeiten. Über Deutsche und Deutschland* (Frankfurt am Main: Suhrkamp, 1993).

steller gewesen. Damit habe man allerdings kein Ruhmesblatt auf-
geschlagen. Dies sei eine "Geschichte in Widersprüchen, die von
Mut und Feigheit handelt, von Soldschreiberei für eine unwürdige
Macht, von Raubbau am eigenen Talent, vom Schaden an Körper
und Geist" (S. 53). Dennoch: Es war der östliche Teil Deutschlands,
der die verjagten Emigranten zur Rückkehr aufforderte, der ihnen
hohe Anerkennung bis hin zur Bekleidung einflußreicher Staats-
ämter zuteil werden ließ. Der heutige Versuch, die Schriftsteller der
DDR als Staatsschriftsteller zu disqualifizieren, sei absurd, denn
Autoren wie Christa Wolf, Heiner Müller oder Volker Braun hätten
ein Schreiben demonstriert, bei dem es um Kopf und Kragen
gegangen sei. Dieses existentielle Risiko fehlte in der westdeutschen
Literatur.

Mit der DDR verband sich für Hans Mayer die Hoffnung auf
eine deutsche Alternative als Konsequenz aus dem Versagen des
Bürgertums vor dem Faschismus. Von einer Schuld der Intellektuellen, genauer gesagt, der bedeutenden Repräsentanten der Literatur, an den Verhältnissen in der DDR mag Mayer deshalb nicht
sprechen. Im Gegenteil ehrte es die Schriftsteller, das Experiment
DDR mit zu unterstützen, bis sie am eigenen Leibe erkennen
mußten, daß dieses Experiment mißlungen war. Daß der "Staat der
Schriftsteller" auch Staatsschriftsteller hervorbrachte, will Mayer für
die herausragenden Autoren von Brecht bis Müller nicht gelten
lassen, da sie dem Staat gegenüber stets kritisch eingestellt waren
und von diesem nicht selten als Staatsfeinde behandelt wurden.
Wenn in der DDR der Versuch, Geist und Macht zu versöhnen,
schließlich scheiterte, so ist dies für Mayer ein Beweis für das
Fortdauern der deutschen Misere, des Leidens an Deutschland und
des unglücklichen Bewußtseins seiner Intellektuellen.

Mayer sieht in dem "permanenten Selbstekel vor dem eigenen
Volk und seinen Verhaltensformen" (S. 277) ein Spezifikum der
deutschen Schriftsteller, das sich geschichtlich auf die Problematik
des nationalen Einigungsprozesses im 19. Jahrhundert zurückführen
lasse. Durch die Nationalstaatsbildung und die damit verbundene
gewaltsame Zentralisierung sei vieles an landschaftlichen und
stammesmäßigen Besonderheiten verlorengegangen. Das gesamt-
deutsche Amalgam habe schlechte Eigenschaften aus ihnen allen
hervorgetrieben. Überträgt man diesen Befund auf die sich gegenwärtig vollziehende Vereinigung, würde dies heißen, daß die Ent-
fremdung von Geist und Macht, von Literatur und Politik sich
weiter vertiefen müßte.

Mayers Interpretation kann leicht dazu verführen, die Realitäts-
blindheit deutscher Schriftsteller in eine politische Tugend umzu-

münzen. Die Staats- und Parteinähe von Autoren wie z.B. Hermlin, Wolf und Braun war an die Prämisse geknüpft, daß die DDR das bessere Deutschland sei. So gesehen war die Parteidiktatur eine Art Protosozialismus, unter dessen Panzer sich "die Gestalt einer freien, humanen, sozialen Gesellschaft"[2] ahnen ließ. Daß dies ein Irrtum war, verrät den Wirklichkeitsverlust der Schriftsteller, der mit der fehlenden Distanz zur politischen Macht zusammenhängt. Der Staat der Schriftsteller, wie ihn Mayer heraufbeschwört, ist ohne das sacrificium intellectus nicht denkbar.

Es gibt inzwischen Anzeichen dafür, daß nicht wenige der ostdeutschen Autoren durchaus um eine genauere Beschreibung ihrer Verstrickung mit dem DDR-Staat und ihrer Situation nach der Wende bemüht sind, als dies Mayer mit seinem historisch weitgespannten Blick auf die deutsche Literatur zu leisten imstande ist. Mit den Formeln "Leiden an Deutschland" und "unglückliches Bewußtsein," gebraucht man sie affirmativ, ist für die Analyse des Zusammenbruchs der DDR und der Mentalität ihrer Schriftsteller nur wenig gewonnen. Sie sind eher geeignet, Ressentiments und liebgewordene Klischees vom ewigen deutschen Zwiespalt zwischen Geist und Macht, von Literatur und Politik zu bestärken. Die von Hans Mayer ins Spiel gebrachten Topoi behalten jedoch ihre Bedeutung, verwendet man sie als kritisches Frageraster, mit dem sich ein wichtiger Aspekt im Selbstverständnis der Autoren in der ehemaligen DDR ermitteln und deuten läßt.

Christa Wolf greift Mayers Formel vom "unglücklichen Bewußtsein" auf, da sie die eigene persönliche Problematik treffend charakterisiere.[3] Wie der bürgerliche Schriftsteller des 19. Jahrhunderts, der an der Nichteinlösung politischer Emanzipationshoffnungen litt, fühle sich nun auch der Schriftsteller in der DDR um seine Hoffnungen betrogen (S. 341). Christa Wolf spricht von einem Verlierergefühl, das sie schon seit 1965, den Tagen des 11. ZK-Plenums,[4] kenne. Dennoch flüchtet sie sich nicht in die Attitüde der selbstgerecht Leidenden, sondern stellt sich und ihren Kollegen die Frage,

> ob wir nicht in Zukunft jene Strömung innerhalb der europäischen Aufklärung, die nicht zu Ideologie, womöglich wieder zu "Heilserwartung"

---

[2] Christa Wolf, "Über Hans Mayer," in Mayer, *Wendezeiten*, S. 341.

[3] Ebenda, S. 337

[4] Auf dem 11. Plenum erfolgte eine Generalabrechnung der SED mit kritischen Künstlern. Vgl. *Kahlschlag. Das 11. Plenum des ZK der SED 1965. Studien und Dokumente*, hrsg. v. Günter Agde (Berlin: Aufbau, 1991).

führt, sondern zu praktischer Vernunft, wahrzunehmen und, selbst in ihren keimhaften, nicht "mehrheitsfähigen" Formen, nach Kräften zu unterstützen haben. (S. 340)

Wolf zitiert den Satz Mayers, daß Identität nur durch Bindung möglich sei. Allerdings dürfe Bindung, so fährt sie fort, nicht zu Abhängigkeit entarten. Sie könne, ja müsse sogar von Fall zu Fall wieder gelöst werden (S. 343).

In einem im Februar 1993 geführten Gespräch mit Günter Gaus wird dieser Gedanke von Christa Wolf wieder aufgenommen. Nicht die Verbundenheit mit dem Leben in der DDR, nicht die dadurch entstandene Identität sei preiszugeben, aber die Bindung an eine Ideologie, eine Heilserwartung, als welche sich die sozialistische Idee darstelle. Auf die Frage von Gaus: "Denken Sie, es wird irgendwann wieder auf etwas wie eine sozialistische Idee hinauslaufen?", antwortet Christa Wolf, wenn sich etwas ändern werde, so werde es wahrscheinlich nicht wieder von einer Idee oder Ideologie ausgehen, sondern nur von unten kommen, von den Menschen, die Ungenügen an den Verhältnissen empfinden.[5] Hier deutet sich eine Tendenz zum politischen Pragmatismus, zu einer Politik kleiner Schritte an, eine Korrektur auch jener von Mayer affirmativ gebrauchten Formel vom "Leiden an Deutschland."

Was bedeutet die Loslösung von der Heilserwartung für die zukünftige Rolle des Schriftstellers im neuen Deutschland? Die Neubestimmung ihrer Rolle ist für die Autoren aus der ehemaligen DDR untrennbar verbunden mit einem Nachdenken über ihr früheres Verhältnis zu diesem Staat, ein Nachdenken, das wiederum nicht zu trennen ist von der Frage nach dem alltäglichen Leben in der DDR und dem Anteil der Intellektuellen an der Legitimation der SED-Diktatur. Allein, der Gebrauch des Wortes Diktatur wird von vielen DDR-Autoren als Zumutung und persönliche Abwertung empfunden. Der geistige Selbstbetrug vieler Intellektueller, die DDR sei im Vergleich zur Bundesrepublik eine historische Epoche weiter gewesen, tritt in dieser Reaktion deutlich zutage. Es ist allerdings ein Unterschied, ob die vielzitierte DDR-Identität eine Identität mit den Menschen in diesem Land oder eine Übereinstimmung mit dem Staatswesen meint. Am Beispiel Christa Wolfs sei dies näher erläutert.

In ihrer Laudatio für den Wissenschaftler und Erzähler Paul Parin rühmt Christa Wolf diesen als ein Beispiel für jene frei von

---

[5] "Auf mir bestehen. Christa Wolf im Gespräch mit Günter Gaus," *neue deutsche literatur*, 41, Nr. 5 (1993), S. 39.

Ideologie Handelnden, die sich bemühen "'Inseln von Vernunft in einer irrsinnig selbstgefährdeten Welt'"[6] zu schaffen. Parin gehöre weder zu den postmodernen Überläufern, noch zu jenen,

> die Eingebundensein, Heimatgefühl, die "Gewißheit, auf der richtigen Seite zu kämpfen und endlich der Gerechtigkeit zum Siege zu verhelfen", dringlich brauchten und in einer streng disziplinierten, hierarchisch aufgebauten und durch beinahe religiöse Gefühle zusammen gehaltenen Organisation fanden. (S. 177)

Christa Wolf hat diese Art der Bindung, der Identität, lange Zeit selbst erlebt und eigentlich erst in der Zeit des Umbruchs 1989 überwinden können.

In ihren Aufsätzen und Reden, die nach dem Zusammenbruch der DDR entstanden sind, wendet sich Christa Wolf immer wieder gegen Versuche, die reale Geschichte der Menschen in der DDR "in einem dunklen Loch des Vergessens verschwinden zu lassen."[7] Anfang 1990 erklärte Christa Wolf es zur Aufgabe des Schriftstellers, "die blinden Flecken in unserer Vergangenheit" zu erkunden und "die Menschen in den neuen Verhältnissen [zu] begleiten."[8] Sie befürchtete, daß in dem geistigen Vakuum, das durch Desorientierung entstehe, eine Dämonisierung der DDR um sich greife. Dagegen müßten die Menschen in Ostdeutschland – und das gelte vor allem für die Schriftsteller – "auf Konkretheit bestehen und aufpassen, daß uns nicht das Leben genommen wird, das wir wirklich geführt haben, und uns statt dessen ein verzerrtes Phantom untergeschoben wird."[9]

Gleichzeitig wird sie jedoch von ihrer eigenen Geschichte – der Verstrickung der jungen Schriftstellerin mit der Staatssicherheit – eingeholt, einem Kapitel, das sie aus ihrem Gedächtnis verdrängt hatte. Das Gefühl des Verlusts betrifft folglich nicht nur die verlorene Hoffnung auf eine andere Art zu leben, es betrifft auch die

---

[6] Christa Wolf, "Auf dem Weg nach Tabou – Versuch über Paul Parin," in dies., *Auf dem Weg nach Tabou* (Köln: Kiepenheuer und Witsch, 1994), S. 184. Erschien zuerst als "Ein Weg nach Tabou. 'Laudatio' auf den Wissenschaftler und Erzähler Paul Parin" in der *Frankfurter Rundschau*, 9.5.1992.
[7] Christa Wolf, "Ein Ort. Nicht irgendwo," *Berliner Zeitung*, 1.10.1991.
[8] Christa Wolf, "Zwischenbilanz. Rede anläßlich der Verleihung der Ehrendoktorwürde der Universität Hildesheim am 31. Januar 1990," *Die andere Zeitung*, 15.2.1990. Der Text wurde mit dem Titel "Zwischenrede" in *Auf dem Weg nach Tabou* (S. 17-22, Zitat: S. 21) nachgedruckt.
[9] Wolf, "Über Hans Mayer," S. 342.

Erschütterung des Selbstbildes, der Identität der DDR-Schriftstellerin Christa Wolf. Im Hinblick auf ihre Anfänge als loyale Parteikommunistin spricht sie von einem Gefühl der Fremdheit sich selbst gegenüber. Beim Lesen ihrer Stasi-Akte stellt sie fest: "Ein fremder Mensch tritt mir da gegenüber. Das bin nicht ich. Und das muß man erst mal verarbeiten."[10] Sie sei frei von Schuldgefühlen, sie seien weggeschmolzen, sie bemühe sich jetzt um die tieferen Einsichten (S. 33). Dafür brauche sie Zeit, und wir dürfen vermuten, daß sich im Verlauf dieses Nachdenkens auch ihr Selbstverständnis als Schriftstellerin verändern wird.

Günter Kunert fragt, ob das unglückliche Bewußtsein, dem eine entzweigebrochene Wirklichkeit entspreche, nicht auch Folge einer ideologischen Trübung, einer Wirklichkeitsblindheit so mancher Schriftsteller in der DDR sei.[11] Als Beleg für Kunerts These sei Werner Heiduczeks Situationsbeschreibung zitiert. Heiduczek sieht die Literatur der DDR im Rückblick zwischen Schamanentum und plattem Journalismus angesiedelt. Der Erwartungsdruck vieler Menschen habe die Autoren in die Ecke des Schamanen gedrängt:

> Ich habe in Kirchen meine Texte von der Kanzel her gelesen oder vom Altar aus. . . . Eben dieses Schamanentum führt unmerklich zu einem Verlust an Realität. Selbst integre Autoren lebten ihr Leben mehr und mehr auf einer solchen Kanzel und schauten von dort herab auf den elenden Zustand der vielen, die nicht im Licht standen.[12]

Die andere Gefahr für das Schreiben sei aus der Misere der Medien erwachsen. Romane, Erzählungen, Theaterstücke dienten vielfach als Medienersatz (S. 170).

Günter Kunert, der 1979 von der DDR in die Bundesrepublik wechselte, betrachtet den zwischen Ostautoren und Westkritikern ausgebrochenen Literaturstreit mit der ihm eigenen Distanz. Es sei dies die erste offene Auseinandersetzung zwischen Intellektuellen aus zwei Systemen, die das sie Trennende ständig überspielten. Kunert sieht die DDR-Schriftsteller weder als Opfer noch als Täter, weder als "Mitläufer" noch als Schmarotzer an. Sie waren dem System ausgeliefert, dem sie sich auf Schwejksche Weise zu entziehen suchten. Jedoch:

---

[10] Wolf, "Auf mir bestehen," S. 33.

[11] Günter Kunert, "Weltfremd und blind. Zum Streit um die Literatur der DDR," *Frankfurter Allgemeine Zeitung*, 30.6.1990.

[12] Werner Heiduczek, "Deutschland – kein Wintermärchen oder Draußen vor der Tür," *neue deutsche literatur*, 41, Nr. 4 (1993), S. 170.

Wo in einem bestimmten Binnenklima, bei einem allgemeinen Konsens, der notwendig ist, den Alltag zu bewältigen, der Grad von Selbstreflexion um des eigenen Lebens willen sich automatisch verringert, wird die künstlerische Selbstbeschränkung nicht mehr wahrgenommen.[13]

Ohne die unerschütterliche Überzeugung von der Wichtigkeit der eigenen Rolle sei ein Leben als Schriftsteller in der DDR nicht möglich gewesen. Daß diese erhöhte Bedeutung und ein dementsprechendes Selbstwertgefühl nunmehr schwinden, verursache Leiden. Das "Leiden an Deutschland" entschlüsselt sich hier als persönliches Gekränktsein infolge des Verlusts des vormals innegehabten gesellschaftlichen Status.

Für Kunert zeigt sich in dieser Haltung ein fragwürdiges Verständnis von der Rolle der Literatur. Der Behauptung, man könne ohne Utopie nicht schreiben, sei die Frage entgegenzuhalten, wie denn wohl Kafka, Proust und Joyce zu ihren Werken gekommen sind. "Ob Sozialismus, welcher Art, irgendwann und irgendwo wiederkehrt, kann einen Schriftsteller kaum kümmern. Für ihn gilt nur, seine Obsession optimal in Literatur umzusetzen."[14] Alles andere sei Selbstbetrug. Kunert übersieht hier freilich, daß Schriftsteller wie Müller, Wolf und Braun in ihrem Schreiben durchaus ihren Obsessionen folgten. Ein wesentlicher Impuls ihres Schreibens war die Vorstellung von einem anderen Sozialismus, ein geschichtsphilosophisch-utopisch geleitetes Schreibmotiv, von dem sich Kunert bereits zu Beginn der 60er Jahre zu verabschieden begonnen hatte.

In einem anderen Zusammenhang wird das Thema des Bedeutungsverlusts der ostdeutschen Schriftsteller von Kunert wieder aufgenommen. "Es geht um die Rolle des Schriftstellers . . . am Ende der Schriftlichkeit in einer umfassend technifizierten Zivilisation."[15] Mit anderen Worten: um den Sturz des Schriftstellers von seinem Sockel. Durch den Kalten Krieg hätten die Systeme ihre "Dichter und Denker" noch einmal aufs Podest gehoben, "um sich durch sie zu legitimieren und die höheren geistigen Weihen verleihen zu lassen."[16] Was Hans Mayer an der Bundesrepublik vermißt, an

---

[13] Kunert, "Weltfremd und blind."

[14] Ebenda.

[15] Günter Kunert, "Der Sturz vom Sockel. Zum Streit der deutschen Autoren," *Frankfurter Allgemeine Zeitung*, 3.9.1990.

[16] Ebenda.

der DDR jedoch schätzt, nämlich, daß letztere ein Staat der Schriftsteller – wenigstens in ihren Anfängen – gewesen sei, wird von
Kunert völlig anders gesehen und bewertet. Die Publizität, die
Schriftstellern im Westen zuteil wurde, ihr Beachtetwerden von der
politischen Macht noch in ihrer Abqualifizierung als "Pinscher," dies
alles seien Indizien dafür, daß Schriftsteller auch im öffentlichen
Leben der Bundesrepublik eine wichtige Rolle gespielt haben.

In größerem Maße treffe dies freilich auf die literarische Intelligenz in der DDR zu, die sich als "Fürstenerzieher" verstand. Die
Folge war ein Realitätsverlust, vollends sichtbar geworden in jenem
Aufruf "Für unser Land" vom November 1989, in dem die Autoren
für einen neuen sozialistischen Anfang plädierten. "Wie um Gottes
willen sollte eine gedemütigte und mental ruinierte Bevölkerung am
Rande der ökologischen und ökonomischen Katastrophe zu realisie-
ren suchen, was selbst unter den besten materiellen Bedingungen
unmöglich ist,"[17] fragt Kunert, um selbstkritisch – seine Bestands-
aufnahme beendend – fortzufahren: "Haben wir, haben die Schriftsteller ihre wahre Verantwortung verkannt, weil sie auf dem ihnen
fremden Felde der Politik agierten und auch agitierten?" Die über-
mäßige Politisierung der Literatur in der DDR und partiell auch in
der Bundesrepublik sei zu Lasten der Menschen- und Welterfahrung
der Schriftsteller gegangen. Mit dem Ende des Kalten Krieges, der
Teilung Europas und der Spaltung Deutschlands sei der Bedarf an
politischer Aktivität von Schriftstellern unvermittelt erloschen. So
sei der Sockel, auf dem sie bisher standen, praktisch über Nacht
zerbröckelt. Von jetzt an sei Literatur nichts anderes mehr als
Literatur und die deutschen Schriftsteller hätten nun denselben
Status wie andere westeuropäische Schriftsteller. Das Tröstliche an
dieser Entwicklung sieht Kunert darin, daß nun so etwas wie
Normalität im Verhältnis von Literatur und Politik in Deutschland
einkehren könne.

Kunert verkennt, daß eine Zurücknahme der Überpolitisierung
nicht bedeuten muß, daß Schriftsteller in Zukunft ihre Rolle als
Intellektuelle nicht mehr wahrnehmen werden. Der Kalte Krieg ist
zwar zu Ende, doch von einem Ende der Spaltung Europas, ja selbst
der Spaltung Deutschlands kann in sozialer, kultureller und mentaler
Hinsicht kaum die Rede sein. Daß der Sockelsturz der Schriftsteller
in Ost- und Westdeutschland, wie ihn Kunert konstatiert, politische
Abstinenz zur Folge haben werde, muß deshalb bezweifelt werden.
Mit der Diskreditierung sozialistischer Alternativkonzepte ist freilich
den linksintellektuellen Autoren der gesellschaftsutopische Impetus

---

[17] Ebenda.

verlorengegangen. Das schließt jedoch nicht aus – und Kunert selbst ist ein Beispiel dafür –, daß Schriftsteller sich auch in Zukunft engagiert zu Fragen der Zeit äußern. Der völlige Rückzug in den Elfenbeinturm wird vermutlich nur wenigen gelingen. Die neue Rolle, in die sich viele DDR-Autoren hineinfinden müssen, hängt mit der bereits angesprochenen Frage nach der Identität zusammen. Günter Kunert bezweifelt, daß sich vor 1989 außer den Funktionären jemand zu einer DDR-Identität bekannt habe.[18] Erst als dieser Staat verschwand, habe das Verlustgefühl bei einigen zu einer posthumen DDR-Identität geführt. Kunert hält diese für etwas Vorgeschütztes, hinter dem sich statt Selbstbewußtsein Lamento und Larmoyanz verbergen. Zweifellos gebe es neben der individuellen auch eine Identität in der Gruppe, doch wenn die Gruppe, hier verstanden als der Staat, das Individuum überwältige, könne der Prozeß der Individuation nicht gelingen. Es entstehe eine von der Gruppenidentität abhängige Person. Das Einbekenntnis einer persönlichen "DDR-Identität" verweise auf eine Abhängigkeit von diffusen Gefühlen, die sich bisher nicht in Worte fassen ließen. Kunert meint, "würde man den ehemaligen Unrechtsstaat hundertprozentig verdammen, wäre es auch mit der 'DDR-Identität' vorbei, die der Ressentiments bedarf, um existieren zu können."[19]

Was Kunert hier thematisiert, hat Christa Wolf des öfteren vor und nach der Wende selbstkritisch ausgesprochen. In ihrer Dankrede für den Geschwister-Scholl-Preis im November 1987 nannte sie den Zwang zur Ein- und Unterordnung, die Übereinstimmungssucht, die Angst vor dem Ausgeschlossenwerden aus der Gruppe als ein für viele Angehörige ihrer Generation kennzeichnendes, von frühen Prägungen herrührendes Verhalten.[20] Im Gespräch mit der Literaturwissenschaftlerin Therese Hörnigk ist Sommer/Herbst 1988 die Rede davon, daß die eigene Ablösung von ideologischen Fixierungen und intensiven Bindungen an festgelegte Strukturen noch kaum gelungen sei.[21]

Betrachtet man Christa Wolfs Reden und Aufsätze nach der Wende, so wird die Frage nach der Gruppenidentität, der Identität mit der DDR, von ihr immer wieder gestellt. Es ist dies zum einen die Frage nach dem wirklich geführten Leben und dessen nach-

---

[18] Günter Kunert, "Homunculus kehrt zurück. Das Rätsel der DDR-Identität," *Frankfurter Allgemeine Zeitung*, 11.12.1991.

[19] Ebenda.

[20] Christa Wolf, "Dankrede für den Geschwister-Scholl-Preis," in dies., *Ansprachen* (Darmstadt: Luchterhand, 1988), S. 71-81.

[21] Therese Hörnigk, *Christa Wolf* (Göttingen: Steidl, 1989), S. 9.

träglicher Bewertung und der Ausprägung und dem Ausmaß dieser Identität. Christa Wolf begreift sie als eine Identität derjenigen, die sich in diesem Staat selbst behauptet und gewehrt haben. Das heißt jedoch nicht, daß sie sich als eine Widerstandskämpferin verstanden wissen will. Vielmehr ist beides zu sehen: die loyale "Staatsdichterin," die die DDR als das bessere Deutschland verteidigt, und die von der Partei beargwöhnte, von der Staatssicherheit bespitzelte kritische Schriftstellerin, deren Identität sich von einem Freundeskreis gleichgesinnter, reformsozialistisch eingestellter Künstler und Intellektueller herleitet. Im Falle Christa Wolfs mögen beide Ebenen eine Rolle gespielt haben. Der Verlust der DDR als auch des vertrauten Lebenszusammenhangs, der damit verbundenen Hoffnungen und Erwartungen, hinterläßt ein Vakuum, das nicht durch eine forsche Distanzierung von der DDR, sondern nur durch mühselige Erinnerungsarbeit und Selbsterforschung überwunden werden kann. Das heißt, "daß man eine Identität ja nur weiterentwickeln und eine neue erwerben kann, wenn man die alte nicht einfach wegwirft."[22]

Nach der Wende hat sich auch der Dramatiker Heiner Müller wiederholt zur Lage der Nation und zur Befindlichkeit der Intellektuellen geäußert. Anders als die meisten reformerisch eingestellten DDR-Schriftsteller bestreitet er, daß er der Illusion der "Fürstenerziehung" jemals verhaftet gewesen sei.[23] Im Unterschied zu Christa Wolf sieht er auch nicht die Aufgabe des Schriftstellers darin, als Sprecher für die Interessen der breiten Bevölkerung zu wirken. Vielmehr ist sein Verhältnis zum "Volk" wie das seines Lehrers Brecht durch ein tiefes Mißtrauen geprägt. Aufgewachsen in der NS-Diktatur und hineingewachsen in den SED-Staat, den er als eine Gegendiktatur anerkannte, geht es ihm als Dramatiker darum, diese Erfahrung als Material auszuwerten. "Gerade diese schwarze Folie der Diktatur und dieses gebrochene oder ambivalente Verhältnis zum Staat war für mich ein Movens, also eine Inspiration zum Schreiben."[24] Daß die DDR-Bevölkerung in einem Status von Kolonisierten lebte, habe ihn, so sagt er heute, nicht gestört. In Abgrenzung zu anderen Autoren begründet Müller seine Haltung mit einer strikten Trennung von Kunst und Moral. Indem er den Materialwert der Diktatur betont, riskiert er es jedoch, die Grenzen zwischen der Rolle des Künstlers und der des Intellektuellen zu

---

[22] Wolf, "Auf mir bestehen," S. 38.
[23] "'Jetzt ist da eine Einheitssoße'. Der Dramatiker Heiner Müller über die Intellektuellen und den Untergang der DDR," *Der Spiegel*, Nr. 31, 30.7.1990, S. 137.
[24] Ebenda, S. 138.

verwischen. Im Spannungsfeld zwischen den divergierenden Rollen zieht sich Müller stets dann auf sein Künstlertum zurück, wenn ihn sein antidemokratischer Affekt als Intellektuellen zu kompromittieren droht. Einzig interessiert an der Tragödie des Sozialismus, kann Müller der deutschen Vereinigung, der Etablierung bürgerlich-demokratischer Verhältnisse in Ostdeutschland wenig abgewinnen. Aus der Sicht des marxistischen Intellektuellen Müller hat die Demokratie in der Bundesrepublik keine Wurzeln. Freilich trägt Müller seine Demokratieverachtung auch als Maske, die es ihm erlaubt, das gesellschaftliche Geschehen aus der Perspektive des scheinbar Unbeteiligten zu betrachten. Unter den namhaften ostdeutschen Schriftstellern stellt dieser Autor zweifellos einen Sonderfall dar.

Schließlich sei noch Christoph Hein erwähnt, der Kunerts Prognose des Rückzugs des Schriftstellers aus der Politik zu bestätigen scheint. Schon unmittelbar nach der Wende konstatierte Hein eine Entlastung der Literatur von der Politik, da sich nun die Zeitungen damit befaßten. Kunst werde wieder auf ihre eigentliche Aufgabe zurückgeführt. "Es ist für die Literatur völlig unwichtig, Neuigkeiten zu reportieren. Literatur ist, wenn Proust mitteilt, wie er Tee trinkt."[25] In einem Gespräch mit Günter Grass hat Hein seine Neigung, sich in den Elfenbeinturm zurückzuziehen, unterstrichen. Während Grass den absoluten Rückzug des Schriftstellers aus der Politik angesichts der deutschen Vergangenheit für unverantwortlich hält, ist das Opfer der Überpolitisierung, als das sich Hein empfindet, entschlossen, sich dem "Dauergeräusch von Öffentlichkeit" zu entziehen.[26] Hier prallen zwei Schreibpositionen aufeinander. Zwischen beiden Polen – so ist zu vermuten – wird in Zukunft der Meinungsstreit über die Rolle des Schriftstellers im vereinigten Deutschland ausgetragen werden.

[25] Christoph Hein, "Weder das Verbot noch die Genehmigung als Geschenk. Gespräch mit der 'Berliner Zeitung', 4./5. Nov. 1989," in ders., *Die fünfte Grundrechenart. Aufsätze und Reden* (Frankfurt am Main: Luchterhand, 1990), S. 193.
[26] "Es gibt sie längst, die neue Mauer! Ein ZEIT-Gespräch mit Günter Grass und Christoph Hein," *Die Zeit*, 7.2.1992, S. 21.

In the Shadow of the Rainbow:
On Christoph Hein's *Exekution eines Kalbes* and Christa Wolf's *Auf dem Weg nach Tabou*

Christiane Zehl Romero

This essay takes its title from Helga Königsdorf's novel *Im Schatten des Regenbogens* (1993). To date, the book is the last in a rapid succession of publications – fictions, letters, protocols, essays, and speeches – through which Königsdorf, an author who was highly respected in the East and West during GDR times, has tried to record and come to terms with the changes taking place around her since the fall of 1989. Her attempts, particularly the fictional *Gleich neben Afrika* (1992) and *Im Schatten des Regenbogens*,[1] strike even the sympathetic reader as more and more desperate and unsuccessful – perceptive insights, brilliant flashes of grotesque humor, and suggestive titles notwithstanding. Neither work has found much resonance, something my allusion to *Im Schatten des Regenbogens* cannot and does not intend to change. Rather, the metaphor of Königsdorf's title, and her name, shall serve to suggest the general issue which interests me, namely the difficulties being encountered by once well-established, (more or less) critical GDR authors – they have also been called "kritisch-loyal"[2] – who are trying to continue writing after German unification and to contribute creditably to a literary landscape which has changed considerably.

---

[1] Both novels were published by Aufbau-Verlag, Berlin.

[2] Horst Domdey, "Die DDR als Droge. Wie kritisch war DDR-Literatur?" *Deutschland Archiv*, 26, No. 2 (1993), p. 169.

Much has been written on these changes. To recall and summarize them briefly, I would group them into three large, interrelated categories: first, in the West, and to a certain degree in the East as well, attitudes toward such writers switched from the so-called "GDR bonus," which more or less guaranteed interest and benevolent reception, to a "GDR penalty," which on the part of its most severe proponents denied literary merit to all works of writers who had remained and been recognized in the GDR. The "Literaturstreit" of 1990-91, which centered on the publication of Christa Wolf's short novel *Was bleibt*, and the ancillary debates made this amply clear.[3]

Secondly and ironically, these heated controversies, which, ostensibly at least, focused on literature, marked the end of the anachronistically inflated and perhaps altogether unique importance granted literature in the East and, by extension but to a lesser degree, in the West as well. Not only did literature have to serve as a substitute for the public or scientific discourse on everyday life and social issues in the GDR which the media and the social sciences did not provide, it also played a significant and complex role in the competition between East and West. "As in the early nineteenth century, literature was the terrain where national unification could be played out or fought over, and judgement on literature, be it the academic judgement in the university or the critical judgement in the press, became a matter of national concern," is the bird's eye view of the American critic Russell Berman.[4]

From this perspective it is not surprising that the "Literatur-

---

[3] For an overview including some of the most important voices in the debate see: *Der deutsch-deutsche Literaturstreit oder Freunde, es spricht sich schlecht mit gebundener Zunge*, ed. Karl Deiritz and Hannes Krauss (Darmstadt/Neuwied: Luchterhand, 1991). See also the *GDR Bulletin* issue on *Was bleibt*, 17, No. 1 (1991), pp. 1-18; William H. Rey, "'Wo habt ihr bloß alle gelebt.' Christa Wolfs Dilemma in ihrem Verhältnis zur DDR," *The Germanic Review*, 66, No. 2 (Spring 1991), pp. 89-95; Andreas Huyssen's more broadly based essay "After the Wall: The Failure of German Intellectuals," *New German Critique*, 52 (Winter 1991), pp. 109-43; and Wolfgang Emmerich, *Die andere deutsche Literatur. Aufsätze zur Literatur aus der DDR* (Opladen: Westdeutscher Verlag, 1994), esp. the "Vorrede" and the essays "Für eine andere Wahrnehmung der DDR-Literatur" and "Im Zeichen der Wiedervereinigung: die zweite Spaltung der deutschen Literatur."

[4] Russell Berman in a lecture given at the Center for European Studies at Harvard, spring 1994.

streite," which had begun as debates about the place in a united Germany – if there was to be one at all – for GDR literature and its authors,[5] culminated in the by now well-known proclamation of the end of post-war German literature, East *and* West, and of the "Gesinnungsästhetik" which supposedly had been its common characteristic. While proponents of this "end" did not dismiss literature altogether but rather called for "true" literary art in which aesthetic rather than moral and political concerns would dominate, they rejected all those authors – Heinrich Böll, Günter Grass, and Christa Wolf among them – who were the great, well-known representatives of German writing since 1945. The argument was that they fell short of the – supposedly – new aesthetic standards which were more appropriate to a united, forward-looking Germany than their moral stance with its fixation on the German past. At the same time, the call for a new start also disregarded the wide range of authors – and writing styles – that existed in addition to the more prominent practioners of a "littérature engagée" in its distinctively German post-war mode.

In effect, the "Literaturstreite" can be seen as the last gasps in that East-West competition for which literature had served as an important arena, with the West "winning" and nolens volens putting literature "in its place," i.e., the less privileged position it has been holding in the contemporary Western world. This does not mean that writers no longer write and – some – readers no longer read, but it does mean both a deflation of the importance of literature and a "relative dedifferentiation": literature is less separate and less special; other modes of artistic expression as well as other symbolic practices compete successfully for attention. In academic circles, for example, cultural studies have gained considerably in significance vis-à-vis literary studies, certainly at US universities. Germanists, particularly

---

[5] The term itself is vague; there are many GDR literatures. The debate centered on Christa Wolf and authors like her who had managed to find a modus vivendi for living, publishing, and gaining recognition in the East while at the same time earning respect as "critical" authors in the West. Writers like Hermann Kant or Erik Neutsch, who had in fact been faithful "Staatsdichter" *and* "Staatsdiener," to use Marcel Reich-Ranicki's distinction, played no role, nor did the "junge Wilde" from Prenzlauer Berg, at least not until the Stasi infiltrations into their supposedly autonomous circles were discovered. However, a number of GDR writers who had been forced to leave or had left the country before 1989 (Wolf Biermann, Monika Maron, Jürgen Fuchs, Klaus Poche, to name but a few with quite different points of view) participated in the debates in ways which suggested that they were the "true" representatives of GDR literature.

those who worked on GDR or more generally twentieth-century literature, also tend to turn to larger, more inclusive questions.[6]

In addition to what Günter de Bruyn has called their "Bedeutungsverlust,"[7] GDR writers must also face the fact that the called-for shift in aesthetic sensibilities seems indeed to be "happening" in the Germany of the mid-1990s, even if it does not appear to be very forward-looking. Its symbol and focus is the hundred-year-old Ernst Jünger, whose work spans nearly an entire century of war and violence and glorifies both as man's (i.e., the male's) true proving grounds. More generally, there is talk again among German intellectuals of a "Conservative Revolution." These changes do not exclude East Germans; Heiner Müller is an acknowledged admirer of Jünger, and Hans Castorf, also an Easterner and director of (East) Berlin's currently most successful stage, the Volksbühne, is a provocative exponent of the ascendant sensibility.[8] But it is not a welcoming climate for a tradition of writing which identifies with Anna Seghers' early, perceptive rejection of the Jüngerian fascination with "gefährliches Leben" and makes the everyday concerns of ordinary men *and* women and the need for peace its main focus. Many of the GDR's "critical writers," including many of its women writers, belong to this tradition.

In the following I will focus on two of the most important among these authors, Christoph Hein and Christa Wolf, both of whom were highly regarded in the GDR and in the West, were politically prominent and active at the time of the *Wende*, and in very different ways have dealt or had to deal with the issue of "Bedeutungsverlust" and the changed critical climate since then. They have not stopped publishing and both have come out with new books at the five-year mark since the opening of the Wall, Hein with

---

[6] See, e.g., Wolfgang Emmerich, "Heilsgeschehen und Geschichte – Nach Karl Löwith," *Sinn und Form*, 46, No. 6 (1994), pp. 894-915; Bernd Hüppauf, "Krieg, Gewalt und Moderne," and Andreas Huyssen, "Wider den negativen Nationalismus," both in *Gewalt – Faszination und Furcht. Jahrbuch für Literatur und Politik in Deutschland 1*, ed. Frauke Meyer-Gosau and Wolfgang Emmerich (Leipzig: Reclam, 1994), pp. 12-40 and pp. 172-92.

[7] "'Die Sehnsucht nach der schöneren DDR.' Günter de Bruyn über ostdeutsche Gefühle und die Rolle der PDS," SPIEGEL-Gespräch, *Der Spiegel*, No. 30, 1994, p. 39.

[8] For a brief summary in English see Denis Staunton, "Young Germans go back to Nazi basics," *The Observer*, 1 January 1995, p. 17.

Exekution eines Kalbes[9] and Wolf with *Auf dem Weg nach Tabou. Texte 1990-1994.*[10] Both works directly or indirectly respond to and reflect their authors' position, their writing "im Schatten des Regenbogens." I will contrast these very different books (from very dissimilar authors) in order to gain insight into the continued literary production – its limitations and achievements – of writers whose past work I still respect, even if I read it differently, and whose further development under changed conditions warrants critical study.

Wolf herself uses the image of the rainbow. In one of the pieces collected in *Auf dem Weg nach Tabou*, "Abschied von Phantomen. Zur Sache: Deutschland," a speech held on February 27, 1994 in the course of the so-called "Dresdner Reden," she describes her perception of Germany after returning from an extended stay in Santa Monica, California:

> Was ich sah, war ein in innere Widersprüche und Kämpfe verwickeltes Land, über dem sich, wie ein Regenbogen, erklärend die Losung DEUTSCHE EINHEIT wölbte. Die endlich "erkämpfte" oder ausgehandelte, oder wiederhergestellte, oder vollbrachte, oder herbeigeführte, jedenfalls nun vorhandene deutsche Einheit. Das höchste Gut. Von Leuten in der DDR gefordert: Wir sind ein Volk!, von den Politikern der Bundesrepublik durchgeführt, ohne die Westdeutschen zu fragen, was man heute manchmal von ihnen als Vorwurf hören kann. (pp. 327-28)

This rainbow also "casts a shadow."[11] Even if Wolf claims that her American experience, the fact that in the United States she had to answer for "die Untaten in Rostock *und* die in Mölln" (p. 327), made her see herself "als deutsche Schriftstellerin" (p. 327) (not in the sense of her own ill-conceived and ill-received identification with the past – the exiled writers of the Third Reich who found refuge around Santa Monica – but because of her hosts' present, undifferentiated concern about resurgent fascism in Germany), she clearly identifies with the East. Along with her (former) countrymen and particularly countrywomen she is living in "the shadow of the rain-

---

[9] Christoph Hein, *Exekution eines Kalbes* (Berlin/Weimar: Aufbau, 1994). All page numbers after quotations in the text refer to this edition.

[10] Christa Wolf, *Auf dem Weg nach Tabou. Texte 1990-1994* (Cologne: Kiepenheuer & Witsch, 1994).

[11] If one takes the phrase literally, one could think of the part of the landscape which is still in the shadow of rain clouds while another part is already in the sunshine.

bow" of unity.

Wolf's rainbow does connect the two parts of Germany, but the collection of speeches, essays, letters, diary entries, and prose texts which constitute *Auf dem Weg nach Tabou* reflect Wolf's own experiences of the shadows, which are presented as those of a – very special but still exemplary – Easterner. She wants to write without self-pity and without the "Larmoyanz" she and other "Ossis" have often been accused of, although many critics did not credit her with succeeding. German unification is accepted as a given; GDR nostalgia in the sense of a longing for and an embellishing of the GDR past is absent, but as a whole the book has a certain wistfulness. "Selbstbefragung und Selbstprüfung" (p. 180) are attempted by someone whose belief in herself has not only been profoundly shaken – at one point Wolf speaks of experiencing a "Totaldemontage des Selbstbewußtseins"[12] – but also by someone who is keenly aware that her time is running out. *"Kindheitsmuster* habe ich 20 Jahre nach Ende des Krieges geschrieben. So lange habe ich jetzt nicht mehr Zeit, um das, was wir erlebt haben, aufzuarbeiten,"[13] she remarks in an interview on the occasion of her sixty-fifth birthday. The earnest self-reflexivity which has always been a characteristc of Christa Wolf's writing has become more pronounced because age adds a sense of urgency to her poignant attempts at probing and proving herself anew and to her demand: "Wir müssen auf Konkretheit bestehen und aufpassen, daß uns nicht das Leben genommen wird, das wir wirklich geführt haben" (p. 28). This life after all makes up the biggest part of the time on earth she can expect to have. Under the weight of a past which must be reexamined in the light of a radically different present, memory, truth, and language, the central categories in Wolf's understanding of herself as a writer, have become ever more elusive at the same time that the search for them has become more desperate.

In contrast, Hein's stance in *Exekution eines Kalbes* is anything but self-reflective, nor can one accuse this writer of "Larmoyanz." His book, also a collection, contains stories which, we are told, stem from the years 1977 to 1990. By publishing these tales – almost all of them set in the GDR – Hein picks up where he left off

---

[12] "Ich bin eine Figur, auf die man vieles projizieren kann," *Freitag*, 18 March 1994, p. 9. Interview with Detlev Lücke and Jörg Magenau. Excerpts from the interview were reprinted under the title "'Allergie aus Unkenntnis'" in *Profil*, 28 March 1994, pp. 100-01.

[13] "Ich bin eine Figur, auf die man vieles projizieren kann," p. 10.

in *Einladung zum Lever Bourgeois*, his first collection of tales from 1980, with seemingly old-fashioned story-telling, in which he records "das, was ich gesehen habe,"[14] and asserts continuity. "Schreiben," he maintains in an interview from 1991, "hat nichts mit Moral zu tun, höchstens was mit der Genauigkeit, mit der ich einen Bericht geben kann von einer Geschichte . . . ."[15] He is intentionally calling attention to his work as literature, claiming relief that its "Ersatzfunktion" has become obsolete. Hein always regretted the importance of this function in the GDR, even when he felt that the exigencies of the political moment demanded his participation. "Schreiben" means storytelling or, for that matter, playwriting, an aesthetic endeavor, as opposed to writing for the purpose of raising issues, which is a task for the media. Since unification Hein has drawn this distinction clearly for himself by also serving as *Herausgeber* (along with Günter Gaus and others) of *Freitag. Die Ost-West-Wochenzeitung.*

While his first major return to storytelling since unification, *Das Napoleonspiel*, which with its "Psychogramm eines Zynikers"[16] represented an imaginary, but abstract and unconvincing foray into the Western milieu, was not well received by critics, *Exekution eines Kalbes* for the most part won considerable, if not unanimous praise. "Es gibt sie noch, die alte deutsche Erzählkunst!"[17] was, with variations, the resumé of a number of critics who liked to draw connections between Hein and Hebel and Kleist.

> Hein legt Meistererzählungen vor, auch im Handwerklichen. In diesen Geschichten wirkt sich zum Guten aus, daß man in der DDR die Erzählkunst nicht neu erfinden mußte. Klassisches Erzählen war ein Vorbild und Stachel, und daran wollte man sich messen. Das gibt der Prosa von Hein den im besten Sinne traditionellen Anstrich.[18]

At the same time that critics praised the traditionalist Hein, whose

---

[14] *Christoph Hein. Chronist ohne Botschaft*, ed. Klaus Hammer (Berlin/Weimar: Aufbau, 1992), p. 26.

[15] Ibid, p. 46

[16] Christine Cosentino, "'Die Gegensätze Übergänge': Ostdeutsche Autoren Anfang der neunziger Jahre," *The Germanic Review*, 69, No. 4 (1994), p. 148.

[17] Gustav Seibt, "Krach in der Mastrinderbrigade," *Frankfurter Allgemeine Zeitung*, 19 February 1994, p. 28.

[18] Beatrice von Matt-Albrecht, "Christoph Heins Erzählband *Exekution eines Kalbes*," *Neue Zürcher Zeitung*, 10 February 1994.

stories appeared to come "aus den Tiefen des 19. Jahrhunderts,"[19] some also gave him credit for developing and continuing his own personal and contemporary style. This lifted him from being a skillful epigone into the realm of art. "Das ist große Kunst," is the conclusion of a critic writing for the *Neue Zürcher Zeitung*.[20]

Some reviewers saw the GDR background in the stories as incidental, neither a drawback nor a plus, but a "Hintergrund, wie es viele andere gibt in der Literatur."[21] What counted was the "unerbittliche Genauigkeit"[22] with which it was drawn. Referring to the fact that most of the stories were written in the GDR – presumably Hein could not publish them there, but then waited longer than necessary to bring them out – a French critic also speaks of the (reader's) distance "par rapport à une situation historique bien réelle, mais révolue," which in his view adds to the charm "d'un livre que l'Histoire à émancipé, et qui vit maintenant sa propre vie."[23] Ironically, the French critic's geographic distance comes into play as well, for charm was not an attribute the Germans chose for Hein's book. Indeed, negative remarks centered on a quality which one critic called "das Edel-Dröge der altmeisterlichen Heinschen Erzählkunst."[24] Ostensibly this referred to the tone of voice, but included the subject matter, which for some German critics was "gray" and still not far enough away. Perhaps lack of distance also played a role in the difficulties reviewers had assessing the merits of individual stories; here opinions varied widely.

Christa Wolf fared much less well. In general, critics took care not to repeat the vehement attacks and polemics which *Was bleibt* had elicited. Their reserve probably reflected a certain shamefacedness at earlier excesses as well as Wolf's already diminished stature and the nature of her book, a collection of varied pieces, of which few lay claim to being poetic texts. Reception in the major newspapers and magazines was relatively low-key; praise, on the whole, scant; and harsh criticism not unusual. Two extremes are represented

---

[19] Andreas Isenschmid, "Nachrichten vom beschädigten Leben," *Die Zeit*, 18 March 1994.

[20] Matt-Albrecht, "Christoph Heins Erzählband *Exekution eines Kalbes*."

[21] Ibid.

[22] Detlev Grumbach, "Christoph Heins *Exekution eines Kalbes*," *Deutsches Allgemeines Sonntagsblatt*, 1 April 1994.

[23] Jean-Luc Tiesset, "Christoph Hein: La RDA en negatif?" *Allemagne d'aujourd'hui*, 130 (October/December 1994), p. 140.

[24] Seibt, "Krach in der Mastrinderbrigade."

by old connoisseurs of GDR literature, Konrad Franke and Marcel Reich-Ranicki. The former describes *Auf dem Weg nach Tabou* as "Ein Buch des gezielten Erinnerns" and Wolf's "Selbsterklärungen ein literarisches Denkmal deutscher Aufrichtigkeit."[25] The other speaks of "Mutter Wolfen," as he calls Wolf in ironic allusion to her repeated references to fairy tales and German children's books, e.g., *Der Struwelpeter*: "eine Volksschullehrerin aus der Provinz . . . , eine tüchtige und sendungsbewußte, die sich unentwegt bemüht, uns die Augen zu öffnen, uns zu warnen und ermahnen."[26] He calls her book "ein Buch der Klage und Anklage" (p. 194) which betrays her political "Unbelehrbarkeit" and contains pure and simple "Kitsch" (p. 197). Again, as they did with *Was bleibt*, some critics raised the question of why *this* book *now*, suggesting that Wolf should wait until she had a major new work to present. Wolf was also contrasted with Sarah Kirsch, who published *Das simple Leben*,[27] poetic texts about the everyday, which, it was implied, demonstrated much more talent than Wolf's attempts along similar lines and a much more mature, i.e., ironic and contemptuous, attitude towards the GDR, das "Ländchen," as Kirsch calls the country she had to leave in 1977.[28]

Considering the differences between Wolf and Hein in age, gender, style of writing, and the nature and critical reception of these particular books, it is striking that reviewers claim to detect a basic protestant moralism in both. Even Hein, who insists that literature has nothing to do with morals, was admonished "[sich] von der Gesinnung ab- und der Ästhetik zu[zu]wenden."[29] It appears that once the distinction between "Moral und Ästhetik" has been reintroduced into the critical discourse and is used to demarcate generational and political divides, the actual literary praxis of the pastor's son and the grocer's daughter become irrelevant.

The critics' reactions give an immediate impression of the gen-

[25] Konrad Franke, "'. . . aber graben müssen wir.' Die Selbsterklärungen Christa Wolfs," *Süddeutsche Zeitung*, 17 March 1994.

[26] Marcel Reich-Ranicki, "Tante Christa, Mutter Wolfen," *Der Spiegel*, No. 14, 1994, p. 194.

[27] Sarah Kirsch, *Das simple Leben* (Stuttgart: DVA, 1994).

[28] "Auf der Flucht vor der Geschichte" in *Die Welt* (17 March 1994) contains reviews by Ulrich Schacht (on Wolf) and Kurt Drawert (on Kirsch) under that heading. See also Iris Radisch, "Deutschdeutsches Gewese," *Die Zeit*, 18 March 1994, pp. 11-12.

[29] Isenschmid, "Nachrichten vom beschädigten Leben."

eral cultural climate and the level of acceptance accorded each writer and work at the moment. But how do the authors and the books themselves respond to the new situation? Are they attempting what Wolf in *Auf dem Weg nach Tabou* remarks to her audience after a reading: "'die Wahrheit' über diese Zeit und über unser Leben müsse wohl doch die Literatur bringen" (p. 295)? Are they in any way trying to fill what in reference to contemporary West German literature has been called "ein 'Schwarzes Loch' in der Wahrnehmung der Gegenwart,"[30] a failure of the literary imagination "unter der neuen Situation sich etwas vorzustellen, was so weder ist noch war"?[31] Do they in some way contribute to an integration of Germany?

At the height of *Wende* euphoria in the GDR, at the mass demonstration on the 4th of November 1989 at Alexanderplatz in Berlin, Christoph Hein still spoke of democracy *and* socialism as the only alternative. Shortly thereafter, however, he refused to sign the ill-fated appeals to the GDR population by intellectuals such as Christa Wolf, "Fassen Sie Vertrauen" and "Für unser Land," because he no longer saw any chance that the people of the GDR would consent to an "anti-kapitalistisches Modell."[32] He accepted unification with equanimity and claimed relief about his release from the "Ersatzfunktionen" of literature. "Von diesen Ersatzfunktionen, vor denen ich die Literatur auch immer gewarnt habe, fallen einige weg. Das ist mir ganz lieb, das kostete mich Arbeitszeit, und mußte doch gemacht werden, gar keine Frage. Es gab keine Sache, der ich mich damals entzogen habe."[33] The new rule of the market does not much concern Hein either, mostly because it does not appear that new to him: "Als Freischaffender unterlag man der Marktwirtschaft ohnehin, ein paar Schwierigkeiten sind weggefallen, ein paar Schwierigkeiten sind hinzugekommen."[34] Even the loss of readers, who now have more of a choice as to what to do with their leisure, is seen as an "Entlastung der Literatur."[35]

Hein's imperturbability regarding his place as a writer and the role of literature in the new Germany – at first glance, at least – is

---

[30] Frauke Meyer-Gosau, "'Was war das? Was haben wir gemacht? Warum sind wir nicht mehr froh?' Deutschland-Bilder in der westdeutschen Literatur nach 1989," *Gewalt – Faszination und Furcht*, p. 214.

[31] Ibid., p. 194.

[32] *Christoph Hein. Chronist ohne Botschaft*, p. 42.

[33] Ibid., p. 45.

[34] Ibid., p. 44.

[35] Ibid., p. 45.

rooted in a sense of continuity and tradition which looks to the 18th and 19th centuries and still bears the imprint of the GDR's "Erbepflege." His position is both modest and elitist in the sense that literature is not for everybody; only some will appreciate it. Unification does not change much for Hein, the author. While he sees "enorme psychische Probleme für die DDR-Bevölkerung, die Anforderungen zu bewältigen hat, die fast das Fassungsvermögen eines Individuums überschreiten,"[36] as a writer he can only profit from the tremendous transformations around him; they mean a potential "Erfahrungsgewinn." "Als Schriftsteller in diesem Land haben wir eine Chance, die es weltweit ganz selten gibt: daß man in seiner kurzen Lebenszeit zwei Leben führen kann. Die alten Themen habe ich noch; jetzt kommen noch neue dazu."[37] "Insofern ist die DDR oder dieser Teil Deutschlands schon ganz spannend,"[38] he concludes.

His is the cool stance and gaze of the chronicler: "Ich habe mich immer als Chronist verstanden, ich schreibe doch nur das auf, was ich erfahre."[39] As such he is carrying on an old tradition and expects to continue in it. He has time and has taken it with the publication of the stories in *Exekution eines Kalbes*, which no longer offer actuality and thus invite a more sophisticated literary, rather than a simplistically political or sociological, reading. On one level, this book, precisely because it contains GDR material which consciously lends itself to a refracted, post-unification reading, can be seen as a contribution toward the integration of German literature and – modestly – German conciousness, an integration based on an understanding of the place of literature and a literary praxis that affirm their roots in the great narrative traditions of a common German past. In the process, his perspective, that of a former citizen of the GDR, and his material, GDR reality, become part of that tradition.

However, this affirmation of past traditions contains an ironic edge. The stories and anecdotes of *Exekution eines Kalbes* with their multiple echoes of and references to Hebel, Kleist, and Brecht display a cultivated artificiality, a studied anachronism. This distances the material even more than the passage of time already had at the time of publication. Hein's distancing devices make clear that for

---

[36] Ibid., pp. 44f.
[37] *Christoph Hein. Texte, Daten, Bilder*, ed. Lothar Baier (Frankfurt am Main: Luchterhand, 1990), p. 39.
[38] *Christoph Hein. Chronist ohne Botschaft*, p. 44.
[39] Ibid.

him, as for Heiner Müller, although from very different perspectives, the GDR is literary material. Hein's method playfully yet purposefully blurs the boundaries between past and present. Figures and incidents are drawn with such precision and care that the reader does get a sense of "Aufarbeitung," of working through and gaining insights into GDR reality, but at the same time the texts suggest a pervasiveness of human failure and societal ills. Coldness, opportunism, betrayal of self and others, the lack of freedom to live fully thrive in, and contribute to, the ills and the fall of "really existing socialism," but we are made to recognize that they exist close to home as well.

It should be said that, although for the purposes of this paper I stress the commonalities, the texts in *Exekution eines Kalbes* vary considerably in length, structure, and style, representing narrational "études." They range from the title story, a "Novelle" about the frustrations of life on a collective farm, in which the gratuitous killing and burial of a calf in protest against the stupidities of the "plan" furnish the GDR-specific "besondere Begebenheit" characteristic of the German novella, to the wonderful, phantasmagoric tale "Ein älterer Herr, federleicht," which concludes the volume. The latter, a kind of love story between Methusalah and a young woman, which is set in the decaying no-man's-land of a contemporary, probably East German city, is one of the few tales in which Hein actually envisions transcending the limitations of time, individual character, and societal conditions which usually stifle his figures. Despite their seeming simplicity none of the stories can be summarized without serious falsification. In terms of content many can be seen as what my students call "depressing," a verdict which a number of the critics shared, but Hein's literate playfulness and mystifying ironies lighten them without trivializing his material – human beings, human aspirations and failures.

A "Gegenwelt," as Hein calls it, shines through, a refusal to let shabbiness and misery close in on the world without deftly and ironically exposing them for what they are and thus keeping alive the idea of something different. "Ohne utopisches Denken ist Denken gar nicht möglich," Hein maintained in 1991 in the face of general proclamations that the fall of Communism had completely discredited and put an end to utopian thinking. "Ich glaube, es hat etwas mit Gegenwelten zu tun. Wenn ich keine Gegenwelten mehr entwickeln kann, dann bin ich eigentlich tot."[40] These "Gegenwelten," however, do not have a concrete shape; they exist only

---

[40] *Christoph Hein. Chronist ohne Botschaft*, p. 47.

through the cool depiction of a status quo which is wanting.

In one of the tales in *Exekution eines Kalbes*, "Moses Tod," Hein speaks of this "Gegenwelt" as "Himmel" in the double and interconnected meaning the word has in German: of sky as atmosphere which, among other things, protects us from the deadly rays of the sun; and of heaven, a projection of wishes and dreams earthly life does not fulfill. He also draws a self-portrait, the chronicle-writer and his relationship to that sky/heaven. As he has done on occasion before, most notably in his play *Die Ritter der Tafelrunde* (1989), and as was increasingly common in the latter years of the GDR, Hein uses a mythological, here biblical, context to present a situation close to home. Moses, we are reminded in this short parable, died before he could lead the Israelites to the promised land. We are then offered an alternative report about why Jahwe was so angry with Moses that he not only let him die on the mountain Nebo beforehand, but even left his corpse unburied. It comes from a "Schrift, die man, nachdem die Israeliten das versprochene Land betreten hatten, öffentlich verbrennen mußte, da der Schreiber des Berichtes sich als starrköpfig und verlogen erwies und daher nicht weiter in dem hohen Amt eines Chronisten verbleiben konnte" (p. 121).

According to this document, Moses and his fourteen scouts began to have doubts about setting out for the promised land because on an exploratory trip the latter had discovered "daß sich über dem guten Land kein Himmel wölbte" (p. 122). As punishment they must all die before reaching it, except for one scout, Kaleb, who, no matter which of the two versions is proposed, suggests they put their trust in Jahwe and venture forth anyway. Each time his suggestion is followed by the narrator's comment: "Und Jahwe fand Gefallen an ihm" (p. 122). The narrator does not explain how the information survives and falls into his hands – apparently that is taken for granted – nor does he claim that the report "jenes unwürdigen Chronisten, dessen Name mit seinen Schriftrollen ausgelöscht und vergessen wurde" (p. 123) is the true story. However, in conclusion to his tale he does confirm offhand that there is no sky/heaven over the promised land, a deficiency which does not bother the Israelites: "Und es verstörte sie nicht, daß sich kein Himmel über ihrem Land wölbt. Denn keiner vermißt ihn, wo der Himmel auf Erden ist. Wie Kaleb es ihnen gesagt hatte" (p. 123).

"Jener unwürdige Chronist" – the old-fashioned word echoes Brecht's "unwürdige Greisin": is this an ironic reference to Hein's position and to censorship during GDR times or does it allude to the *Wende*-period and project into the future? From the perspective of

1995 I would argue that the tale, irrespective of when it was originally written, spans past and present, and expresses the continuity which Hein is claiming for his writing. Whether the promised land is GDR socialism or the market economy of a united Germany, he suggests, an insistence on inopportune knowledge, on doubting any promise of heaven on earth, while at the same time refusing to live without a sky/heaven above – in an ecological interpretation and in the meaning of dreams that go beyond what exists – will be unpopular. Efforts will be made to silence this chronicler, yet somehow his story will survive, next to the others, which are officially sanctioned and propagated by Kalebs. The chronicler, however, is not telling *the* truth; his version only counters and subverts whatever is commonly proposed and accepted as truth, because it records the willfully forgotten or blithely ignored information and facts which do not "fit."

With his emphasis on the subversive nature of the literary text, with his refusal to dignify the "unwürdige Chronist" by showing him to be in possession of the master narrative, Hein, despite his seeming traditionalism, connects to a contemporary, dare one say postmodern, view of literature along the lines of Michel Foucault. It was Foucault who accorded (modern) literature a special place among discourses, which as a rule were repressive and affirmed a particular order. Since its relationship to language was different and allowed room for fear, utopian visions, and playfulness, it had the potential of carrying on *a* counter-discourse[41] to the leading discourse(s).

During GDR times Hein, I would argue, saw himself as participating in the – to use Wolfgang Emmerich's words – "subversiven Artikulation von Zwängen und Sinnkrisen"[42] which engaged many of the better writers in the latter years, a project that centered on the GDR, but was not delimited by the Wall. It was part of a more comprehensive "Zivilisationskritik," which no longer really believed in socialism as the answer.[43] A united Germany, Hein seems to

---

[41] Michel Foucault, *Die Ordnung der Dinge* (Frankfurt am Main: Suhrkamp, 1971), pp. 365f.

[42] Emmerich, *Die andere deutsche Literatur. Aufsätze zur Literatur der DDR*, p. 201.

[43] For a brief and good, if one-sided, discussion of the role of "Zivilisationskritik," see Richard Herzinger, *Masken der Lebensrevolution. Vitalistische Zivilisations- und Humanismuskritik in Texten Heiner Müllers* (Munich: Wilhelm Fink Verlag, 1992), pp. 78-80.

think, will not change his basic task. He will continue to be "jener unwürdige Chronist" to those who carry on the main discourse(s) – and perhaps even to a part of himself. It will place him on the margin and expose him to the danger of being silenced and forgotten. Playfully and seriously, it seems, Hein is prepared for the worst in terms of reception. However, it also remains to be seen whether his future "chronicles," particularly if they concern the new Germany, will have the same precision and sureness of touch which characterize his past work, including *Exekution eines Kalbes*, whether the continuity of stance and perspective which Hein claims for himself will actually work for him. For the moment he has returned to the theater.[44]

Auf dem Weg nach Tabou, Christa Wolf's collection of 29 varied prose pieces, does not contain a single story. In one of her diary entries in the book, she puts her finger on this absence:

> Ich habe mir aus der Buchhandlung ein Buch mitgenommen, das gerade im Gespräch ist, habe darin geblättert, eine ganz und gar ausgedachte Geschichte, ich beneide die Autorin. Wann werde ich, oder werde ich überhaupt je noch einmal ein Buch über eine ferne erfundene Figur schreiben können; ich selbst bin die Protagonistin, es geht nicht anders, ich bin ausgesetzt, habe mich ausgesetzt. (p. 298)

Wolf lacks Hein's belief in the tale, his ironic distance, and his sense of certainty and continuity. Yet, like him, she is determined to go on writing. Her contribution will not be the tale as chronicle of the times, but the exposure of the self in crisis as chronicle.

In this project, Wolf, again like Hein, holds on to some notion of utopia. The title essay "Auf dem Weg nach Tabou – Versuch über Paul Parin" (on the occasion of his receiving the Erich Fried Prize in Vienna) contains a key passage of the book. Referring to Parin's description of a trip to Tabou on the Ivory Coast of Africa (in his travel book *Zu viele Teufel im Land*[45]), Wolf creates her own vision:

> Tabou, ein Ort, den es nicht gibt, dessen Name immer wieder aufleuchtet, lockend, verführend, bis sie sich aufmachen müssen, ihn zu suchen; ein Ort, den man, wie billig, nur unter äußerster Anstrengung aller körperlichen und geistigen Kräfte erreichen kann. Den man "verges-

---

[44] His play *Randow*, about life in the provinces of unified Germany close to the Polish border, had its world premiere in Dresden in the winter season of 1994/95.
[45] Paul Parin, *Zu viele Teufel im Land* (Hamburg: Europäische Verlagsanstalt, 1993), pp. 99-108. The first edition of the book appeared in 1985.

sen" muß, damit er einem endlich "entgegenkommt", in einem "duften-
den Windhauch". (pp. 186-87)

As so often in *Auf dem Weg nach Tabou*, somebody else's work
serves as a starting point and prop for Wolf's own reflections. This
kind of connective writing, trying to understand oneself through the
interpretation of another, has always been characteristic of Wolf's
essays and even her fictional writing, in fact blurring the lines
beween the two, but it becomes more important in this collection,
partly because of the many occasional pieces in it, mainly however
because it is Wolf's way of fighting criticism and self-doubt, which
have been massive and seriously disorienting. *Auf dem Weg nach
Tabou* has rightly been called "ein Protokoll des Suchens"[46] and as
such it draws on other writers and artists as guides. Their selection
is never only a matter of circumstance and may sometimes, as in the
case of Friederike Mayröcker, be surprising, at least at first glance.

To return to the specific case of Paul Parin, it was Wolf who
proposed him for the Fried Prize. Via this Westerner,[47] she resur-
rects the GDR topos Africa, which, along with India, had been the
symbolic locus for utopian hopes – originally clearly socialist, later
more diffuse – for dreams of escaping a gray, over-industrialized,
and oppressive (GDR) reality.[48] Significantly, Paul Parin himself
does not mention the word utopia in his travelogue. As a psychoanalyst he is interested in playing on the words and meanings of
"tabu," forbidden, untouchable, and Tabou, the mysterious, hard to
reach, and beautiful town at the edge of an almost impenetrable rain

---

[46] Thomas Wohlfahrt, "Der ungestalte Abgrund. Sprachvertrauen und Sprach-
mißtrauen im Werk von Christa Wolf," in *Christa Wolf*, Text + Kritik 46, 4th
edition (Munich: Edition Text + Kritik, 1994), p. 110.

[47] Paul Parin, who was born of a Jewish family in Slowenia in 1916, is a
psychoanalyst and writer who lives in Switzerland. Between 1955 and 1971 he
made a series of ethno-psychoanalytic research trips through West Africa.

[48] The most sophisticated treatment is Volker Braun's poem "Das innerste
Afrika," in, e.g., *Luchterhand Jahrbuch der Lyrik 1984*, ed. Christoph Buchwald
and Gregor Laschen (Darmstadt/Neuwied: Luchterhand, 1984), pp. 26-28. For
discussions see Frauke Meyer-Gosau, "'Linksherum nach Indien!' Zu einigen
Hinterlassenschaften der DDR-Literatur und den jüngsten Verteilungskämpfen der
Intelligenz," in *Literatur in der DDR. Rückblicke*, ed. Heinz Ludwig Arnold
(Munich: Text + Kritik, 1991); Irma Hanke, "Wendezeiten: Deutsche Schrift-
steller in der Übergangsgesellschaft," in *Deutschland. Eine Nation – doppelte
Geschichte*, ed. Werner Weidenfeld (Cologne: Wissenschaft und Politik, 1993),
p. 310; and Christine Cosentino, esp. pp. 147f.

forest. Only Christa Wolf makes the association:

> Und auch das gehört zu den Eigenheiten endlich erreichter Sehnsuchts-
> ziele, zu den Gesetzen von Utopia: Was der Reisende dort erfährt, ist
> eigentlich nichts ganz Besonderes, "nur" das gesteigerte Normale, das
> konzentriert Menschliche, ein "Licht", das die Zukunft, die dunkle
> Wolkenwand, die heraufzieht, von fern her "erleuchtet". (p. 187)

Utopia has become an individual "Sehnsuchtsziel" which can
indeed be attained with great effort and perseverance, but only
unexpectedly. And while Wolf uses the example of an exotic place,
she stresses its "ordinary" qualities. Utopia, it seems, is the concentration and intensification of positive elements which already exist in
everyday life. It is a trust in life and living which lights up an otherwise threatening future. This version of utopia is modest, individualized, and "domesticated" in contrast to the grand visions which had
provided the impetus and foil for the social criticism of *Kein Ort
Nirgends* and *Kassandra*. However, Christa Wolf does not give up
on what she calls "das konzentriert Menschliche," that richer, more
fulfilling, interconnected life which has always been central to her
concepts of utopia. But she now looks for moments, intimations, in
present existence. They are the end, not the basis for larger expectations. To the reader who is familiar with Parin's original description,
the transformations Wolf performs on his text are striking. Her
interpretation and careful selection of quotations leave out the inhumanity (including Parin's) and the exploitation which he records
finding in beautiful Tabou as elsewhere in Africa.

These changes show how strongly Wolf is still committed to the
concept of utopia, modest as it now is. It holds great motivational
power for her, a power she also hopes to communicate to her
readers, especially women. In an interview for *Freitag* from March
1994 Wolf says: "Das gehört zu meinem jetzigen Konzept, daß
Leute zum Selbstbewußtsein gebracht werden müssen. Frauen sind
weitgehend die Verlierer der Einheit. Es tut mir in der Seele weh,
was mit den Frauen passiert und wozu sie sich bringen lassen."[49]
On one level she thus persists in seeing herself as an author whose
work provides "help" to others, and her sympathy continues to go to
"losers," people whose human potential a given society is casting
aside. By sharing more radically than ever before her own predica-
ment, her own doubts, her own struggles for self-awareness and
self-confidence, she may assist others.

---

[49] "Ich bin eine Figur, auf die man vieles projizieren kann," p. 10.

However, Wolf's adaptation of her past role to the new circumstances represents only one tentative and shaky attempt to find a foothold in the torturous process which *Auf dem Weg nach Tabou* records. The change in social paradigm with the related negative reviews of *Was bleibt* and the – sometimes ad feminam – attacks associated with the subsequent debate, the even more unsettling discovery that she, for a short time and before she herself became a long-standing target, had been a collaborator, an IM for the Stasi, a fact which she claims to have completely forgotten – all this has shaken her so profoundly that she needs to find a stronger antidote against the permanent loss of identity which threatens. The idea of a role in the new society, however modestly conceived, can no longer be the core of her existence as a writer and individual. Just as Wolf's beginnings as a writer in a socialist state were shaped by her dialogue in essays with Anna Seghers and with the sense of "Auftrag," of mission, which had motivated her great Communist role model, she now resorts to a very different mirror, the "Schreibexistenz Friederike Mayröcker" and her "Zwang zu *schreiben bis zur Erschöpfung*" (p. 205). She identifies with Mayröcker's statement:

> *es geht um das Schreiben als Leben, es geht um die Schreibexistenz, die Seele auf dem Papier, die eigenen Verdammungen und Verteufelungen in Empfang zu nehmen, es ist eine Entscheidung auf Leben und Tod, nämlich mein Schreibzwang, diese torkelnde Pilgerschaft . . . .* (p. 207)

Wolf, whose need to belong had been so strong and whose emphasis on "Erinnerungsarbeit" had given her work so much of its distinctive tone, is deeply troubled by the attacks on her and even more so by her failures of memory and of courage. Knowing full well "daß mein Name entwertet ist" (p. 203), she makes an existential leap, committing herself to language as a faltering, stumbling pilgrimage, to (experimental) writing for its own sake, in order to overcome the loss of faith in her own words, her work, and herself. Language has helped her in the past. After her IM activity was made public, she says in "Rückäußerung," her response – in the form of an experimental, rhapsodic prose collage – to a supportive letter from Anne and Volker Braun:

> Gewiß
>   Ernstlich hab ich mich der Sprache anvertraut
> die mir die Türen sprengte
>   zu jenen Innenräumen
>   in die sie nicht vorgedrungen waren. . . . (p. 275)

However, she did not go far enough. She never did kill "den Fremden in mir" (p. 275), a kind of inner censor who was tied to what had remained of her need for and fear of authority, her complicity with the GDR state. Thus Wolf is plagued by doubts about "the truth of writing," doubts which recur as a leitmotif in a number of the texts in *Auf dem Weg nach Tabou*. She fights for

> ein winziges bißchen Mut, so daß etwas wie der Hauch eines Gedankens daran aufkommen kann, daß ich irgendwann diesem beharrlichen Selbstverdacht der Unaufrichtigkeit vielleicht doch wieder Worte abringen kann oder, frage ich mich, werde ich nie mehr die Lust und die Unverfrorenheit aufbringen, die Verzerrungen und die Verfälschungen in Kauf zu nehmen, die bei der Umwandlung von Erfahrung in geschriebene Sätze unweigerlich entstehen . . . so daß ich endgültig den Abgrund scheuen werde, als der mir der Spalt zwischen dem vorgedanklichen aufrichtigen wortlosen Wissen und dem geschriebenen Text heute erscheint . . . . (p. 203)

"Unruhe bei Selbstbefragung und Selbstzweifel" (p. 9), "Stücke, also Bruchstücke" (p. 10), this is how Wolf herself characterizes *Auf dem Weg nach Tabou* in the "Selbstanzeige" with which she introduces the volume – in ironic analogy to Anna Seghers' "Selbstanzeige" from 1931. Then the young Seghers, who had only recently joined the Communist Party, advertised and defended her first collection of stories to the new comrades who would not really appreciate them. Now the sixty-five-year-old Wolf presents herself to a world from which Communism is being erased, aware that her texts are exercises in writing under a new system which will find fault with them. Yet she insists on showing what she has done, on "exposing herself" (p. 298). The act of writing – about herself without recourse to fiction – is the only way to a post-1989 voice and identity.

The "exposure" of *Auf dem Weg nach Tabou* involves many incidental pieces, especially speeches, starting with Wolf's "Rede" at Alexanderplatz on November 4, 1989 and ending with "Abschied von Phantomen," the Dresden speech from 1994. There are exchanges of letters, e.g., with Jürgen Habermas, Efim Etkind, Günter Grass, and diary entries about her everyday life in Mecklenburg and Santa Monica. There are attempts at looking back and "setting the record straight," such as "Rummelplatz 11. Plenum 1965 – Erinnerungsbericht," which complements Wolf's other contemporaneous efforts to document her past, such as the publication of the short file on her activity as Stasi informant and, more importantly, her exchange of letters with Brigitte Reimann between 1964 and 1973.[50] Finally, as has been mentioned, reflections on other writers and artists, among them Max Frisch, Grace Paley, Parin, Mayröcker, and Nuria Quevedo.

Poetological questions are existential ones and provide the common thread throughout the book, from the reenactment of a public role in the – very different – speeches from 1989 and 1994, which serve as an outer frame, to the most private fears of speechlessness in "Befund." It has been suggested that the collection as a whole takes its aesthetic lead and justification from Friederike Mayröcker's last books, particularly *Stilleben* of 1991.[51] In her essay on Mayröcker, Wolf characterizes the Austrian avantgardist's writing practice as one that she finds so congenial "daß ich innerlich ganze Seiten lang bei der Lektüre JA JA JA vor mich hindenken muß" (p. 206):

> dieser Sprach- und Gedankenstrom, der alles mit sich führt, was ihm in den Weg kommt, Gefühle und Papierfetzen und Eindrücke und Regungen und Sinneswahrnehmungen in schier unvorstellbarer Feinheit und sprachliche Wendungen von erregender Neuheit, und Kleidungsstücke und Briefe und Redeweisen, aber auch Menschen, Landschaften, Blumen, Tiere, wirkliche und imaginierte, ein Motiv nach dem anderen wird aufgerufen, tritt auf, verschwindet, wird aber nicht fallengelassen wie die Masche in einem Strickzeug, sondern wird wieder hochgeholt . . . eine Art *Gedankenflucht*, heißt es, *vieles läßt sich nur in Analogien begreifen*, sagt sie, ein atemloses Jagen nach dem geringsten Schnipsel Wirklichkeit, zugleich ein Beschlossensein in einem Kreis, Rituale, Schreigebete, zahllose Stimmen, gerufene und ungerufene . . . .
>
> (pp. 205-06)

Wolf finds (or perhaps hopes to find) that "ein ähnlich starker, allerdings anderslaufender Strom" (p. 206) is opening up in her, although she herself probably knows better than any critic how far away *Auf dem Weg nach Tabou* with its varied pieces ultimately is from a book like *Stilleben*, artistic success being not the least among the differences. However, this is *a* path she looks to, a "road to Tabou," where "das Gelingen von Leben und Werk" may again become conceivable, in the sense in which she had envisioned it long ago in an essay on Max Frisch: "Angenommen, ein Autor

---

[50] *Brigitte Reimann/Christa Wolf. Sei gegrüßt und lebe. Eine Freundschaft in Briefen 1964-73*, ed. Angela Drescher (Berlin/Weimar: Aufbau, 1993).

[51] Heidi Gidion, "Nagelexerzitien. Beobachtungen am Textstück Nagelprobe," in *Christa Wolf*, Text + Kritik 46, pp. 114f.

macht, von früh an, das Gelingen von Leben und Werk voneinander abhängig, . . . was er am tiefsten ersehne, sei nicht das Meisterwerk (das auch, gewiß), sondern das Lebendigbleiben . . . ."[52]

There are two texts in *Auf dem Weg nach Tabou* in which Wolf actually follows Mayröcker further into experimental prose. One is "Nagelprobe" from 1991, first published in a catalogue for an exhibition of Günther Uecker, an artist in whose work nails figure prominently; the other is the "Rückäußerung" from 1993, which has already been mentioned. They constitute the most interesting and important contributions to the volume. As Heidi Gidion points out in an excellent reading of "Nagelprobe,"[53] they are linked to each other, to other pieces in the book, to Wolf's earlier work, to the work of others, and, in "Rückäußerung," to the writings of colleagues who share a similar political past. With these dialogic texts, Wolf makes her heretofore most concerted and successful efforts at finding a poetic voice in which to speak of the pain of facing her own failures and the willingness to tap that pain to get at the truth, her truth, about them.

"Nagelprobe" uses a discontinuous, associative style of writing which centers on the meanings and actual and metaphoric uses of nails. The title itself refers to a custom among drinkers, a way to show that a cup or glass has been emptied completely, a bottoms up. In listing and detailing her associations with the word – nails as fasteners and nails as instruments for piercing and inflicting pain, functions which are joined most vividly in the iconography of crucifixion – Wolf is performing her own "Nagelprobe." The short text with its obsessive – one is tempted to say masochistic – concentration on images of suffering concludes with the description of a terrifying, apocalyptic vision which reveals the identity of perpetrator and victim. Earlier books, such as *Kindheitsmuster*, *Störfall*, and *Was bleibt*, had given intimations; now, in analogy to the piercing and painful thrust of a nail, Wolf goes deeper:

> all unser Wohltun und Unschuldig-bleiben-Wollen ist ja vergeblich, die dunkle wilde Jagd ist ja, womöglich in unserer Gestalt, über dem Land, und die steile feste Burg im Hintergrund wird sie nicht abwehren, ganz im Gegenteil, da kommt sie schon über uns, mit Spießen und Stangen, und wir hören den Hetzruf, und der heiße Atem schlägt uns in den

---

[52] Christa Wolf, "Max Frisch, beim Wiederlesen," in her *Lesen und Schreiben. Neue Sammlung* (Darmstadt/Neuwied: Luchterhand, 1980), p. 202.

[53] Gidion, "Nagelexerzitien," pp. 114-28. The following discussion owes much to Gidion's more detailed analysis.

Nacken, und wenn wir uns umsehn und in ihre Gesichter blicken, er-
schrecken wir vor unserem Ebenbild, das wir nicht erkennen wollen ....
(pp. 166-68)

This vision of guilt and punishment is cloaked in an interpretation of
Lukas Cranach the Older's painting "Melancholie,"[54] and comes at
the end of "Nagelprobe" just before the final prose poem, which
refers to Ernst Bloch and represents the head of the text as nail:

> *Prinzip Hoffnung*
> Genagelt
> ans Kreuz Vergangenheit.
>
> Jede Bewegung
> treibt die Nägel
> ins Fleisch. (p. 169)

In "Nagelprobe" Wolf speaks figuratively, and in a passage like
the one quoted above uses a very general "we." In the later
"Rückäußerung," which, it should be remembered, follows the
revelations about her IM file, Wolf becomes more concrete and
direct. Through insistent questions, she carries on a fragmented
dialogue with herself, with Braun, and with quotations from herself,
Braun, Heiner Müller, and Bert Brecht. When she says "we" she
specifically means people like them and herself, intellectuals who at
some point had held to that "Prinzip Hoffnung":

> Aber
>   wie oft und wann
>   war Hoffnung Selbstbetrug
>   DIE HOFFNUNG LAG IM WEG WIE EINE FALLE
> Und warum konnten wir uns
>   so schwer aus ihr befrein
> Warum und wie lange haben wir
>   die erdichteten Fragen des lesenden Arbeiters

---

[54] Wolf's choice of Cranach's "Melancholie," with a woman as centerpiece, uses
a striking and perhaps intentional counter-image to Albrecht Dürer's "Melancolia
I," which the literary historian Wolfgang Emmerich has chosen as centerpiece of
his interpretation of the development of GDR literature. Cf. Wolfgang
Emmerich, "Status melancholicus. Zur Transformation der Utopien in vier Jahr-
zehnten," in *Die andere deutsche Literatur*, pp. 175-89. The essay is from 1991
and contains ideas that Emmerich expressed even earlier, so Wolf could easily
have been aware of his discussion.

```
dem nichtlesenden Arbeiter
            in den Mund gelegt . . . .
Da fallen dir Gesichter ein    Namen . . . .
Da ging es doch um etwas
Oder
    soll das alles nichts gewesen sein
    Selbstbetrug und Sinnestäuschung
    Paule Bauch    Rolf Meternagel         (pp. 266-67)
```

However, this "we" which shared her illusions and is still somewhat comforting must be left behind for the "I" that has to face its own actions:

```
Ich Volker hätte damals eine Wahl gehabt
                Warum hab ich mich nicht geweigert
                                        (p. 273)
    Ich nahm den eigenen Namen und verdarb ihn mir
    Ich schrieb den Bericht   (p. 274)
```

The "I" which accepts its mistakes can then provide its own explanations; it can emphasize the passing of time, the development away from "jenes andere Sprechen / in Floskeln Anschuldigungen Fertigteilen / und ich vergaß . . . / (Vergaß nicht ganz . . .)" (p. 275). No matter what explanations it finds, it also finds that they are inadequate. Still the "I" must make them; it must be prosecutor and counsel for the defense if it is to reclaim life and art:

```
Das sagt sich so    Es war mein Leben
Jetzt gilt das alles nichts   (p. 276)
```

"Rückäußerung" suggests that Wolf wants to do herself what she, elsewhere in *Auf dem Weg nach Tabou* as well, refuses to accept from others:

```
Den Prozeß
        den ich gegen mich eröffnet habe
        muß ich ohne Beistand führen
                Ausgang ungewiß
Mir schwant
        daß unrecht haben
                mir gut tun kann
        daß ich kein fremdes Urteil
                akzeptieren muß   (p. 278)
```

Auf dem Weg nach Tabou is an uneven book, the quality of the pieces, their language and interest for the reader, depending of course on who she or he may be, vary. Wolf herself speaks of it as "eine Art Chronik der letzten Jahre als innerer und äußerer Prozeß."[55] Her chronicle however, unlike Hein's, cannot contain stories about others; more than ever she concentrates on herself, performing her own "Vivesektion" in order to "stay alive" in the meaning she gave it in the essay on Max Frisch: a union of life and work, a "Gelingen von Leben und Werk." Whether she will succeed under the new conditions and how she will proceed, whether the "Prozeß," in the sense of process and trial, will continue in fictionalized form, as Wolf's first public reading[56] from her work in progress, "Medea," seems to suggest, remains to be seen.

In conclusion then, Christa Wolf and Christoph Hein with their recent works, contribute to and directly or indirectly reflect upon literature "im Schatten des Regenbogens" in very different ways, suggesting two poles in a continuum of possible ways of "coping." While Hein's sense of himself and his work as subversive witnesses to any time remains as secure under the new circumstances as it can for any German writer in the late 20th century, Christa Wolf is searching anew. Gender, I would maintain, plays a role in their different ways of writing and dealing with the changes wrought by unification, but this is a question for a much longer study. Neither author can at this point satisfy expectations for *the* book about the GDR or the *Wende*, nor do they have imaginative projections about the future in a united Germany. Both, however, insist on having their voices and their Eastern perspectives available. In their different ways the two books at hand bring aspects of the GDR past, its disappointed hopes and damaged lives, into present view so that they will not be suppressed and forgotten, thus contributing to an integration which is based on self-knowledge. Their works are thoughtful and deserve what Wolf asks for "auf dem Weg nach Tabou": "Das Höchste, was ich mir erhoffen kann, sind nachdenkliche Leser"[57] – on both sides of the former Wall.

---

[55] "Ich bin eine Figur, auf die man vieles projizieren kann," p. 9.
[56] On January 29, 1995 at the Hebbel Theatre in Berlin.
[57] "Ich bin eine Figur, auf die man vieles projizieren kann," p. 10.

Apocalypse Now?
Reading Volker Braun's *Böhmen am Meer*

Theodore Fiedler

Published in June 1992 after an unsuccessful March première at the Schiller Theater in (West) Berlin, the drama *Böhmen am Meer* is Volker Braun's first major literary work to appear since the historic events of the summer and fall of 1989 and the formal demise of the GDR a year later.[1] Characterized in a blurb opposite the title page as "ein heiteres Trauerspiel" concerned primarily with the plague of ideology in this century, Braun's play features an international cast of characters that is the stuff of geopolitical allegory. At its center stands the Czech emigré couple Pavel and Julia, whose dubious refuge on the Italian coast of the polluted Adriatic is the drama's

---

[1] Volker Braun, *Böhmen am Meer. Ein Stück* (Frankfurt am Main: Suhrkamp, 1992). All references to this text will be cited parenthetically by page number. In the meantime a significantly revised version of *Böhmen am Meer*, accompanied by a series of related short texts, has appeared in Volker Braun, *Texte in zeitlicher Folge*, 10 vols. (Halle: Mitteldeutscher Verlag, 1993), 10, pp. 61-115. All references to this version, which will be discussed later, will be cited parenthetically by volume and page number. For the record it should be noted that Braun's book-length publications during 1992 also included *Die Zickzackbrücke. Ein Abrißkalender* (Halle: Mitteldeutscher Verlag), a collection of poems and short prose spanning the years 1987-1991, and *Iphigenie in Freiheit* (Frankfurt am Main: Suhrkamp), a dramatic text dating from the same four-year period. In contrast, Braun dates his work on *Böhmen am Meer* from 1989 to 1993 (*Texte in zeitlicher Folge*, 10, p. 211).

setting. They are joined by Pavel's invited guests, the dark-skinned American industrialist Bardolph, "ein Chicano vielleicht" (p. 11), and the Russian journalist Michail, the one wracked by disease, the other by alcohol. The younger generation is represented on the one hand by the twosome Raja and Robert, she Michail's runaway daughter and at the same time possibly an allegorical representation of the GDR, he a German physics student who has rescued her from the shambles of Soviet communism. On the other hand, there is the brooding adolescent Vaclav, Pavel's social and Bardolph's biological son, and an ostensibly promiscuous young thing – "ein Flitt-chen" Braun calls her though the text does not bear out this designa-tion – who literally (and figuratively) "hangs around" on an exercise bar. Finally, there are Assia, Pavel and Julia's Arab housekeeper, an unspecified number of "dark figures" with hidden ties to Assia who haunt a majority of the play's ten *Bilder*, and a mysterious stranger of color who joins the play's final scene, presumably to be engulfed with the rest by the play's apocalyptic closure: "*Die Sturmflut tritt auf*" (p. 62).

I propose to read this decidedly anti-naturalistic play in the Brechtian tradition with reference to the three main contexts it thema-tizes explicitly or implicitly: contemporary history both in itself and in its relation to the early modern era; literary tradition; and chaos theory. Among the questions shaping my reading are: What aspects of contemporary history are represented, how are they represented and why? Is Braun in control of the gender and political stereotypes that mark his play or do they control him? Does Braun's use of literary tradition ranging from Shakespeare's *The Tempest* and *The Winter's Tale* to Franz Fühmann's novella *Böhmen am Meer*, Ingeborg Bachmann's poem "Böhmen liegt am Meer," Brecht's poem/duet "Die Liebenden" from *Mahagonny*, and Milan Kundera's novel *The Unbearable Lightness of Being* add up to something more than a superficial pastiche? Does chaos theory provide a meaningful way of making sense of the represented world of the play or is it relativized in turn as yet another ideology masquerading as scientific truth in the face of entropic cultural reality?

Let me first of all pursue some of the implications of the title of Braun's play. It has a venerable tradition that reaches from Füh-mann's *Böhmen am Meer*[2] and Bachmann's "Böhmen liegt am

---

[2] Originally published as a single volume with illustrations (Rostock: Hinstorff, 1962), Fühmann's *Böhmen am Meer* is reprinted in his *Erzählungen 1955-1975* (Rostock: Hinstorff, 1977). I am indebted to my colleague Phillip McKnight for bringing the work to my attention.

Meer"[3] back in time to Shakespeare's late play *The Winter's Tale*. Braun's reception of these two radically different German texts of the early 1960s reflects their difference. Written at the time of the construction of the Berlin Wall, Fühmann's narrative is apologetic in character and legitimizes the GDR in opposition to both precommunist Czechoslovakia and postwar West Germany as "eine menschliche Gemeinschaft" (p. 317) that readily integrates the ethnic Germans expelled from the Bohemian region of Czechoslovakia following the Second World War, one that ostensibly creates a Bohemia on the Baltic for some of these refugees in the process. In appropriating its title for his delegitimizing critique of both socialism and capitalism thirty years later, Braun implicitly unmasks and subverts the ideological character of Fühmann's transparently and superficially affirmative narrative.

Braun's use of Bachmann's far more complex text, her subtly differentiated affirmation of the act of writing *despite* the human condition and the destructive course of history, is correspondingly more difficult to delineate. Braun, it seems, would have his readers associate Pavel at more than one juncture of his play with the lyrical persona of Bachmann's poem, though there are clearly categorical differences between these two literary creations. Thus, taken out of its original context, the tenth line of Bachmann's poem – "Ich will nichts mehr für mich. Ich will zugrunde gehn" – succinctly captures Pavel's mood as he departs in silence at the end of the play's ninth *Bild* and appears as well to underlie his unresolved death as reported in the final *Bild*. And in the play's closing scene Julia says of the dead Pavel, "Er hatte nichts. Er hatte nichts. Er wollte nicht recht haben" (p. 62), words which echo at least in part the self-characterization of Bachmann's lyrical persona, in the penultimate line of the poem, as "ein Böhme, ein Vagant, der nichts hat, den nichts hält." What Braun's play as a whole necessarily negates however is the critically affirmative utopian thrust of the final line of "Böhmen liegt am Meer": "begabt nur noch, vom Meer, das strittig ist, Land meiner Wahl zu sehen." Apocalypse after all does not

---

[3] Bachmann's poem first received wide attention with its publication in *Kursbuch 15*, November 1968, pp. 94f. some three months after the Soviet-led invasion of Czechoslovakia. It is reprinted in her *Werke*, ed. Christine Koschel, Inge von Weidenbaum, and Clemens Münster, 4 vols. (Munich/Zurich: Piper, 1978), 1, pp. 167f. My understanding of the poem is based in part on Ulrike Schellhammer's reading of it in "Spatial Dynamics in Poetry: A Topographical Approach to Poems by Rilke, Hölderlin and Bachmann," Dissertation, Rice University, 1992.

tolerate affirmation, no matter how carefully qualified.

In the final analysis Braun's reception of Fühmann's *Böhmen am Meer* and Bachmann's "Böhmen liegt am Meer" points beyond these texts to their common literary origin in Shakespeare's *The Winter's Tale*. In that play Antigonus, a member of the court of Leontes, King of Sicily, is charged by the insanely jealous king to dispose of the unnamed child his wife Queen Hermione has just borne, a child whose father Leontes takes to be not himself but his friend Polixenes, King of Bohemia. Though he opposes his king's suspicions and related action, Antigonus nonetheless carries out the order "to commend it strangely to some place, / where chance may nurse or end it" (II, iii, ll. 180-81).[4] That place turns out to be the geographically nonexistent but poetically realizable coast of Bohemia, as we learn from Antigonus' question to the mariner who has brought him to it: "Thou art perfect then our ship has touched upon / The deserts of Bohemia?" (III, iii, ll. 1-2).

To make a long story short, the babe Perdita, as Antigonus calls her at the behest of her ostensibly dead mother, who appears to him in a dream, grows up in a bountiful natural setting, the foundling of a shepherd who recognizes her to be of noble birth, and is herself striking in her naturalness and knowledge of her environment. She is found a second time in the full bloom of maidenhood by Florizel, Prince of Bohemia, a chance encounter that leads initially to the apparent disorder of a class-transcending love but finally results in the reconciliation of Florizel's father and Leontes as well as of Leontes and his restored queen.

Aside from ultimately owing its title to *The Winter's Tale* Braun's play, it seems to me, presupposes and asks to be read against Shakespeare's in several crucial respects. Where Shakespeare represents in the "deserts of Bohemia" an unspoiled if sometimes dangerous natural order that is the ultimate source of cultural regeneration, Braun's *Böhmen am Meer* lies on an Adriatic that is hopelessly polluted – in particular by the largely unchecked and untreated wastes of the Po River basin, as Pavel informs his guests with a pointed reference to the city of Parma: "Die Gülle von Parma. Sie kommt den Po herunter. Parmaschinken" (p. 24). Significantly it is the unsuspecting *Ostler* Raja who is the tragicomic victim of this

---

[4] Although Braun's reception of Shakespeare is presumably based primarily on German translations, I have chosen to cite the original English text (as published in Penguin Books' Signet Classic editions of *The Tempest* (2nd ed., 1987) and *The Winter's Tale* (2nd ed., 1988) since my argument is nowhere dependent on Braun's use of a specific translation.

literal and figurative mess, which Braun gives the specific form of
the "Algenpest" that did indeed plague the Italian Adriatic during the
summer and fall of 1990. Thus Raja appears on stage for the first
time wearing a bathing suit and covered from head to toe in a sticky
green substance. "Wie eine Hexe. Das geht nicht mehr ab!" (p. 19),
she notes of her state, alternately laughing and crying. "Sie ist ins
Meer gegangen," explains Julia to one and all. "Sie hat gebadet hier.
Sie weiß nicht, daß die Algenpest – Die Urlauber sind alle abgereist." Robert, too, has a comment, one loaded with geopolitical
implications and sarcastic on a personal level in keeping with the
strained relationship that is shown to exist between him and Raja:
"Dein westliches Kostüm. Ja, ohne Anprobe, das ist ein Risiko" (p.
20).

What is of course fundamentally dishonest about this representation of human-caused natural disorder in the contemporary world
is that Braun here (and elsewhere in his play) attributes such disorder solely to Western capitalism when in fact, as every East
German school child surely knew by 1992 if not sooner, some of
the worst environmental destruction of the Cold War period came
about under socialism, not least on the territory of the GDR. The
underlying culprit, if there is a primary one, is that of a mindlessly
instrumentalized rationality, a way of looking at and dealing with the
natural world, one might argue, that has its intellectual origins in the
writings of Shakespeare's contemporary Francis Bacon and that is
certainly common as praxis to both systems at issue in *Böhmen am
Meer*.

If we now look at the social world as represented in the two
plays, it is evident that another "sea change," to borrow a phrase
from *The Tempest*, marks the passage of time from 1611 to 1992.
The *Winter's Tale*, whatever the reality of Jacobean England,
depicts a stable and benign hierarchical social order, temporarily
troubled at the top to be sure, but solidly grounded in the self-
sufficient and culturally intact rural world of the shepherd. What
thievery there is is confined to the petty exploits of the comic rogue
Autolycus. Braun's play, on the other hand, entails a social world
sharply divided into rich and poor, and features in addition to its
major individualized characters marginal dark figures engaged in
theft of a social character at every opportunity. As Pavel puts the
situation in the midst of a discussion of failed ideologies: "Der
Hunger, der Hunger ist die Gewalt. Die Hungerrevolten, die ins
Haus stehen. Man braucht ein Gewehr. Die Verteilungskriege, wenn
der Tisch gedeckt wird" (p. 25).

One can certainly take issue with Braun as to whether his representation of the North-South conflict here and elsewhere in the play stands up to critical scrutiny. Yet given the projected state of affairs, it is hardly surprising that unexplained gunfire punctuates a number of the play's *Bilder* while Pavel disarms his son in an early scene and is himself shown shooting or poised to shoot from the rooftop of his house (p. 36). In the end he dies from gunfire, although it is unclear from the initial published version of the play, given the conflicting testimony of the *Flittchen* and the housekeeper Assia, whether he in effect commits suicide by forcing himself on an armed group or is killed in a shootout with that group. To cite yet another possibility, Robert concludes: "Er hat sich erschossen" (p. 61). Significantly, in director Thomas Langhoff's staged version of the play at the Schiller Theater Pavel is murdered by a group of black-clad figures representing the impoverished South, an act suggestive of class warfare on a global scale. Indeed, the staged version appears to have ended with this scene.[5] If Braun gave his approval for this departure from the initial published text of the play or perhaps even authored it, I can only conclude that the revolutionary romantic in him is alive and well.

There is a third thematic complex, namely love and sexuality, that connects *Böhmen am Meer* and *The Winter's Tale*, but I want to defer my discussion of it in order to focus for a moment on the simultaneous presence of the best known of Shakespeare's late plays, *The Tempest*, in Braun's drama. The commanding figure of *The Tempest*, in several senses of the word, is Prospero, the rightful Duke of Milan, who as a man of learning had become so preoccupied with his studies that he was usurped by his brother Antonio to whom he had delegated his political authority. While living with his daughter Miranda in hiding on an island in the Mediterranean, he has with the aid of his books penetrated the secrets of the natural order to the point of being able to manipulate its forces at will via the spirits that inhabit it. Creating the storm with which the play opens, he brings the passengers of a passing ship to his island in an apparent shipwreck, among them his brother

---

[5] As reported by Franz Wille in *Theater heute*, 33, No. 4 (1992), p. 39: "Nachdem das Stück schon über eine Stunde auf der beliebigen Stelle tritt, beendet eine letzte apokalyptische Vision das Spektakel. Der Wolf kommt aus dem Süden, hat Heiner Müller schon längst prophezeit, und Volker Braun bemüht konsequent schwarzgewandete 'Arbeitslose', um Pavel zu ermorden. Der Aufstand der verarmten Massen wirkt im Staatstheater wie eine Erlösung. Ordentlich gekleidete Komparsen betreten und verlassen diszipliniert die Bühne. Ein letzter Sturmwind aus Bühnenblitz und Donner verheißt das gnädige Ende."

Antonio, Antonio's fellow conspirator Alonso, King of Naples, and Ferdinand, Alonso's son and heir to the throne. After putting all three of them, but especially Antonio and Alonso, through various trials and tribulations, he not only gives Miranda and Ferdinand, who meet and fall in love, his blessing if they remain chaste until their wedding vows but also takes steps toward reconciliation with Alonso and his brother after being chided for his unrelenting punishment of them by Ariel, the chief spirit at his beck and call:

> Hast thou, which art but air, a touch, a feeling
> Of their afflictions, and shall not myself,
> One of their kind, that relish all as sharply,
> Passion as they, be kindlier moved than thou art?
> Though with their high wrongs I am struck to th' quick,
> Yet with my nobler reason 'gainst my fury
> Do I take part. The rarer action is
> In virtue than in vengeance. They being penitent, the sole
> Drift of my purpose doth extend
> Not a frown further. Go release them, Ariel. (V, i, ll. 21-30)

That Braun would have us see Pavel as a late twentieth century Prospero becomes clear in the second *Bild* of the play when Pavel's monologue, in which he begins to reflect on his life at the age of fifty, is not so much interrupted as continued by an offstage voice reciting Prospero's penultimate speech (V, i, ll. 301-12) in a prose translation whose one liberty is the substitution of Prague for Milan in its closing sentence:

> Herr, ich bitte Euch und Euer Gefolge in meine ärmliche Zelle, wo Ihr Euch zur Ruhe legen sollt für diese Nacht. Ich werde sie zum Teil mit solchen Erzählungen verkürzen, daß die gewiß im Flug vergehen wird: mit der Geschichte meines Lebens und den verschiedensten Ereignissen, die geschehen sind, seitdem ich auf dieser Insel landete. Am Morgen bringe ich Euch zu Eurem Schiff; und dann auf nach Neapel, wo ich zu erleben hoffe, wie die Vermählung unseres innig geliebten Paares feierlich begangen wird. Von dort ziehe ich mich dann nach Prag zurück, wo jeder dritte Gedanke mein Grab sei. (pp. 14f.)

How does Pavel, represented as a financially successful, yet thoughtful member of the technical intelligentsia of our day, fare in his quest for closure and a meaningful life in the disenchanted world he inhabits? I have already indicated that his life ends violently in his "Böhmen am Meer" (p. 19), as he calls his retreat, a fact that preempts the exile's return to his native Prague and precludes the grand resolutions both presupposed and projected by Prospero's transposed speech. Benign, enlightened patriarchy of a Christian cast, complexly embodied in Shakespeare's knowing and caring figure and *The Tempest* as a whole,[6] is clearly not to be reaffirmed as a metanarrative despite Pavel's efforts in that direction. His primary effort is directed at the American industrialist Bardolph and the Russian journalist Michail, as we learn in his abbreviated account of his life to his son Vaclav in the second *Bild*, a scene structurally reminiscent of Prospero's recounting of his life at the hands of

---

[6] I do not mean to gloss over the troubled master/slave, colonizer/colonized relationship between Prospero and the "wild man" Caliban, the one, anagrammatically renamed native inhabitant (cf. Canibalis, Columbus' Arawakan-based name for the man-eating inhabitants of Cuba and Haiti) of the island where Prospero takes refuge with his daughter Miranda. This relationship, as Prospero reminds Caliban, comes about after Caliban, who is nurtured by and assimilates the civilizing influence of the newcomers to a point, "didst seek to violate / The honor of my child" (I, ii, ll. 347f.). As Stephen J. Greenblatt has shown in his 1976 essay "Learning to Curse: Aspects of Linguistic Colonialism in the 16th Century," reprinted in *Learning to Curse: Essays in Early Modern Culture* (New York/London: Routledge, 1992), pp. 16-39, Shakespeare's representation of that relationship implicates him and his character in the linguistic colonialism of 16th and early 17th century Europe. Nonetheless, he overstates his case when he argues that "[w]ith Prospero restored to his dukedom, the match of Ferdinand and Miranda blessed, Ariel freed to the elements, and even the wind and tides of the return voyage settled, Shakespeare leaves Caliban's fate naggingly unclear" (p. 26). On the contrary, Prospero, in a gesture that exemplifies benign patriarchy at the dawn of a new age ideally governed by reason and reasonableness, explicitly extends to Caliban the opportunity to redeem himself after engaging in a conspiracy with servants of Alonso to gain control of the island: "Go, sirrah, to my cell; / Take with you your companions. As you look / To have my pardon, trim it handsomely." A chastened Caliban responds:

> Ay, that I will; and I'll be wise hereafter,
> And seek for grace. What a thrice-double ass
> Was I to take this drunkard for a god
> And worship this dull fool. (V, i, ll. 295-98)

Of course this resolution entails Caliban's submission to Prospero's rational order and superior wisdom and begs the question of his sexual aggression/ transgression which Shakespeare, drawing on the discourse on witchcraft of his day, implicitly relates to his origins: "Thou poisonous slave, got by the devil himself / Upon thy wicked dam, come forth!" (I, ii, ll. 319-20). I am grateful to my colleague Joan Hartwig for facilitating my access to the scholarship on Shakespeare, *The Tempest*, and colonialism.

Antonio and Alonso to his daughter Miranda in Act I, Scene ii of *The Tempest*. Recalling that "Michail, mein Freund aus Rußland, hat uns in Prag besucht: 68, als wir Prag verließen. Du warst noch nicht geboren. Den andern, Bardolph, kenn ich geschäftlich: ich hab ihm vor – wie alt bist du? – fünfzehn Jahren die Fabrik entworfen," Pavel goes on to outline what he has in mind for these now broken individuals (one should of course also think of them as systems):

> Nun weiter: Bardolph ist bankrott und krank und lebensmüde. Für Mischa bricht die Welt zusammen, seine verliebte Tochter ist ausgereist. Dein Vater, ich, wohlinformiert von beiden, lädt beide ein, die er herzlich haßt. Wir haben uns genug gestritten: jetzt sollen s i e das tun; und sich selber widerlegen beide, indem ich beide liebe. (p. 13)

Pavel's appended rationale for his elaborate plan – "Das ist ein kleiner Stern, der verlöschen kann, und wir verstehn uns nicht? Wir nehmen uns nicht wahr. Hier in dem Licht. Hier wollen wir uns sehn. Hier zeige ich mein Leben" (p. 13) – is at once subjective and intersubjective in character and appears to put his moral authority beyond dispute, much as Prospero's is. Yet as if to anticipate Pavel's coming failure to achieve mutual understanding and personal resolution, Braun immediately undermines his character's moral authority by dramatizing his unwillingness to "see" certain things, be it his son's dark skin – "Sitz nicht in der Sonne, du wirst ein Neger. . ." (p. 13) – or the *Flittchen*, whom he stigmatizes as "todkrank," suspects of sexually compromising his son, and banishes from his sight: "Hast du mit ihr geschlafen. . . . Ich will sie nicht mehr sehen. Nie mehr im Leben" (p. 14).

Whatever one might wish to say about Braun's evenhandedness in presenting the shortcomings of capitalism and socialism in the series of devastating self-assessments uttered by Bardolph and Michail in the further course of the play and in Pavel's summary accusations in the seventh *Bild*, it should come as no surprise that Pavel derives little satisfaction from having brought his two "friends" together to argue with one another and to refute themselves. At the end of the seventh *Bild*, having charged Bardolph with scorching the West – an extrapolation from the American use of napalm in Vietnam – and Michail with shooting socialism to death in Prague and elsewhere, his grand design to achieve mutual understanding has clearly gone awry as he concludes bitterly: "Ihr seid Faschisten. Beide, beide. *Lacht*: Ich hasse euch. Ich hasse euch" (p. 43). No thoughts of human solidarity or the primacy of reason over vengeance here to motivate reconciliation as a necessary step toward the reenactment of order. Instead, two *Bilder* later, after Michail and Bardolph shirk any responsibility for dealing with the present disorder that is their joint legacy by mouthing aphoristic sayings which at least appear to privilege inaction,[7] Pavel utters his final words of the play: "Ihr habt recht, und ich habe nicht recht. Nicht der Mörder, der Ermordete ist schuldig. Euer Pavel" (p. 54).

Having delivered himself of this signed utterance of ultimate resignation, articulated in terms of the inversion of the most elementary principle of justice, Pavel stands *"abgewandt"* (p. 55) while his two "friends" finally begin to sample the banquet that, in allusion to both of Shakespeare's plays and as an image of the *Überfluß* of the North, has been spread before them for some time. As they joke about the need to call a spirit to set things right in the world – Ariel obviously not being at their disposal, they ostensibly call "unsern Geist" by singing *"wie einen selbst gefundenen Choral"* the line "STEHT NICHT LÄNGER TIEFGEBEUGT" (p. 55) – Pavel finally leaves. His departure, that of the only father figure with some moral authority intact, provides the necessary space, as it were, for a social storm to descend on the stage even as Michail – "Wie wird das wieder sauber?" – and Bardolph in response – "Nur durch einen Sturm" – muse naively about how the banquet is to be consumed. In the words of the stage directions: *"Ein Haufe dunkler Gestalten, dringt selbstherrlich in das Gelände, raubt die große Tafel leer, enteilt geräuschvoll"* (p. 55).[8]

Having presented some evidence of the relevance of *The Tempest* to a reading of *Böhmen am Meer*, I now want to return to a discussion of the thematic complex of love and sexuality in Braun's play with reference to both *The Tempest* and *The Winter's Tale*. Like Shakespeare's two late plays *Böhmen am Meer* features two generations related by blood and marriage but with some significant differences that reinforce the historical and ideological tensions already seen to determine the interrelationship of these plays. Unlike Shakespeare's two young couples, the younger generation in Braun's play clearly does not embody an unquestioning reaffirmation and regeneration of a preexisting ideal order, nor does it

[7] The sayings – "Wenn man uns nicht direkt umbringt, sterben wir nicht an den Tatsachen" and "Unser Rollenbuch muß von der Geschichte erst geschrieben werden" (p. 54) – are attributed respectively to Hungarian-born Swiss author Agota Kristof and Shakespeare scholar Kiernan Ryan.

[8] Earlier in the *Bild* Braun presents Pavel mindlessly feeding three of the dark figures "Zuckerstücke" (p. 52) instead of inviting them to partake of the banquet, a paternalistic gesture with geopolitical implications.

anticipate some "brave new world" (Miranda in *The Tempest*, V, i, l. 183) or another, lesser projected alternative to the natural and social disorder that marks the parental world it is going to inherit. By the end of the play Robert and Raja appear no closer to resolving the questions of economic dependency, free choice, desire, and fidelity that trouble their relationship. Vaclav, characterized in an early stage direction as *"dunkelhäutig, ein Halbstarker"* (p. 12), speaks for the most part in one-word utterances – "steil," "perfid" – in sharp contrast to the learned discourse of a Miranda. When he finally does have something more to say in an exchange with the *Flittchen*, who craves nothing so much as his affection, he uses language to assert his toughness and dominance and goes on to rape her, an act and its rationalization that recall Caliban's reported attempted rape of Miranda (I, ii, ll. 344-62):

> VACLAV   Sie sind alle krank. Sie streiten sich um nichts, um die
> kaputte Welt.
> DAS FLITTCHEN   Wenn ich in der Welt bin!
> VACLAV   Meine Haut ist schwarz. Faß sie an. Wie die von Bardolph.
> Das ist kein Mensch. Ich will kein Mensch sein. *Vergewaltigung*.
> (p. 50)

Vaclav's momentary articulateness reveals that he has come at this point in the play to recognize Bardolph as his biological father, a fact Braun infuses with a further critique of capitalism as he has Vaclav see in the "nonhuman" character of this newly discovered father an alternative role model to Pavel, a compelling excuse for not being "human" in a disordered, "kaputte Welt." Of primary interest in the present context, however, is the issue of paternity as a manifestation of the sexual and emotional entanglements of the parental generation in *Böhmen am Meer*. Unlike the cruelly obsessive Leontes, whose suspicions of his wife's infidelity and pregnancy are utterly groundless and tyrannical in their consequences, Pavel is oblivious to the question of his son's paternity despite his awareness and apparent tolerance of his wife Julia's affairs with both Michail and Bardolph. Indeed, he intimates that he has relied on their lingering feelings for her as their underlying motive for accepting his invitation (p. 16). And once they are on the scene he gently acknowledges what appears to be her own at least momentary vulnerability to such feelings:

> PAVEL   Ich meine, du mußt nicht aufgeregt sein.
> Es sind ausgetrocknete Flußbetten.

JULIA
    Ich werde ihnen Limonade
PAVEL
    Du
    Bist eine, die es jedesmal erwischt.
JULIA
    Oder Wasser.
PAVEL
    Beim ersten Anblick, aber
    Dann ist es ausgestanden. Dieses Wasser
    wischt ihr die Augen
    Mußt du ihnen nicht bringen. Limonade.
    Umarmen sich. (p. 17)

When Julia solicitously rejects his conjecture – "Entschuldige. Ich freue mich für d i c h" – Pavel both concedes and disputes her point: "Du hast zu mir gehalten, ja. Das Meer / Zu seiner Küste. Wenn kein Sturm war – / *Ein Windstoß im Sonnensegel*" (p. 17).

In the context of the play as a whole Pavel's metaphorical rejoinder, punctuated here by a gust of wind, a brief manifestation of the very elemental force he ascribes to Julia's unbounded sexuality, resonates with allusion and implication. "Sturm," after all, recalls *Der Sturm,* the title in German translation of Shakespeare's *The Tempest,* and it marks both the beginning and ending of Braun's play. It is the threat and promise of "Sturm" in its several senses which underlie the action of the opening *Bild,* driving off the tourists in a state of chaos reminiscent of the disorder experienced by the victims of the doubly staged shipwreck that opens *The Tempest* while attracting Julia's former lovers, who have, as Braun makes abundantly clear, themselves experienced "shipwreck" in their dual roles as individuals and as allegorical representations of competing sociocultural systems. And it is nothing less than the staged reality of "Sturm" as a destructive natural event with geopolitical and possibly even anthropological implications that signals the closing apocalypse.

Julia's own understanding of her sexuality, articulated in the play's eighth *Bild,* both presupposes and deviates from Pavel's metaphorical characterization. Midway through her attempted seduction of Robert, who, following his latest quarrel with Raja, has been keeping his aroused hostess at bay by reframing her amorous advances in terms of chaos theory, Julia counters his intellectualizing by baring her breasts and noting: "Hier ist das Chaos" (p. 49). Julia's startling response is multilayered. It reiterates in a new context the verbally identical utterance of a woman in the opening

Bild. While that utterance is naively matter of fact in its explicit reference to the disorder occasioned by the departing tourists, it does implicitly thematize the geopolitical chaos at issue in the opening *Bild* as well as in the play as a whole. Julia's reiteration of it thus appears to link her sexuality to this central issue, an issue recalled in turn by Vaclav's "Ein Chaos hier" (p. 59) amidst the disorder of the closing *Bild.*

In its immediate context Julia's gestural and verbal concretization of chaos in terms of her own body and sexuality effectively ends Robert's diversionary excursion into chaos theory, leaving him virtually speechless in his ambiguous, if temporary, dual role as Robert *and* Pavel: "WAS SOLL PAVEL SAGEN" (p. 49). Julia herself, as one might expect, is not at a loss for words. After suggesting that Robert/Pavel might speak with his hands – "Sag etwas, Pavel. Hast du keine Hände" – she attempts to overcome his scruples about responding to her desire by revisioning the image of the cloud that he introduces in his cautionary account of chaos theory: "Julia. Es gibt einen Begriff für das chaotische Ergebnis der immer gleichen Operation, das sich als eine Wolke von unendlich vielen Punkten darstellt: die Julia-Menge" (p. 48). The mathematical entity to which Robert refers is by no means a convenient fiction Braun invents to capture the ostensible implications of its namesake Julia's sexual desire but is indeed named after its discoverer, French mathematician Gaston Julia. Moreover, Benoît Mandelbrot's computerized visualization of the Julia Set as a cloud-like formation surrounding a hole, an aspect of the image that Braun did not make explicit despite its potential sexual connotations in the present context, has come to figure prominently in chaos theory as an icon of "ordered chaos."[9]

For Julia, on the other hand, a cloud is nothing more nor less than "ein schönes Bild" and its natural referent, a phenomenon she uses to describe to Robert her experience of her sexuality as a kind of "ordered chaos" in its own right:

> Siehst du die Wolke dort.
> Pavel vertraut mir, und ich durfte leben.
> Wie sie den ganzen Himmel überzieht.
> *Robert sieht gepeinigt zuboden: während die Wolke dahinjagt.*
> Ohne Plan, in einem Augenblick.
> Nicht denkend, was draus wird . . . und nichts bedauernd.

---

[9] See *Fractals: An Animated Discussion. With Edward Lorenz and Benoît B. Mandelbrot. Animations – Experiments*, a film by Heinz-Otto Peitgen, Hartmut Jürgens, Dietmar Saupe, and C. Zahlten (New York: W.H. Freeman, 1990).

Mit jedem bin ich anders und bin ich.
Sonst wär ich tot. Ich lebe ohne ihn.
Das ist entsetzlich, Pavel, das ist gut. (pp. 49-50)

At this juncture Julia clearly appears to have the last word in this matching of "theoretical" and "natural" wits, not least in her paradoxical and provocative valorization of her lived sexuality as "entsetzlich" and "gut." Yet Braun goes on to undermine her position as well by revealing a sense of quiet desperation of apocalyptic proportions behind her desire when Robert/Pavel fails to respond:

Pavel, was machst du.
Schweigen.
Was soll aus uns werden.
Bardolph und Mischa sind nicht abgereist.
Ruhig: Wenn nicht etwas passiert, gehn wir alle unter,
Robert steht reglos. Herausfordernd:
Was machst du mit mir. (p. 50)

As in Brecht's "Die Liebenden," a poem which metaphorizes love in terms of cranes and clouds as natural phenomena in a manner anticipating Julia's musings, "scheint die Liebe Liebenden ein Halt" without ultimately being so.[10] Whether Robert in the end responds to Julia's overtures is left unsaid, as is their presumed exit from the stage to make way for Vaclav and the *Flittchen*. But Julia's "Sturm," her unbounded desire, implicitly merges via stage directions with the multivalent "Sturm" that frames and permeates the play, thus setting the stage for Vaclav's rape of the *Flittchen*.

Yet it is not just love and sexuality that are illusory or brutal. There is in fact *nothing* to hold on to in the represented world of *Böhmen am Meer*, something Braun, whom the poet Uwe Kolbe not so long ago called the "schrecklich aufrichtige marxistische Student auf Lebenszeit,"[11] appears to go out of his way to insist on. In the opening exchange of the play reason itself, the cornerstone of Western thought, science, and "progress" since the early modern period, is called into question as a viable foundational principle: "Vernunft, Vernunft. Kommen Sie doch nicht mit der Vernunft. Vernunft braucht Gründe, Gründe gibt es für alles. . . . Aber keinen

---

[10] Bertolt Brecht, *Gesammelte Werke*, 20 vols. (Frankfurt am Main: Suhrkamp, 1967), 2, p. 536.

[11] Quoted by Michael Braun in his brief commentary on Braun's poem "Marlboro is Red. Red is Marlboro" in the Berlin weekly *Freitag*, 9 April 1993.

vernünftigen, der alles rechtfertigt" (p. 9). In the ensuing intellectual banter, carried on oddly enough only by the men in the crowd of fleeing tourists (the women have immediate practical concerns or express emotional needs), a syllogism emerges equating reason, chaos, and politics: "Das Chaos ist die Summe der Vernunft." "Die Politik ist das Chaos." "Die Anarchie der Vernunft" (pp. 9-10).

While the "chaos" at issue here is not (at least not explicitly) that of chaos theory, the physicist Robert's version of the latter is hardly more comforting, illustrating as it does his founding theorem – "Die Welt ist physikalisch unberechenbar" (p. 48) – and supporting aphorism – "'Eine gewalttätige Ordnung ist Unordnung. Eine große Unordnung ist Ordnung'" (p. 48) – in an extreme form:

> Kleine Handlungen können gigantische Folgen haben. Seit hundert Jahren weiß man, daß die Gleichungen Newtons unlösbar werden, wenn man nicht nur die Bahnen von z w e i Körpern sondern von dreien und mehr in ihrem Verhältnis . . . zueinander untersucht. Die geringfügigste Anziehung durch die Schwerkraft eines dritten kann einen Planeten dazu bringen, auf seiner Bahn wie betrunken herumzutorkeln und sogar völlig aus dem Sonnensystem fortzufliegen. (p. 48)

Whether or not the physical world is as "unberechenbar" as Robert and quite possibly his author would have us believe,[12]

---

[12] The "Three-Body Problem" was formulated by French mathematician Henri Poincaré in 1890 in response to the question "Is the solar system stable?" that King Oscar II of Sweden had posed for a competition. On the basis of his work, which seeks to determine the orbit of a hypothetical small planet acted on by two suns of equal size, Poincaré concluded that the solar system is not likely to be stable since in complex nonlinear systems very small irregularities could in principle lead at some point in time to immense consequences. In the second installment of his critical three-part series on chaos theory in *Der Spiegel* (4 Oct. 1993, pp. 232-41) Peter Brügge juxtaposes two computer visualizations of Poincaré's work. One, the product of chaos theorists Heinz-Otto Peitgen and Peter H. Richter, is in Brügge's apt description "ein Bild . . . auf dem der kleine Planet gleich einer wahnsinnigen Stubenfliege im Kraftfeld der beiden 'Sonnen' herumfährt" (p. 239). The other, produced by a team under Ernst Adams at the University of Karlsruhe's Institut für angewandte Mathematik with the aid of a self-checking procedure for computer calculations, pictures the hypothetical planet's orbit as a symmetrical triple loop. Of the Karlsruhe team's work Brügge notes: "Beim 'Dreikörperproblem' kamen sie zu dem Ergebnis, so eine 'chaotische' Laufbahn des kleinen Planeten entstehe immer dann, wenn für ihre Entwicklung im Computer falsche 'Zeitschritte' gewählt werden. Wählte man angemessen kleine Intervalle, so kurvte ein solcher Trabant schön regelmäßig" (p. 239).

Braun apparently has come to see a similar principle at work in the sociocultural world.[13] I am thinking here specifically of the two reports of sociocultural chaos external to the action of the play that he inserts in a Brechtian manner in the fifth and seventh *Bilder*. The first report relates an incident in present-day Beirut that began as a dispute over a kite that had gotten away from some children and ended with three people dead and three wounded:

ZU DER AUSEINANDERSETZUNG KAM ES ZWISCHEN DEM VATER DER KINDER UND EINEM AUTOFAHRER, DER DEN DRACHEN FÜR SEINE IM WAGEN SITZENDEN KINDER BEANSPRUCHTE. UNBEKANNTE MIT AUTOMATISCHEN WAFFEN SCHRITTEN EIN, UM DEN KAMPF ZU SCHLICHTEN, WOBEI SICH EINE SALVE AUS EINER DER WAFFEN LÖSTE. ZU DEN TOTEN GEHÖRTEN BEIDE VÄTER. (p. 26)

The second reported incident involves two New Guinea tribes whose meeting to enact a peace ritual degenerated into a battle lasting several days that resulted in five deaths, dozens of injuries, and the destruction of houses and other property. "VERURSACHT WURDE ALLES DURCH EINEN DISPUT ÜBER DIE ZUBEREITUNG VON SPEISEN" (p. 40).

Clearly, both instances of sociocultural breakdown can readily be viewed as illustrations of the notion that small actions can have enormous consequences. Moreover, it is presumably no coincidence that Braun should select these incidents from two diverse nonwestern cultures, as if to underscore the universal character and applicability of the illustrated principle. Indeed, Braun appears in *Böhmen am Meer* to be groping his way, however grudgingly, toward a kind of political anthropology to replace the comforting certainties of Marxism-Leninism that translated all too concretely into the lived reality of really existing socialism with its privileged nomenclatura and court intellectuals, its placated and withdrawn masses, and its disaffected dissidents.

The sociocultural reality of the contemporary West is of course

---

[13] Braun's fascination with chaos theory as an explanatory model for the sociocultural world is further borne out by the following reflection on Gorbachov in his "ARBEITSNOTIZEN" to the revised version of the play: "auch die rettende idee kann zur materiellen katastrophe werden; in erstarrten verhältnissen hat die konkrete utopie eine diffuse sprengkraft. der neue denker gorbatschow in seinem gebäude verschüttet; er will die eine welt: und ist der zerstreuer seines reiches. von der wissenschaftlichen weltanschauung bleibt die chaostheorie" (*Texte in zeitlicher Folge*, 10, p. 106).

anything but an alternative ideal order, as Pavel's newscast-like account of human strife in Italy at the start of the penultimate *Bild* makes abundantly clear:

> In der Nähe von Neapel haben sich die Geschäftsleute bewaffnet, mit Flinten, wegen der Plünderungen, nachdem ein Wirbelsturm die Läden zertrümmerte. In Florenz machten sechzig Maskierte auf Nordafrikaner Jagd. Ein Marokkaner wurde mit Messerstichen verletzt, zwei Tunesier mit Baseballschlägern zusammengedroschen. Estracomunitari. Die Passanten applaudierten. (p. 51)

Michail's ironic quip in response – "Gibt es Neuigkeiten?" – leads in turn to Assia's addendum: "Immer noch kein Trinkwasser im untern Viertel. Aber ein Stadion bauen sie" (p. 51). Both Bardolph and Pavel offer an anthropological perspective on what has been reported. Bardolph formulates his in universal human terms: "Es handelt sich um die ganz gewöhnliche menschliche Dummheit, Trägheit, Gier." Pavel gives his perspective – "Herrschen ist besser als ficken, sagen die Sizilianer" (p. 52) – an ethnic spin, but there is little doubt as to the intended generality of the referent. As far as I can tell, Braun makes no moves to relativize either utterance.

What are we to make of all this? What does Braun himself make of all this? His more obvious response is to make good on the storm that threatens more than once in the course of the play. "Eine Sturmflut ist angesagt," Pavel notes laconically after delivering himself of his Sicilian maxim, and the play, as I have already noted, ends with its destructive appearance, an apocalyptic closure entirely in keeping with Braun's sense of betrayal and outrage toward all parties involved in and responsible for the *Wende*. Braun, the spurned prophet, returns, it would appear, in the role of avenging author.

Yet the play also contains another, less obvious response in the form of a self-contained dream narrative that follows on the climactic plundering of the banquet table in the ninth *Bild* and is thus, in effect, situated between the final two *Bilder*. Indeed, this unattributed first-person dream narrative, which reads like nothing so much as an oblique authorial monologue on the events of 1989 and their consequences for displaced intellectuals such as Volker Braun, has at the very least something of the character of an alternative ending to the play, if not in fact that of an alternative text altogether. Spoken to African music in contrast to the classical music specified for the Pavel/Prospero monologue at the close of the second *Bild* – presumably we are to see and hear in this juxtaposition musical icons of elemental disorder as opposed to superficial order – it invokes the Julia Alps of Slowenia and neighboring Italy as its primary setting and thematizes radical discontinuity, uncertainty, and unpredictability in a truly nightmarish manner.

In this appropriately sublime setting, the narrating self, "vom Weg abgewichen," an indeterminate figure of deviation, finds itself "sofort, im Taumel, aus der Straße geweht" (p. 55). The structurally synonymous double agency of this displacement – dictatorial repression and consumer capitalism – manifests itself in the following interwoven visual and acoustic imagery: "das Geräusch der Panzerketten erlosch im Dröhnen des Autoverkehrs" (p. 55). Exposed to the elements in "eine fremde große Landschaft," the narrating self is stripped of its material and intellectual possessions, in short its identity: "der Luftstrom riß meine Taschen und Koffer auf und verstreute meine Sachen, alles was mir gehört hatte, und auch die Gedanken flogen mir aus dem Kopf und zerklirrten auf dem Asphalt" (p. 55). This moment of liberating dispossession, "DRAUSSEN, im FREIEN," of nonidentity between past and future, leaves the narrating self deeply ambivalent, exhilarated, to be sure, at experiencing its shattered thoughts as laughter, indeed as its own laughter, yet pained by the difficulty of thinking the future new and frightened at the prospect of admitting to being alive "ohne schon vorhanden zu sein" (p. 56). In a momentary shift to a domestic dreamscape the narrating self recounts its efforts to remain inconspicuous "mit meinen ungelenken Bewegungen, mit denen ich Nahrung faßte und mich im Bett herumwarf" (p. 56). Yet these efforts are subverted by its "Sucht" to throw itself against "Wände," presumably an allusion to oppositional behavior, by the desire to touch "irgendwelche Personen" and thus, by implication, break out of its isolation. The anxiety such impulsive behavior entails is that of being pointed out, held against one's will, pinned down in several senses of the word. Reverting to the original dreamscape, the narrating self then goes on to outline its strategy for survival in this alien region, alluding in the process to the central concept of Kundera's *The Unbearable Lightness of Being*.[14]

---

[14] Kundera's novel, whose primary setting is Prague before, during, and after the Soviet-led suppression of "socialism with a human face" in August 1968, was published in Susanna Roth's German translation by Hanser Verlag, Munich and Vienna, in 1984, the same year the author copyrighted the original Czech version in Paris. Braun's allusion seems negatively valorized in keeping with the ambivalence that permeates the dream narrative and possibly in reaction to the incomparably sharper and much more detailed critique of socialism to be found in Kundera's novel. Far from championing "lightness" himself, Kundera juxtaposes

ich konnte mich nur so flüchtig zeigen, beschwingt, mit der Leichtig-
keit, für die die Gegend konstruiert zu sein schien, und mußte mich nur
zusammenhalten, meine Kleider, die sich in den Warmluftschleusen
bauschten, die Sohlen auf den Weg konzentrieren, den VORSCHRIF-
TEN FOLGEN (es gab keine Vorschrift, die mir galt; sinnlose Losun-
gen), und mich sogleich losreißen von den Gesichtern, es mußte schnell
jaja oder nein gesagt werden, und ich konnte doch immer erst nach einer
Umarmung einen Gedanken fassen, es blieb mir nur, in der Hast, mich
selbst zu umarmen und auch das durfte ich nicht merken lassen. . . .

(p. 56)

Rounding out this depiction of a "brave new world" radically at
odds with the one Miranda envisions in *The Tempest*, the narrating
self moves associatively from the allegorized mountain terrain of
history – "den Sturm, in der harten Geometrie der Geschichte, die
hellen getünchten Schluchten, und ich sah den Fanatismus ihrer
Faltungen" (p. 57) – to the surreal landscape of contemporary capitalism with its slagheaps and artificial mountain ranges composed of
the debris of stripmining, its directive catchword "PROSPERITÄT,"
its mounds of consumer goods ("die Warenhalde vor Milano, in die
sich die Lastwagen gruben," p. 57), and last but not least its adver-
tising slogans that offer what the narrating self does not itself seek.

The narrating self's subsequent wish for self-destruction, "ein
Verbrechen, rasch, daß ich ins Nichts falle" (p. 57), a longing for
apocalyptic closure all its own, might seem the logical outcome of all
this. And yet, Braun moves the self of the dream narrative away
from the abyss toward a profound experience of its own interiority,
its own primordial chaos, an experience, moreover, that leads in
turn to a paradoxical tranquility: "ich kannte doch etwas Wildes,
Regelloses in meinen Regungen, das keine Form annehmen wollte,
eine Freiheit, die aus einer festen Tiefe kam, aus einem Massiv, das
ich in mir spürte, ich setzte meine Füße darauf, in der Verwirrung,
die mich ruhig machte" (p. 57).

This tranquility amid confusion sets the stage for the hypothetical open ending of the dream narrative. While the self sees "keine
Lösung für mich," the uncertainty about how things might turn out,
it notes, "hatte nichts Lähmendes" (p. 57). Conflicting images, "das
Licht des Tags die zerbrochenen Türen," follow and are juxtaposed
without separation between a pair of commas, as if to emphasize the
ongoing difficulties confronting the narrating self. Perhaps the great-

---

it and "heaviness" in the opening pages of his novel as a profound existential and
axiological dilemma in the life of each individual.

est difficulty for an intellectual such as Braun is to concede the possibility with which the dream narrative closes, namely that the postsocialist future, "das uns nicht Denkbare, das Gefürchtete," is livable: "wir könnten es leben" (p. 57). That the narrating self imagines this possibility while shifting unobtrusively to the collective "uns" and "wir," pronoun signifiers of community and solidarity familiar from its author's previous work but rhetorically and thematically at odds with the dream narrative, underscores Braun's profound ambivalence in formulating this concession.

In "HERAUSGERISSENE SZENE," the last in a series of satellite texts published along with a revised version of *Böhmen am Meer* in the tenth volume of his newly collected works, *Texte in zeitlicher Folge*,[15] Braun has four of the characters from the play, Julia, Assia, Bardolph, and Michail, banter on about various aspects of the play and its performance. Wordplay and disjunctive associations move the dialogue along more than do logical sequentiality and coherence to the point that Julia exclaims in frustration: "Was für eine ausgeflippte Szene" (10, p. 110). Her utterance serves Braun as a prelude to acknowledging his play's failure on the stage:

> BARDOLPH   Sie gehört nicht hier her.
> MICHAIL   Herausgerissen aus der Handlung und ans Ende gespült.
> BARDOLPH   Man hat das Stück verrissen.
> MICHAIL   Zerrissen, wie ich sage. So muß es enden.
> ASSIA   Das Chaos. (10, p. 110)

Whether or not it was undertaken in response to the criticism leveled at the play on its première, Braun's revision of his play, aside from numerous minor deletions, additions, and rewordings, consists primarily of the elimination of Raja and Robert as characters. While they continue to figure peripherally in Michail's (and Bardolph's) references to his daughter, who has been renamed Ludmilla, and her German husband Robert, most of their original dialogue (pp. 27-30, 44-47) now appears with four minor changes as two separate texts under the heading "AUSREISE" (10, pp. 97-100) among the revised version's satellite texts. The remainder of their speeches have been reassigned to other characters and in part relocated in the sequence of the play. Thus the *Flittchen* assumes the role of the unsuspecting Raja in the polluted Adriatic (10, pp. 70f.) – an implausible substitution since both Julia, who in the revised version knows her on a first-name basis as Lucia, and Pavel give us

---

[15] See Note 1.

every reason to believe she is a local girl – and later also that of the initiated Raja who goes for a swim in spite of what she knows about the "Algenpest" (10, p. 91). And Bardolph, who in the revised version is identified as a scientist rather than an industrialist, stands in for Robert in a reframed version of what initially constituted the opening of the seduction scene (10, p. 78). The bulk of the seduction scene itself is transformed into a lengthy and opaque monologue (10, pp. 85f.) that marks Julia, speaking incoherently in multiple voices, as confused and disturbed in contrast to the clear-headed free spirit of the original version.

The only other noteworthy changes involve Pavel and the dream narrative analyzed at length above. Braun removes the latter, without a change in the text of the original version, from the play proper to a position immediately following it under the heading "ZUGEHÖRIGE SZENE" (10, pp. 94-96). He then adds the following note: "Der Kommentar kann in der Mitte oder vor dem Schluß Verwendung finden, sein Ort ist das ganze Stück," an understanding of the dream narrative that is anything but self-evident. The changes involving Pavel are of a different order. Braun deletes Prospero's transposed speech and in its place has an offstage voice interrupt Pavel's incipient monologue with this admonition: "Kein Wörtlein mehr – mein Freund! das dich bedrückt. Kein Sterbenswort. Kein Wort von Politik" (10, p. 67). At play's end Braun revives Pavel instead of presenting him shot to death as in the original version but not without having the offstage voice now hurl the same charge at Pavel that Pavel earlier (10, pp. 84, 85) hurls at Michail and Bardolph: "Du bist ein Verbrecher" (10, p. 94).

In the absence of performances of the recast version of *Böhmen am Meer* it is difficult to judge whether Braun's revision of his play has made it more playable, whether it will lead, in Assia's words in "HERAUSGERISSENE SZENE," to a performance that is "Eine nahegehende. . ." (10, p. 109). One might speculate, for example, that the deletion of the Raja/Robert dialogues, which resist the play's geopolitical allegorization of contemporary sociocultural reality toward apocalypse by suggesting that life, however difficult it may be, goes on in the rising generation and might just be negotiable, helps to streamline the text, making the tragic thrust underlying its comic surface more compelling. The same effect could be attributed to the removal of the dream narrative with its hypothetical open ending and the transformation of the engaging and largely upbeat seduction scene into Julia's somber monologue, her bewildered and bewildering musings on love, sexuality, and the fate of us all.

Yet none of these changes addresses the hard issues that Braun himself raises – not necessarily always intentionally – about his play in a series of dated "ARBEITSNOTIZEN" (10, pp. 104-07) accompanying the revised version. In the first of these, dated November 27, 1990, Braun notes about the setting of his play: "eigentlich müßten sie in der wüste sitzen; der abraum ist unsere adria" (10, p. 104). What follows on this metaphorical equation of environmental destruction under socialism and capitalism is a remarkable categorical critique of GDR socialism primarily in terms of its environmental record and of lingering hopes of a "third way" that persisted in various circles beyond the unification of Germany:

> ich muß noch einmal unter die erde, wo meine wurzeln sind . . . wo wir *schön leben* wollten! wo wir glaubten, es gut zu machen. und nun sitzen wir auf der halde und reden immer noch: als narren. was ist da, was kaputt ist . . . das modell, in grund und boden gewirtschaftet. die trümmer unserer geschichte. die utopie ist zur fata morgana geworden. wasser! wasser! aber es ist alles verseucht und vergiftet. wir haben das land weggegeben und was ändert das. es klebt elend an den händen. es gibt kein anderes modell . . . . (10, p. 104)

One can not help wondering what kind of drama might have emerged if Braun, acting on his insight into the skewed character of its setting, had put his work on *Böhmen am Meer* aside and chosen instead to transform the arresting images and the passion that permeate this passage into literature. As things stand, there is no direct trace in the play that did emerge of either it or the theoretically oriented critique of socialism recorded in the second set of "working notes" dated October 16, 1991. Instead, as the next to last of these notes makes clear, Braun apparently thought he had bigger fish to fry:

> was sind übrigens die sozialistischen vorstellungen, mühsame visionen, gegen die bürgerliche utopie der machbarkeit, der immerwährenden prosperität, der zuwachsraten von adam und eva bis bayer leverkusen? hammer oder sichel waren primitive, aber noch handhabbare werkzeuge. die großindustrie ist eine eigensinnige maschine, in die wir, und alle natur, involviert sind. an den grenzen der welt erfährt sie ihr desaster.
>
> (10, p. 106)

What is objectionable here is not the critique of contemporary capitalism, which is readily understandable and to the point, but the renewed, metaphorically bolstered illusion that socialism in its praxis to date has not exhibited the same tendencies and consequences, as if the "Deckgebirge" (p. 57) the narrating self of the dream narrative envisions are not equally visible in the GDR and the stripmined regions of Kentucky.

There is a final "working note," dated 15 March 1992 and thus written at the time of the unsuccessful première of *Böhmen am Meer*. When I first came across the opening sentences of this note – "die endzeit ist die zuflucht der enttäuschten. das lokale desaster diktiert den weltverdruß; der katastrophengang der geschichte betäubt die eigene wunde" (10, p. 106) – I immediately thought about using them as an epigraph to this paper. They seemed after all to corroborate my own reservations about Braun's use of apocalypse in the initial published version of his play. On a more careful reading of the note as a whole, however, I realized that Braun intended these sentences not as self-criticism of his anaesthetizing recourse to apocalypse but as the first part of a statement of fact justifying his play precisely on the grounds of apocalypse. The "katastrophengang der geschichte," as it turns out, refers not merely to his staging of apocalypse but to the ostensible collapse of modernization: "über die niederlage der maroden planökonomien tröstet der *kollaps der modernisierung*, gedankt sei robert kurz" (10, p. 106).[16]

The hardboiled poetological and existential stance Braun assumes in response to this state of affairs – "wir halten uns aufrecht an den untergängen. nun inszenieren wir sie" (10, p. 106) – is not coincidentally reminiscent of that of the young, pre-Marxist Brecht, whose explicitly autobiographical lyrical persona is determined not to let its cigar go out "Bei den Erdbeben, die kommen werden."[17] Yet unlike the young Brecht, who in the same poem cockily projected a community of like-minded individuals cogniscent of their provisionality and went about his way, Braun does not wear the stance he has assumed here and elsewhere easily. Instead he is at pains to justify himself and his play in terms that undermine that stance, terms the young Brecht would presumably have found alien. Of his play's ending, "das schmutzige meer in böhmen, die sturmflut," he asks rhetorically with some feeling: "aber vielleicht hilft sich die natur selber? und es ist ein reinigender sturm: und der *auftritt* der natur eine versöhnende geste gegenüber dem verrotteten

---

16 The allusion is to Robert Kurz, *Der Kollaps der Modernisierung. Vom Zusammenbruch des Kasernensozialismus zur Krise der Weltökonomie* (Frankfurt am Main: Eichborn, 1991). Here too one must take exception: however disturbing the effects of modernization on nature and culture may be, it proceeds apace worldwide. Kurz's predication of the collapse of modernization is no more likely to prove true than Marx's comparable notions about the end of capitalism.

17 Bertolt Brecht, "Vom armen B. B.," *Gesammelte Werke*, 8, p. 263.

menschen" (10, pp. 106-07). As the counterpart to this anthropo-morphized conception of nature he goes on to ask, again rhetorically and this time obliquely, of his own efforts as playwright: "und er sollte nicht der gleichen gesten fähig sein, in einem ernsthaften spiel?" Having pleaded his case, Braun concludes with a resounding attack on his undoubtedly largely West Berlin audience: "schande. weg von diesem theater" (10, p. 107).

It would be a serious mistake, I think, to see in Braun's aggres-sive reaction to his play's negative reception nothing more than a self-indulgent, peevish outburst, though that element may well be present. Instead, I see it as symptomatic both of the play's prophetic structure, a communicative gesture that wants to be believed and affirmed, and Braun's necessary search via the play for a new audience in the changed sociocultural order of a united Germany, a Germany in which the state apparatus of the GDR that appears to have been among Braun's most avid readers and by its actions in this and many other spheres helped insure an interested audience for his works no longer exists. These two aspects of the play are of course intimately related, and to fail at one is to fail at the other. How Braun ultimately comes to terms with the changed situation in which he finds himself remains to be seen. As his bantering actors in "HERAUSGERISSENE SZENE" seem to suggest, the answer may well lie at his doorstep: "Es muß etwas Naheliegendes sein. / Die nächste Vorstellung. / Eine nahegehende. . ." (10, p. 109). Per-haps in dramatizing rather than anaesthetizing "die eigene wunde" he will find both himself and his audience.

Das Literatursystem der DDR. Kontexte und Voraussetzungen einer neuen Literaturgeschichte

Ulrich Meyszies

Die Selbstreflexion der Sozial- und Geisteswissenschaften in Deutschland wird gegenwärtig von einer Metaphorik des Sehens beherrscht. Im Gefolge von Radikalem Konstruktivismus und Luhmannscher Systemphilosophie erscheint der Wissenschaftler als Beobachter und die Exploration des Gegenstandes als perspektivische Handhabung von Unterscheidungen, die systematisch von jenen blinden Flecken durchzogen sind, die jedem Beobachten innewohnen.[1] Wenn man die epistemologischen Voraussetzungen akzeptiert, dann können wissenschaftliche Theorien, die der Untersuchung eines Objektes explizit oder implizit zugrunde liegen, als "Brillen" bezeichnet werden, die bestimmte Aussagen gestatten und dadurch andere Perspektiven verstellen. Ein kritischer Rückblick auf die Erforschung der DDR-Literatur hätte demzufolge die optischen Instrumente nochmals "vor Augen zu führen," die vor und nach der historischen Zäsur des Jahres 1989 die perspektivische Wahrnehmung des "Gegenstandes" ermöglichten. Ich werde mich deshalb zunächst als Wahrnehmungshistoriker präsentieren, um mich

---

[1] Niklas Luhmann, *Beobachtungen der Moderne* (Frankfurt am Main: Suhrkamp, 1992), S. 98ff. und Siegfried J. Schmidt, *Kognitive Autonomie und Soziale Orientierung* (Frankfurt am Main: Suhrkamp, 1994), S. 20ff.

anschließend durch die Verfertigung einer neuen Brille als Optiker zu empfehlen.

Folgt man der kritischen Reminiszenz Wolfgang Emmerichs, der "Für eine andere Wahrnehmung der DDR-Literatur" plädierend, vor allem die bis 1989 geleistete Forschung aus Ost und West evaluierte, so hat die Perspektive der wissenschaftlichen Beobachter zum Gegenstand vor allem an einer übergroßen Nähe zum Objekt gelitten, die "in einer politischen Bindung oder aber zumindest in einer politischen (Konträr-) Faszination begründet lag."[2] Das Interesse an der Literatur der DDR sei zumeist ein Interesse am Sozialismus gewesen.

Die Gründe für die perspektivischen Probleme, die Literaturwissenschaftler in der Beobachtung von DDR-Literatur hatten, lassen sich auf die Wahrnehmungsverhältnisse in jenem sozialen und kulturellen Raum zurückführen, der bis 1989 durch ein festgefügtes dichotomisches Wirklichkeitsmodell strukturiert war. Die Existenz zweier sich in ihren ökonomischen und politischen Grundlagen ausschließender Gesellschaftssysteme, die in einem jahrzehntelangen geopolitischen Antagonismus befangen waren, hinterließ die Spuren der konfrontativen Semantik noch in den wissenschaftlichen Perspektiven auf die Literatur der DDR.

Deren anfängliche Bewertung im Westen wurde fast gänzlich durch Gegensätze strukturiert, die ihre Herkunft aus dem ideologischen Diskurs kaum verleugneten. Die grundsätzliche Bindung der Beobachter an einen binären Wertungskontext änderte sich auch nicht, als sich die Vorzeichen der Wahrnehmung in den 70er Jahren zu verändern begannen. Typologisch handelt es sich bei Beobachtungen, die Unterscheidungen wie Sozialismus/Kapitalismus, DDR/BRD, Apologie/Kritik, eigentliche/nicht eigentliche DDR-Literatur einen wie immer gearteten ontologischen Status zumessen, um teilnehmende Beobachtung oder, um terminologisch an der eingangs skizzierten Theorie anzuschließen, um sogenannte Beobachtungen erster Ordnung. Beobachtungen dieser einfachen Art konstituieren sich zwar durch Unterscheidungen, erzeugen aber für den, der sie benutzt, noch keine Kontingenz, d.h. sie enthalten keine anderen Bezeichnungsmöglichkeiten. Das Beobachtete erscheint in unmittelbarer Präsenz – als das, was "es ist" oder sein soll. Über diese Form der Wahrnehmung von DDR-Literatur notierte Volker Braun noch 1983: "Westdeutsche Lexika führen mich als Republikflüchtigen; wo

---

[2] Wolfgang Emmerich,"Für eine andere Wahrnehmung der DDR-Literatur," in ders., *Die andere deutsche Literatur* (Opladen: Westdeutscher Verlag, 1994), S. 193.

nicht, dann als 'linientreuen Propagandisten'. Beschreibungsimpotenz."[3]

Vom Ungenügen an den Wahrnehmungs- und Beobachtungsverhältnissen in der DDR-Literaturwissenschaft zeugt der in kritischen Rückblicken mittlerweile zum Standardwerk avancierte Literaturbericht, den Bernhard Greiner 1983 unter dem bezeichnenden Titel "DDR-Literatur als Problem der Literaturwissenschaft" veröffentlichte. Greiners Plädoyer für methodische Erweiterung und theoretische Reflexion der Forschung zur DDR-Literatur, die "an einer Verquickung von Germanistik und Politik"[4] leide, markiert am auffälligsten den expliziten Übergang von einer kontextabhängigen Beobachtung erster Ordnung, die in ihren konstitutiven Unterscheidungen mit dem politischen Unterscheidungsrahmen übereinstimmte, zu einer wissenschaftlichen Beobachtung zweiter Ordnung, die, indem sie ihre eigenen Beobachtungsvoraussetzungen als Literaturwissenschaft hinterfragt, ihren Gegenstand nicht substantiell festzuschreiben sucht, sondern ihn relational als Kommunikations- und Wahrnehmungsverhältnis zwischen Literatur, Kultur und Gesellschaft begründet. Greiner explizierte in seinem Bericht Positionen, die seit Ende der 70er und zu Beginn der 80er Jahre einer ganzen Reihe von Untersuchungen bereits implizit zugrunde lagen.

Ein theoretisches Konzept, mit dem m. E. der Schritt zur Beobachtung zweiter Ordnung am deutlichsten vollzogen wurde, stellte Jörg Schönert, von der Fachwelt leider weitgehend unbemerkt, 1985 unter dem Stichwort "Identität und Alterität zweier literarischer Kulturen in der Bundesrepublik und der DDR" vor.[5] Schönert unterbreitete den Vorschlag,

> von einem relativ selbständigen Sozialsystem DDR-Literatur (als einem kulturellen Teilsystem im gesellschaftlichen Systemzusammenhang der DDR) zu sprechen, das sowohl in historisch variablen Austauschbeziehungen mit anderen Sub- und Teilsystemen der DDR-

---

[3] Volker Braun,"Rimbaud. Ein Psalm der Aktualität," in ders., *Verheerende Folgen mangelnden Anscheins innerbetrieblicher Demokratie* (Leipzig: Reclam, 1988), S. 101.

[4] Bernhard Greiner, "DDR-Literatur als Problem der Literaturwissenschaft," in *Probleme deutscher Identität*, hrsg. Paul G. Klussmann und Heinrich Mohr (Bonn: Bouvier, 1983), S. 20.

[5] Jörg Schönert, "Identität und Alterität zweier literarischer Kulturen in der Bundesrepublik und der DDR als Problem einer interkulturellen Germanistik," in *Das Fremde und das Eigene. Prolegomena zu einer interkulturellen Germanistik*, hrsg. Alois Wierlacher (München: Fink, 1985), S. 212-33.

Gesellschaft steht . . . , als auch – wiederum historisch variable und unterschiedlich intensive – Austauschbeziehungen zu 'Umwelten', zu anderen Gesellschaftssystemen und ihren politischen, ökonomischen und kulturellen Subsystemen zeigt.[6]

In ganz ähnliche Richtung hatte sich die theoretische Reflexion der Literaturwissenschaft in der DDR bewegt, die, ohne sich ausdrücklich auf die Literaturverhältnisse innerhalb des Landes zu beziehen, Literatur als systemischen Prozeß der Produktion, Distribution und Rezeption deutlich von den konkreten Merkmalen des literarischen Lebens in der DDR ableitete.

Die literaturtheoretische Entdeckung des Lesers bot darüber hinaus der im wesentlichen von Manfred Naumann, Dieter Schlenstedt und Hans-Georg Werner entwickelten Kommunikations- und Wirkungsästhetik, die die Eigengesetzlichkeit, Subjektabhängigkeit und Kreativität literarischer Kommunikation betonte, wesentliche Ansatzpunkte.[7] Die DDR-interne Beobachtung hatte selbstverständlich auch ihren blinden Fleck. War die externe Wahrnehmung der DDR-Literatur eher durch eine Omnipräsenz des politischen Wahrnehmungskontextes getrübt, so mußte der politische Bezug der literaturtheoretischen Reflexion innerhalb der DDR ausgespart bleiben. Gegen welche kulturpolitische Restriktion oder ideologische Vereinseitigung der literarische Rezipient oder die literarische Wirkungsästhetik wissenschaftlich ins Feld geführt wurde, blieb weitgehend tabuisiert. DDR-Literaturwissenschaft hatte insofern Anteil an den strukturellen und diskursiven Voraussetzungen ihres Gegenstandes. Auch hier also, wenn auch anders motiviert, übergroße Nähe zum Objekt.

Faßt man die perspektivischen Verschiebungen, die in den wissenschaftlichen Wahrnehmungen von DDR-Literatur in den 80er Jahren stattfanden, zusammen, dann läßt sich ein eindeutiger Trend zur wissenschaftlich reflektierten Beobachtung zweiter Ordnung feststellen. In relativer Übereinstimmung wurde die Literatur der DDR:

• als differenziertes ästhetisches Phänomen innerhalb einer Ge-

---

[6] Ebenda, S. 221.

[7] Vgl. dazu Manfred Naumann u.a., *Gesellschaft. Literatur. Lesen* (Berlin/ Weimar: Aufbau, 1973); Dieter Schlenstedt, *Wirkungsästhetische Analysen. Poetologie und Prosa in der neueren DDR-Literatur* (Berlin/Weimar: Aufbau, 1979); und Hans-Georg Werner, *Text und Werk. Analyse und Interpretation* (Berlin/Weimar: Aufbau, 1984).

sellschaft betrachtet, deren politische Ideologie Anspruch auf Steuerung aller sozialen und kommunikativen Bereiche erhob,
• als sozial-kommunikatives Verhältnis zwischen Autoren und Lesern gedeutet, das an der Etablierung und Veränderung von Strukturen der Öffentlichkeit wesentlichen Anteil hatte, und
• zunehmend als deutsch-deutsches Problem begriffen, das sich nicht ausschließlich in Bezug auf einen teilstaatlichen territorialen oder politischen Raum definieren läßt.

Gleichwohl war der politische Beobachtungsrahmen bis 1989 existent; die Wahrnehmung der Literatur hatte sich jedoch in gewissem Umfang entpolitisiert und, wenn man will, verwissenschaftlicht. Danach wurde, verkürzt gesagt, zunächst einmal alles anders. Durch die unerwartete und vollständige Auflösung des Beobachtungs- und Wahrnehmungskontextes, von Heiner Müller sehr pointiert in dem Satz: "Das Gespenst verläßt Europa" zusammengefaßt, entstand für viele der Eindruck, plötzlich auch sehr viel klarer zu sehen und, um im Bild zu bleiben, überhaupt ohne Brillen auszukommen. Da aber der zuvor in Ost und West verbindlich benutzte Unterscheidungsrahmen als Wertorientierung abhanden gekommen war, konnten die neuen Einsichten oftmals nur als Paradoxien formuliert werden. Bereits der erste Satz jener folgenreichen Rezension von Ulrich Greiner über Christa Wolfs Erzählung *Was bleibt* bietet ein Beispiel für jene paradoxen Formulierungen und Unentscheidbarkeiten, die im Feuilleton verhandelt wurden und mehr und mehr auch Einzug in den wissenschaftlichen Diskurs hielten: "Das ist ja ein Ding: Die Staatsdichterin der DDR soll vom Staatssicherheitsdienst der DDR überwacht worden sein?"[8] An Greiners Formulierung läßt sich der Reflexionsverlust, der in der Wahrnehmung von DDR-Literatur nach 1989 eingetreten war, sehr deutlich ablesen. Nicht nur daß er, jegliche ästhetische Bedeutung der Erzählsituation in *Was bleibt* negierend, die Autorin schlicht mit der Erzählerin gleichsetzte (ein Fehler, der den Studenten der Literaturwissenschaft gewöhnlich im ersten Semester abgewöhnt wird), er identifizierte, die binären Schematismen der 50er Jahre gebrauchend, die Autorin mit dem Staatswesen, das sich in Form der Staatssicherheit selber observiere.[9] Wenn alles eins ist, werden Unterscheidungen über-

---

[8] Ulrich Greiner, "Mangel an Feingefühl," *Die Zeit*, 1. 6. 1990.
[9] Greiner führt hier eine Gleichsetzung zwischen Literatur und Staat aus, die man nach Luhmann als vormoderne Form von "second-order-observations" bezeichnen kann. Der Staat "DDR" übernimmt die Funktion, die Gott in der Reflexion der stratifizierten Gesellschaft erfüllte (Luhmann, *Beobachtungen der Moderne*, S.

flüssig oder paradox – die Beobachtungsverhältnisse näherten sich
dem Versuch unvermittelter Wahrnehmung und Bewertung nach
dem Schema gut/böse, ohne daß ein antagonistischer Orientierungs-
rahmen den Urteilen noch Gültigkeit verschafft hätte. Nach dem
Ende der Diskussion, das Greiner 1993 verkündete, war dann auch
keiner klüger. Daß die Betroffenen sich während der Streitigkeiten in
die Zeit des kalten Krieges zurückversetzt fühlten, was wiederum
den Wortführern der Christa Wolf-, Gesinnungsästhetik-, Stasi-,
etc.-"Debatte" vollkommen unverständlich blieb, kann bei den perspektivischen Verhältnissen nicht verwundern.

Unentschieden blieb: War Christa Wolf ein staatstragendes
Subjekt oder eine kritische Autorin? Waren Sascha Anderson und
Rainer Schedlinski raffinierte IM oder bemerkenswerte Autoren und
Organisatoren der autonomen Literaturszene? Die Reihe der Bei-
spiele, über die unter dieser Optik nicht entschieden werden kann,
ließe sich bis in die literaturpolitische Administration fortsetzen. Die
Preisfrage lautet hier: Hat der "Literaturminister" Höpcke kritische
Literatur gefördert oder behindert?

Da sich wissenschaftliche Beobachter weder mit dem Wahrheits-
kriterium der Medien noch mit einem salomonischen "sowohl-als-
auch" zufrieden geben können, plädiere ich für eine Fortsetzung des
Versuchs, durch theoretische Reflexion der Voraussetzungen
unserer Beobachtung die perspektivischen Verhältnisse in der DDR-
Literaturforschung erneut zu verwissenschaftlichen.

Ich beende mit diesem Appell meinen wahrnehmungshistori-
schen Abriß und wende mich der Verfertigung eines "optischen
Instruments" zu. Die handlungsleitende Frage muß dabei lauten: wie
kann DDR-Literatur wissenschaftlich beobachtet werden?

Als eine erste Antwort empfiehlt sich das Wort: historisch. Die
DDR-Literaturforschung muß den Epochenumbruch 1989 ernst
nehmen und ihr Selbstverständnis als historische Wissenschaft
finden – so schwer das auch durch die Gewöhnung an die bis 1989
synchrone Wahrnehmung des Gegenstandes fallen mag. Bereits
diese Entscheidung hat ernstzunehmende Konsequenzen, die zu
perspektivischen Veränderungen führen müssen, denn in den
heftigen Diskussionen, in denen um Moral und persönliche Verant-
wortlichkeit von Schriftstellern in der DDR ebenso wie um die
Qualität ihrer literarischen Verfahren und ästhetischen Konzepte
gestritten wird, sehen die Beteiligten fast ausnahmslos von den
Voraussetzungen und Bedingungen ab, unter denen die DDR-
Literatur bis 1989 existierte.

106f.).

Akzeptiert man die vorgetragene Argumentation, dann müßte die nächste Frage folgerichtig lauten: Unter welchen Bedingungen und mit welchen Voraussetzungen existierte die DDR-Literatur bis 1989, und mit welchen literaturwissenschaftlichen Kategorien läßt sich das Spezifische der DDR-Literatur beobachten? Bei dem Versuch, die Frage auf kanonische Weise zu beantworten, ergeben sich Schwierigkeiten, die ich an einer zentralen literaturwissenschaftlichen Kategorie, dem literarischen Werk, exemplifizieren will.

Bereits die Anwendung der Kategorie "Werk" auf die Literaturen der sozialistischen Staaten in Osteuropa ist äußerst problematisch, weil eine literaturgeschichtliche Analyse, die das publizierte "literarische Werk" zum Ausgangs- und Fluchtpunkt der Beschreibung macht, die Vielzahl der Mechanismen aus dem Blick verliert, die gerade die Besonderheit und historische Einmaligkeit der "Text-bzw. Werkgenese" in Gesellschaften wie der DDR kennzeichneten. Literarische Texte wurden vor der Publikation in jahrelangen Auseinandersetzungen zwischen dem Autor, dem Lektor, den Repräsentanten der literaturpolitischen Administration etc. ästhetisch modifiziert, politisch lektoriert, zensiert und literaturwissenschaftlich begutachtet, zum Druck empfohlen, von politischen Reizthemen und -worten bereinigt oder nicht, druckgenehmigt oder verboten, bzw. nach erfolgter Buchproduktion aufgrund politischer Erwägungen nicht ausgeliefert oder in den Reißwolf gesteckt.

Vor der "Seinsweise des literarischen Werks" liegt also ein immenser Komplex literarischer und literaturpolitischer Handlungen und Entscheidungen, die maßgeblichen Einfluß auf den existentiellen Status (publiziert bzw. nicht publiziert) und die ästhetische sowie politische Qualität von Literatur haben.

Die Literatur der DDR ist ohne einen systematisch erweiterten Literaturbegriff wissenschaftlich nicht zu beobachten. Neben den literarischen Texten und Autoren müssen die literaturbezogenen Handlungen, die literarischen und literaturpolitischen Institutionen, die Literaturkritik und die kommunikativen Funktionen, die Literatur in der politisch kontrollierten Öffentlichkeit hatte, in die Systemanalyse der DDR-Literatur integriert werden.

Welches Modell erlaubt es, die Vielfalt der skizzierten Bezüge und Aspekte theoretisch darzustellen und empirisch zu erforschen? Als Antwort unterbreite ich den Vorschlag, die Gesamtheit der literarischen Phänomene in der DDR unter dem Oberbegriff des Literatursystems zu beobachten. Meine zweite These lautet, daß es sich zur wissenschaftlichen Erforschung der Literatur der DDR empfiehlt, von einem literarischen System auszugehen, das die sozialen Handlungsbereiche der literarischen Produktion, Rezeption,

Vermittlung und Verarbeitung sowie die Konstituierung und Ver-
änderung eines im Systemzusammenhang erzeugten literarischen
Diskurses umfaßt.[10]
    Um den Begriff des Literatursystems im Kontext der modernen
Gesellschaft historisch zu bestimmen, bietet es sich an, Max Weber
zu folgen, der die Herausbildung einer eigenständigen ästhetischen
Wertsphäre im Zuge der europäischen Modernisierung konstatierte.
Gemäß dieser Annahme kann in Deutschland seit dem Ende des 18.
Jahrhunderts die schrittweise Ausdifferenzierung eines relativ autonomen Literatursystems beobachtet werden, das spezifische Hand-
lungsrollen umfaßt, kommunikative Funktionen in einer funktional
ausdifferenzierten Gesellschaft übernimmt und einen eigenen literarischen Diskurs hervorbringt.[11]
    Die kognitive und kommunikative Funktionsweise des literari-
schen Systems ist durch den Modernisierungsprozeß jedoch keines-
wegs festgelegt, sondern je nach Ausprägung des Modernesyn-
droms von den sozialen und diskursiven Rahmenbedingungen
abhängig, die durch die jeweiligen kulturellen, gesellschaftlichen
und nationalstaatlichen Einheiten seit dem 18. Jahrhundert formuliert
werden.
    Bezogen auf die Situation der DDR nach 1945 würde dies be-
deuten, daß die besonderen Ausformungen von Gesellschaft und
Kultur im Rahmen eines ideologisch integrierten Wirklichkeits-
modells die Funktionsweise und Phänomenologie der ostdeutschen
Literatur wesentlich beeinflußt haben. Dieter Schlenstedt hat in der
Reihe des deutschen P.E.N.-Zentrums Ost, die 1992 unter dem Titel
Gespräche zur Selbstaufklärung stand, auf diesen Umstand auf-
merksam gemacht, als er, nach der Besonderheit der literarischen
Phänomene in der DDR befragt, antwortete: "Wir reden nicht über
Zensur allein, sondern über ein bestimmtes System von DDR-
Literatur, das wir in einer Kurzform 'reglementiert' genannt ha-
ben."[12]
    Die besondere Verfassung und Entwicklung des DDR-Literatur-
systems zwischen 1949 und 1989 lassen sich, wie die seit 1990
geführten Diskussionen in Geschichtswissenschaft und Soziologie

---

[10] Die Empfehlung folgt der Empirischen Theorie der Literatur (ETL), die von
Siegfried J. Schmidt im *Grundriß der Empirischen Literaturwissenschaft* (Frankfurt am Main: Suhrkamp, 1991) systematisch begründet wurde.

[11] Vgl. dazu Siegfried J. Schmidt, *Die Selbstorganisation des Sozialsystems
Literatur im 18. Jahrhundert* (Frankfurt am Main: Suhrkamp, 1989).

[12] Deutsches P.E.N.-Zentrum Ost, *Gespräche zur Selbstaufklärung '92* (Berlin,
1993), S. 126.

zeigen, durchaus auf die Dynamik von Modernisierungsprozessen in einer Gesellschaft zurückführen, die unter dem Primat der politischen Ideologie stand bzw. stehen sollte. Wie Sigrid Meuschel immer wieder betont, beförderte die SED im Verlaufe des politischen und sozio-ökonomischen Umbruchs Ende der 40er und zu Beginn der 50er Jahre die Einschränkung und den schrittweisen Abbau eigenständiger gesellschaftlicher Institutionen zugunsten einer umfassenden mono-organisatorischen Struktur. Die Partei versuchte durch die politisch intendierte gesellschaftliche Entdifferenzierung der im 19. und 20. Jahrhundert dominierenden europäischen Modernisierungstendenz entgegenzuwirken und die spezifische Eigenlogik sozialer Subsysteme durch Funktionskriterien der marxistischen Ideologie zu ersetzen.[13]

Der Versuch einer politischen Steuerung der Literaturverhältnisse ist im Bereich der sozio-strukturellen und -organisatorischen Voraussetzungen für literarische Kommunikation in der DDR am wirksamsten und nachhaltigsten gewesen. Das deklarierte Ziel der politischen Führung, "alle sozialen Organismen in Richtung auf die größtmögliche Gleichartigkeit zu entwickeln,"[14] wurde in der Gestaltung der Gesamtheit von institutionellen und infrastrukturellen Determinanten, die die Literaturproduktion, -distribution, -rezeption und -verarbeitung in der DDR-Gesellschaft steuern sollten, nach den allgemeinen Grundsätzen einer umfassenden Wirtschaftsplanung und politischen Kontrolle realisiert. So unterlag die Buchherstellung von der Themenplanung und -bestätigung über die Papierkontingentierung bis zur Auflagenhöhe zentralen Vorgaben. Der Buchhandel wurde mit der schrittweisen Zentralisierung des Zwischenbuchhandels (Leipziger Kommissions- und Großbuchhandel), der Begründung und kontinuierlichen Erweiterung staatlicher Volksbuchhandlungen (bei stetem Rückgang privater Unternehmen) dem Planungs- und Verteilungsermessen des politischen Kalküls unterworfen. Die Gründung und institutionelle Verfassung des Schriftstellerverbands und der Akademie der Künste entsprachen, wie die Versuche zu ihrer Politisierung, einer gesamtgesellschaftlichen Leitungs- und Kontrollprogrammatik der SED.

---

[13] Vgl. dazu Sigrid Meuschel, *Legitimation und Parteiherrschaft* (Frankfurt am Main: Suhrkamp, 1992), S. 10ff.

[14] Dieter Strützel, "Theoretische Voraussetzungen für die Erklärung vereinheitlichender und differenzierender Prozesse in der sozialistischen Kulturentwicklung," in *Einheitlichkeit und Differenzierung in der sozialistischen Kulturentwicklung*, hrsg. Dieter Strützel und Lali Petzold, Wissenschaftliche Beiträge der Friedrich-Schiller-Universität Jena, 1985, S. 28.

Die sozio-organisatorischen Randbedingungen des Systems "DDR-Literatur" umfaßten darüber hinaus u.a. die materiellen Vergütungen von Autoren (Stipendien, Auftragshonorare der gesellschaftlichen Organisationen), die Modi der schriftstellerischen Nachwuchsentwicklung und -förderung (Schriftstellerseminare, Literaturinstitut Johannes R. Becher, Poetenwerkstätten, Zirkel schreibender Arbeiter, Bezirksliteraturzentren etc.), die Einrichtung von literaturpolitischen Institutionen, die über Dienstvorschriften und Gesetze Aufgaben zugewiesen bekamen (staatliche Kommissionen, HV Verlage und Buchhandel beim Ministerium für Kultur u.a.).

Unter den diskursiven und handlungspraktischen Randbedingungen des DDR-Literatursystems wird die Gesamtheit aller literaturbezogenen Handlungen und Diskurse verstanden, die Einfluß und Wirkung auf die literarische Kommunikation und den literarischen Diskurs haben sollten. Aus der Vielzahl der möglichen Referenzbezüge sollen einige in kurzen Skizzen angedeutet werden: Die literaturbezogenen Handlungen im politischen System und der politisch-ideologische Diskurs stellten die einflußreichsten Randbedingungen für das Literatursystem der DDR dar. So impliziert die kulturpolitische Modellierung der Beschaffenheit, Funktionsweise und Tradition einer "neuen sozialistischen Nationalliteratur" präskriptive ästhetische Normen, vorzugsweise zu gestaltende Wirklichkeitsbereiche und indoktrinierte soziale Faktizität wie Verbote und Tabus in ästhetischen und semantischen Fragen, die gegebenenfalls auch mittels politischer Intervention zur Geltung gebracht werden.

Bereits in den 50er Jahren ist die Entwicklung von "Abwehrmechanismen" des Literatursystems gegen die politisch ideologische Fremdsteuerung deutlich feststellbar. Wie in vielen Dokumenten aus unterschiedlichen institutionellen und politischen Bereichen deutlich wird, war der politisch geforderte Beitrag, den literarische Kommunikation zum ideologischen Diskurs und damit zur Herausbildung sozialistischen Bewußtseins im Staatsvolk der DDR zu leisten hatte, für die literarisch Handelnden, d.h. für die Autoren, Verleger, Leser und Kritiker, kontraproduktiv. Insofern ist es auch kaum verwunderlich, daß, wie unsere Untersuchung[15] über das DDR-Literatur-

---

15 Die Forschungsgruppe der Martin-Luther-Universität Halle bearbeitet seit 1991 ein Projekt mit dem Thema "Das Literatursystem der DDR – ästhetische Autonomisierung und politische Fremdbestimmung." Das Projekt wird durch die Deutsche Forschungsgemeinschaft im Rahmen des trilateralen Forschungsprogramms der Schweiz, Österreichs und der Bundesrepublik Deutschland "Differenzierung und Integration. Sprache und Literatur deutschsprachiger Länder im

system in den 50er Jahren zeigt, die Literatur, die unter dem Einfluß ideologischer Fremdsteuerung stand, vom literarischen Distributionsapparat aus kommerziellen Gründen behindert und vom Leser schlicht negiert wurde.

Dafür ein Beispiel: Bodo Uhse benutzte während einer Vorstandsdiskussion des Deutschen Schriftstellerverbands, die den Mängeln bei der Verbreitung der neuen literarischen Werke gewidmet war, ein metaphorisches Bild, das sowohl die systemische Dimension des Problems als auch die Konflikte zwischen ideologischen und literarischen Kriterien in allen Bereichen des Literatursystems deutlich macht:

> Wir haben die Bibliotheken fertiggemacht. Wir haben schärfste Kritik am Buchhandel geübt. Jetzt sind wir auch noch auf die Leser gekommen und haben auch sie fertiggemacht. Und schließlich haben wir auch die Schriftsteller fertiggemacht. Damit scheint mir aber der Kreis geschlossen, und die Schlange beißt sich in den Schwanz.[16]

Die Auswirkungen der ideologischen Einflußnahme auf die schriftstellerische Produktion ließ die Autoren zu Bestandteilen einer "ideologischen Maschine" (Brezan) werden, deren "Konstruktionsfehler" in den 50er Jahren zum einen im Widerstand des zum Teil noch nach kommerziellen Prinzipien funktionierenden Distributionsapparates lag, zum anderen in der grundlegenden Divergenz bestand, die zwischen ideologisch konstruiertem literarischen Publikum (dem hypothetischen Leser) und den Präferenzen und literarischen Wertvorstellungen des realen Lesers in der DDR existierte.

Am Beispiel des Literatursystems der DDR in den 50er Jahren wird die Notwendigkeit der wissenschaftlichen Doppelperspektive von sozialer und diskursiver Systemreferenz der Literatur auf nachhaltige Weise bestätigt: Die diskursive Fremdbestimmung, deren textuelle Umsetzung sich im Bereich der literarischen Produktion über die Akzeptanz des ideologischen Primats vollzog, bringt eine schwere Funktionsstörung im literarischen Handlungssystem mit sich – der Buchhandel und die Leser verweigern Anschlußhandlungen.

Bereits für die 50er und 60er Jahre können demzufolge nicht vorbehaltlos Rückschlüsse aus den überlieferten Proklamationen der

---

Prozeß der Modernisierung" gefördert.

[16] Protokoll der Sitzung des Vorstands des Deutschen Schriftstellerverbands v. 25. 8.1955, Akademie der Künste. Archiv des Deutschen Schriftstellerverbands, o.Sign.

Politik auf die Realität und Funktionalität des literarischen Lebens und der literarischen Kommunikation gezogen werden. Autoren und Distributionsapparat widersetzen sich ebenso wie das Publikum auf unterschiedliche Weise den ideologischen Vorgaben und literaturpolitischen Interventionen. Besonders in den 70er und 80er Jahren mehrten sich die Anzeichen und Voraussetzungen einer Autonomisierung des Sozialsystems Literatur und des literarischen Diskurses.

Das analytische Potential des Modells vom "Literatursystem der DDR" soll abschließend anhand eines konkreten Falls überprüft werden. Als Ausgangspunkt soll ein persönlicher Brief von Kurt Hager an Erich Honecker vom 24. April 1980 dienen, in dem Hager die bevorstehende Publikation des dritten Bandes von Erwin Strittmatters Romantrilogie *Der Wundertäter* thematisiert. Der Text lautet:

> Lieber Erich
>
> Anbei einige Überlegungen zu Strittmatters Buch. Bei der Lage der Dinge bleibt m. E. keine andere Wahl als in den sauren Apfel zu beissen, also Variante 2 zu akzeptieren (Erscheinen, begleitet von kritischen Rezensionen im ND, Wochenpost, NDL und Sonntag).
>
> Von der bereits dem Autor bekannten 1. Auflage von 60 Tausend Exemplaren wäre ein "Abkauf" von 20 000 Exemplaren möglich ohne dass es auffallen würde. Weitere Massnahmen zur unauffälligen Reduzierung der Wirkung des Buches halte ich für möglich.
>
> Ich bitte Dich um Mitteilung ob Du mit diesem Vorgehen einverstanden bist.[17]

Unter der Perspektive des "Sozialsystems Literatur" ist auffällig, daß Hager tatsächlich alle literarischen Handlungsbereiche thematisiert. Neben dem Autor, mit dem in den Jahren zuvor natürlich intensiv diskutiert und verlegerisch gearbeitet wurde, stehen die Kritiker, welche nach Erscheinen durch kritische Rezensionen die kommunikative Wirkung des Textes in die richtigen Bahnen lenken sollten. Der Handlungsbereich literarischer Vermittlung wird durch eine quantitative Regelung berührt, wenn Hager empfiehlt, die Auflagenhöhe von 60 000 Exemplaren durch "Abkauf" von 20 000 Exemplaren unauffällig zu verringern. Die Wendung "ohne dass es auffallen würde" steht für die Vernichtung von 20 000 Exemplaren, die aus den Lagern des Zwischenbuchhandels offenbar auf direktem

---

[17] Kurt Hager, Brief an Erich Honecker, 24.4.1980, Stiftung Archiv der Parteien und Massenorganisationen der DDR im Bundesarchiv, Zentrales Parteiarchiv, IV B 2/2.024/98.

Weg in den Reißwolf kamen. Der literarische Rezipient ist schließlich angesprochen, wenn der Verfasser die Möglichkeit in Erwägung zieht, Maßnahmen zur unauffälligen Reduzierung der literarischen Wirkung des Textes in die Wege zu leiten.

Oberflächlich betrachtet, könnte der Text als Ausdruck der Omnipotenz des politischen Machtapparats gegenüber dem Literatursystem gelesen werden; bereits eine etwas schärfere Beobachtung verdeutlicht, daß sich die Verhältnisse zwischen Literatur und Politik seit den 50er Jahren spürbar verändert haben. Die Formulierung, daß es sich bei Variante 2 um eine "saure-Apfel-Lösung" handelt, verweist auf eine Zwangssituation, mit der sich das politische System in seiner Entscheidungsfindung konfrontiert sieht. In den "Überlegungen zum Erscheinen bzw. Nichterscheinen des Wt.," die in der Abteilung Kultur des ZK der SED ausgearbeitet worden waren, um die verschiedenen Handlungsmöglichkeiten mit ihren Konsequenzen vor einer Publikationsentscheidung gegeneinander abzuwägen, ist von 3 Varianten die Rede: "1. Nichterscheinen; 2. Erscheinen, begleitet von kritischen Rezensionen in ausgewählten Organen; 3. Erscheinen bei totaler Ignorierung in der Öffentlichkeit und eventuell begrenzter Zahl."[18]

Die als Konsequenzen aus "Variante 1" prognostizierten öffentlichen Reaktionen werden von den Kulturpolitikern als so katastrophal angesehen, daß eine politische Entscheidung für die Veröffentlichung fällt, obwohl das Buch eigentlich als nicht publizierbar gilt. Würde das Buch nämlich nicht erscheinen, wären der Bruch zwischen Autor und Partei, eine komplizierte Lage unter den Künstlern und Schriftstellern der DDR, Fragen und Probleme der Leserschaft sowie die gegnerische Propaganda der Massenmedien zu befürchten.[19]

Das beschriebene Beispiel beweist meines Erachtens, daß sich die Literatur in kommunikativer und sozialer Hinsicht zu Beginn der 80er Jahre durch die Politik nicht mehr steuern ließ. Allein Hagers Absicht, die bereits produzierte Auflage von 60 000 Exemplaren durch "Abkauf" von 20 000 zu verringern, verdeutlicht, daß die politischen Direktiven im literarischen Vermittlungsbereich nicht mehr ohne weiteres durchzusetzen waren. Man entschied sich im Politbüro lieber für Unauffälligkeiten. Sehr viel schwerer wiegt der Umstand, daß das Literatursystem der DDR schon zu Beginn der

---

[18] Abteilung Kultur, Überlegungen zum Erscheinen bzw. Nichterscheinen des Wt., 18.04.1980, Stiftung Archiv der Parteien und Massenorganisationen der DDR im Bundesarchiv, ZPA, IV B 2/2.024/98.

[19] Ebenda.

80er Jahre auch in kommunikativer Hinsicht für die Parteipolitik kaum noch beherrschbar war. Insbesondere die Integration von Texten und Autoren der DDR in den Literaturbetrieb der Bundesrepublik, spätestens seit Anfang der 70er Jahre, zählte zu den Faktoren, die literarische und literaturpolitische Handlungen in der DDR immer stärker beeinflußten. Die restriktiven Rahmenbedingungen der sozialen Organisation und ideologischen Determination von Literatur führten nach dem neuralgischen Datum vom November 1976, der Ausbürgerung von Wolf Biermann aus der DDR, bei denjenigen Autoren, die sich auf die Definitionen und Setzungen des politischen Systems nicht mehr verpflichten ließen, zur immer stärkeren Orientierung an den sozialen und diskursiven Bedingungen der literarischen Kultur Westdeutschlands.

Diese Tendenz wurde durch unterschiedliche Umstände und Faktoren befördert. Die Rahmenbedingungen des Literatursystems der Bundesrepublik Deutschland boten die Chance,

- ein ausdifferenziertes Mediensystem und eine vergleichsweise freie Öffentlichkeit zur literarischen Arbeit und zur politischen Meinungsäußerung zu nutzen,
- die zunehmende unerträgliche Belastung der administrativen Kontrolle von Literatur schon im Arbeitsprozeß außer acht lassen zu können, denn für den Originaltext bestand die Chance einer Publikation in Westdeutschland,
- die ideologischen und ästhetischen Hemmnisse zu negieren, die vor allem als ästhetische Dogmen und referentielle Tabus im Literatursystem der DDR in Kraft waren.

Die Konflikte zwischen den Strategien der politisch-ideologischen Steuerung und Diskurskontrolle und der notwendigen Integration bedeutender Autoren in die DDR-Gesellschaft mußte aus der Sicht des politischen Systems in dem Maße zu Kompromißlösungen führen, in dem den Autoren Alternativen offen standen, deren Wahrnehmung politisch unangenehme Rückwirkungen in der DDR nach sich ziehen konnte (vor allem durch die Berichterstattung der westdeutschen Medien). Bei Entscheidungen über Druck- und Reisegenehmigungen innerhalb des politischen Systems und selbst in Reflexionen innerhalb des MfS spielten solche "autorenpolitischen" Erwägungen eine maßgebliche Rolle. Sie trugen beispielsweise dazu bei, daß die eigens geschaffenen institutionellen und juristischen Voraussetzungen zur Kriminalisierung nicht genehmigter Veröffentlichungen in der Bundesrepublik (Büro für Urheberrechte, Devisengesetzgebung) nur in wenigen Fällen konsequent zur Anwendung kamen (u.a. gegen Stefan Heym). Prominente Autoren konnten diese Konstellation sogar als Druckmittel nutzen, um die Realisierung geforderter Überarbeitungen von Manuskripten einzuschränken oder ganz abzulehnen. Als weitere literaturhistorische Indikatoren, die eine fortschreitende Autonomisierung des Literatursystems bezeichnen, können folgende Merkmale und Charakteristika der DDR-Literatur dienen, die mögliche Forschungsfelder einer systemorientierten Geschichte der DDR-Literatur darstellen:

- die seit Beginn der 60er Jahre schrittweise vollzogene Entkoppelung von ideologischem Normativ und schriftstellerischer Produktion (Strittmatter, Fühmann, Christa Wolf etc.),
- die paradigmatische Bedeutung der literaturästhetischen Mittel und Verfahren von Bertolt Brecht, der in den 50er Jahren die einzige moderne literarische Konzeption gegen die Vereinnahmung der Parteiideologie behauptet hatte, für eine Vielzahl von repräsentativen Autoren (Heiner Müller, Günter Kunert, Volker Braun, Karl Mickel etc.),
- die "Modernisierung" der erzählenden Literatur in den 60er Jahren (Abbau der auktorialen narrativen Instanz zugunsten einer Pluralisierung und Subjektivierung der Stile),
- das Entstehen des literaturhermeneutischen Problems zu Beginn der 70er Jahre, das zu einer extensiven Diskussion über die interpretatorische Methodik der Literaturwissenschaften und zur schrittweisen Eliminierung eines ideologisierten Modells von Literaturgeschichte und literarischer Textbedeutung führt,
- die zunehmende theoretische Unschärfe des Begriffs "sozialistischer Realismus," dessen "Weite und Vielfalt" oftmals nur die ideologischen Probleme bei der Reflexion einer ausdifferenzierten literarischen Praxis signalisiert,
- die Entdeckung des Lesers als sinnstiftenden Faktors in der literarischen Kommunikation,
- die Liberalisierung der literaturvermittelnden Tätigkeit in den Verlagen und Redaktionen, die mit der nominellen Aufhebung des Druckgenehmigungsverfahrens 1988 ihren Höhepunkt findet,
- die Verwendung ästhetischer Mittel der Moderne in den 70er und 80er Jahren (Beckett, Rimbaud, surrealistische und dadaistische Schreibweisen, Nouveau Roman, Beat Generation), und schließlich
- die Entstehung einer eigenständigen literarischen Bewegung

der "autonomen Literaturszene," die expliziten Anschluß an poststrukturalistische Diskurstheorien herstellt.

Die vielfältigen Themen und Forschungsmöglichkeiten, die eine systemorientierte literaturhistorische Beobachtung der DDR-Literatur eröffnet, werden seit einigen Jahren von Literaturwissenschaftlern in Ost- und Westdeutschland mit durchaus unterschiedlichen theoretischen Ansätzen bearbeitet. Die Publikation erster Forschungsergebnisse[20] und die Vorstellung neuer Projekte,[21] die system- und kommunikationstheoretischen Modellen verpflichtet sind, beweist, daß die Systemanalyse der DDR-Literaturgeschichte zu neuen Einsichten verhilft und auf innovative Perspektiven hoffen läßt.

---

[20] Vor allem die Studien des Forschungsprojekts "Struktur und Funktion literarischer Öffentlichkeit in der DDR," die von Siegfried Lokatis, Simone Barck und Martina Langermann in *Historische DDR-Forschung. Aufsätze und Studien*, hrsg. Jürgen Kocka (Berlin: Akademie, 1993) publiziert wurden, wären zu nennen.

[21] Zum Beispiel, die Projektvorstellung von Birgit Dahlke, Frank Hörnigk, Martina Langermann und Thomas Taterka, "Kanon und Zensur. Zur literarischen/ kulturellen Kommunikation in der SBZ/DDR," *Zeitschrift für Germanistik*, Neue Folge, 5, Nr. 1 (1995), S. 74-81.

Buchenwald: Symbol and Metaphor for the Changing Political Culture of East Germany

David A. Hackett

High on a mountain in Thuringia overlooking the Autobahn from Frankfurt to Leipzig and mainline railroad tracks that parallel it, is a massive marble monument clearly visible to all those passing below. The mountain is the Ettersberg, 1578 feet high, not the highest mountain of central Germany, but high enough to be visible from all directions for many miles. In a joke typifying the black humor of the Third Reich, it was said that it was the highest mountain in Germany because it took a man ten minutes to go up, but two years to come down.[1] The reference, of course, is to the concentration camp Buchenwald, built on the Ettersberg in 1937. The marble monument is the *Mahnmal*, erected by the East German government in the mid-1950s to commemorate the concentration camp victims of the Third Reich and to serve, as the name suggests, as an admonition to future generations.

Nestled at the base of the Ettersberg, just five miles away, is the picturesque city of Weimar, famous as the home of Goethe, Schiller, Herder, and Wieland, as well as Liszt and Nietzsche. Today the city is filled with museums that make it a shrine to German classicism. To the people of Weimar, the existence of Buchenwald has been both a blessing and curse for almost two generations now. In the last thirty years of the GDR period, the prison camp became a major tourist attraction, a national memorial

---

[1] Manfred Overesch, "Ernst Thapes Buchenwalder Tagebuch von 1945," *Vierteljahrshefte für Zeitgeschichte*, 29, No. 4 (1981), p. 634.

(*Gedenkstätte*) that drew steady streams of domestic and foreign travelers, most of whom came from East bloc countries.

Today, after German unification, the stream has become a trickle. Buchenwald Camp once again appears to be more of a nuisance and embarrassment to the neighboring city of Weimar, much as it had been in its early days in the late 1930s. That feeling of embarrassment is probably even greater in regard to the great stone monument on the Ettersberg.

After unification a controversy broke out in Germany over what was to become of the site that the Berlin newspaper *die tageszeitung* described in 1991 as "the red Olympus" and one of "the pilgrimage places of official GDR antifascism."[2] The article's author, Vera Gaserow, spoke of the growing debate over the "positioning" (i.e., political interpretation) of the monuments of East German antifascism. Complicating this debate was the new public awareness of the existence of a Soviet camp at Buchenwald (Lager II), which in the immediate postwar period had contained thousands of people charged with being Nazi party officials, as well as numerous others categorized as "class enemies" or potential opponents of the regime. The history of this second camp had been kept secret during the GDR regime, but after 1989 it began to come into the open.[3] The debate that began was over what group or groups ought to be commemorated in Buchenwald.

Visitors who traveled up the Ettersberg in the early 1980s would typically ride on a crowded city bus.[4] It might be full of Russian soldiers from the barracks at the bottom of the hill, of young people from the Free German Youth, tourists from East bloc countries, and a few Western tourists. The parking lot at the top was usually full,

---

[2] Vera Gaserow, "Buchenwald wird 'neu positioniert,'" *die tageszeitung*, 5 June 1991. My translation here and throughout. See also Bernd Faulenbach, "Von der Gegenwärtigkeit des Vergangenen: Zur Neukonzeption von Gedenkstätten in der ehemaligen DDR," *Weltspiegel, Sonntagsbeilage des Tagesspiegels*, 7 February 1993, p. 1. The author wishes to thank Margy Gerber for calling these articles to his attention.

[3] See *Recht oder Rache? Buchenwald 1945-50, Betroffene erinnern sich*, ed. Hanno Müller (Frankfurt am Main: dipa, 1991); Gerhard Finn, "Wieder einmal nichts gewußt: 'Vergangenheitsbewältigung' in Buchenwald," *Deutschland Archiv*, 23, No. 8 (1990), pp. 1251-59.

[4] These comments are based on the author's personal impressions on two visits to Buchenwald and the *Mahnmal* in July 1980 and July 1992. Similar impressions are also recorded by Ian Buruma, "Buchenwald," *Granta* 42 (Winter 1992), pp. 67-75.

crowded with cars from Poland, Czechoslovakia, Yugoslavia, Bulgaria, and the GDR, as well as France and the Netherlands. A hotel, a youth hostel, and a cafeteria on the grounds catered to the visiting throngs. Inside the camp, groups and clusters of tourists, many with tour guides, walked around the camp and streamed through the museum exhibit.

A few years after unification, the same surroundings gave a rather forlorn impression. In 1992 city buses no longer traveled the route to the camp and monument. A private bus line took a handful of tourists and employees up the mountain on an irregular schedule of four roundtrips a day. On the days I was there, the parking lot was mostly empty; few of the cars were German and none were from East bloc countries. In July 1992 the hotel had been closed for over a year; the youth hostel contained only one small group of students; and the inexpensive cafeteria was mostly empty at lunch time. Organized tours were conspicuously absent and tourists wandered aimlessly about in small groups on self-guided tours. The nearby *Mahnmal* was usually totally deserted. On most days no tourists boarded or left the bus at the designated stop there.

How can one explain this precipitous loss of interest in what remains, in theory at least, an important site of contemporary German history? (In contrast, Wartburg castle, a short distance away at Eisenach, has been flooded with tourists since unification.) Obviously the painful memories associated with Nazism and the Third Reich are part of the reason for German tourists staying away. But it could also be argued that the *Mahnmal* and Buchenwald Camp have lost their past significance because they have lost their present and future meaning. Although at first glance this sounds anachronistic, historians have demonstrated that past, present, and future are interlocked in subtle and interesting ways.[5] This is especially true of public monuments, which have always been deliberately created by governments and groups of citizens as ways of linking future and past. Therefore it is in this diachronic sense that public monuments must be studied by historians.

Over the last decade a new methodology of history has begun to develop: the study of "political culture." Unlike earlier studies of monuments which were largely antiquarian in nature, newer studies see the building of monuments as expressions of political values and goals, either on the part of the state and its official culture, or of

---

[5] See for example the work of Reinhart Koselleck, *Futures Past. On the Semantics of Historical Time* (Cambridge, MA: MIT Press, 1985), originally published in Germany as *Vergangene Zukunft* (1979).

groups of citizens expressing themselves as a subculture.[6] George
L. Mosse recognized the importance of this field of study in two
pioneering works: *The Nationalization of the Masses* (1975) and
Fallen Soldiers (1990).[7] These works and one on American monuments, *Remaking America* by John Bodnar (1992),[8] have inspired
the present attempt to deal with Buchenwald as a monument.

Symbol

In GDR times the official name of the historical monument at
Buchenwald was the Nationale Mahn- und Gedenkstätte Buchenwald, an entity which after 1961 was administered by the Ministry
of Culture in East Berlin. It included both the monument on the
Ettersberg (the *Mahnmal*) and the concentration camp itself (*Gedenkstätte*).[9] Today its official letterhead reads simply "Gedenkstätte
Buchenwald" and the greatly reduced staff is employed by the CDU-
governed state of Thuringia. The relative lack of interest of the
Landesregierung in supporting this historical monument is no doubt
influenced by an awareness of the highly political role that Buchenwald played in the old East German state. A brief historical sketch of
the camp and monument will help make this clear.

As late as 1953, the German Democratic Republic had taken no
concrete steps to create an official historical site at Buchenwald
concentration camp. Recent accounts reveal that as late as 1950
political prisoners were still kept there by the Soviets and the new
GDR state.[10] No doubt, local residents had little reason to create a
celebratory monument on the Ettersberg in the early 1950s.

Evidence for this assumption can be found in an official guidebook, published by the City Council of Weimar in 1953, which

---

[6] On the concept of political culture, see *Rites of Power. Symbolism, Ritual
and Politics since the Middle Ages*, ed. Sean Wilentz (Philadelphia: University
of Pennsylvania Press, 1985). The author wishes to thank Sean Wilentz for the
ideas and inspiration that came from a seminar he conducted on political culture
at the University of Texas at El Paso in March 1993.

[7] George L. Mosse, *The Nationalization of the Masses. Political Symbolism
and Mass Movements in Germany from the Napoleonic Wars through the Third
Reich* (New York: Howard Fertig, 1975); *Fallen Soldiers. Reshaping the Memory of the World Wars* (New York: Oxford University Press, 1990).

[8] John Bodnar, *Remaking America. Public Memory, Commemoration and Patriotism in the Twentieth Century* (Princeton: Princeton University Press, 1992).

[9] *DDR Handbuch* (Cologne: Wissenschaft und Politik, 1979), p. 753.

[10] *Recht oder Rache? Buchenwald 1945-50*, pp. 9-16.

devoted only four of its 118 pages to the camp, emphasizing the city's classical heritage instead.[11] The camp itself is described as "having remained in part in its previous condition" (p. 106). The guidebook also takes note of the "Ehrenhain" on the slope facing Weimar, where 7,000 to 8,000 victims of the Nazis were buried in mass graves, but it makes no mention of a monument there. In the way of directions, the booklet advises tourists to walk up the Ettersburger Landstraße from the train station "about one to one and a half hours on foot" (p. 107).

This rather complacent attitude toward the historical significance of Buchenwald was shaken by the tumultuous events that culminated in the June 17, 1953 uprising. A few days earlier, the East German regime had eased its hardline economic policies, initiating a series of changes, known as the "New Course," designed to shore up popular support for the regime.[12] The uprising proved that more energetic measures were called for to build loyalty to the new socialist state.

One outgrowth of the uprising was the decision to create a Ministry of Culture, which was then headed by Johannes R. Becher, the noted poet and literary critic. Clearly one of its goals was to build a new national political culture in order to create emotional attachments to the state. In a wide-ranging plan dating from October 1954 and titled "Aufgaben und Ziele bis zum Jahre 1960 bei dem Aufbau einer demokratischen und nationalen Volkskultur in der Deutschen Demokratischen Republik," Becher outlined fifteen specific goals covering all areas of culture, including film, literature, art, music, museums, and libraries. Point 14 relates specifically to the subject of this paper: "14. Creation of suitable national memorials of the workers' movement and of the antifascist struggle, in particular at Buchenwald, Sachsenhausen, Ravensbrück, Gotha, and Erfurt."[13] Point 14 of the program was in fact carried out – in the case of Buchenwald within the following four years.

An official history of the city of Weimar states that the government of the GDR had passed a resolution as early as 1951 to build a

---

[11] *Weimar. Ein Führer durch seine Kultur und Geschichte*, ed. Rat der Stadt (Weimar: Thüringer Volksverlag, 1953). See pp. 104-07.

[12] The official GDR history, Rolf Badstübner et al., *Geschichte der Deutschen Demokratischen Republik* (Berlin: Deutscher Verlag der Wissenschaften, 1981) states that these changes began with resolutions passed on June 9 and 11, before the "counter-revolutionary putsch" attempt (p. 157).

[13] *Dokumente zur Kunst- , Literatur- und Kulturpolitik der SED*, ed. Elimar Schubbe (Stuttgart: Seewald, 1972), pp. 346-47.

Mahnmal honoring the victims of fascism as the central theme of a large historical monument on the Ettersberg.[14] It appears, however, that nothing was done to implement this resolution until after the June 1953 uprising. The first step towards a memorial, taken on August 18, 1953, was the placement of a plaque honoring Ernst Thälmann, the prewar Communist Party (KPD) leader, who was murdered at Buchenwald on that day in 1944. The plaque was unveiled by Paul Wandel, Central Committee secretary in charge of education and culture, in the presence of Thälmann's daughter, Irma.

One year later, on the tenth anniversary of Thälmann's death, a Museum of the Resistance Movement and a Thälmann Memorial were opened on the grounds of the former camp. An even larger commemoration was held the following year, on the tenth anniversary of liberation, April 11, 1955. At that ceremony, thousands of "antifascists" gathered on the former roll call square to remember those who died at Buchenwald. In the ceremony, earth of Buchenwald was mingled with that from sites of other martyrdoms: Oradour, Lidice, Warsaw, and Maidanek, as a gesture of the international solidarity of the victims of fascism. Nevertheless, despite increased publicity, it appears that relatively few visitors came to the memorial in the early years: 95,000 in 1954; 174,500 in 1955; and 191,000 in 1956.[15]

The massive monument adjoining the camp on the east slope of the Ettersberg, though begun in 1954, was not actually completed until 1958. The agency building the monument was the Curatorium for the Construction of National Memorials to the Antifascist Resistance Struggle. According to the official history of Weimar, the completion of this vast building project required in the months before its formal dedication some 400 "volunteer" workers a day from the city of Weimar. It was formally dedicated by Otto Grotewohl, President of the Council of Ministers, on September 14, 1958, in the presence of "antifascist" spokesmen from twenty-one countries and a crowd of 100,000 onlookers. "This monument should become a place of commemoration for the friendship with the great Soviet people that liberated our nation and Europe," Grotewohl told the

---

[14] Gitta Gunther and Lothar Wallraf, *Geschichte der Stadt Weimar* (Weimar: Hermann Böhlaus Nachfolger, 1976), p. 733. See also the most complete East German guide to the Buchenwald monuments: Ingrid and Lothar Burghoff, *Nationale Mahn- und Gedenkstätte Buchenwald* (Berlin/Leipzig: Tourist, 1978), pp. 40-41.

[15] *Geschichte der Stadt Weimar*, p. 733.

audience. Antifascism should be subordinated to Bolshevism, "because the antifascist resistance struggle can only be successful, where the people are solidly united under the leadership of the working class."[16] The official Weimar history comments that "peace-loving humanity saw in the new memorial a symbol of the fulfillment of the legacy of the Buchenwald heroes by the German Democratic Republic."[17]

The site chosen for the *Mahnmal* was consciously symbolic in several senses. First, it was on the location of the mass graves dug by the Nazis in the last few months of the war, the site called the "Ehrenhain" in the 1953 pamphlet. Second, a 130 foot high Bismarck tower had stood at the same spot since the turn of the century.[18] The older monument symbolized not only Bismarck's Second Reich, but was linked as well to the extreme nationalism of the Nazis, because SS camp guards used to celebrate their monthly comradeship evenings there.[19] Thus it must have seemed doubly appropriate to the planners of the *Mahnmal* that a monument to the new international socialist solidarity should replace one that symbolized both bourgeois German nationalism and the worst excesses of Nazi barbarism.

The symbolism implicit in the *Mahnmal* can best be explained by a brief description of the completed monument.[20] The central feature is the 164 foot high bell-tower made of cut stone in the spare neoclassical style also favored in the Third Reich. In front of it is a massive stone statue of eleven prisoners by the well-known East German artist Fritz Cremer. The eleven prisoners, though unarmed,

---

[16] *A bis Z. Ein Taschen- und Nachschlagebuch über den anderen Teil Deutschlands* (Bonn: Deutscher Bundesverlag, 1969), p. 439.

[17] *Geschichte der Stadt Weimar*, p. 733.

[18] East German sources do not actually identify it as precisely the same spot, but circumstantial evidence suggests that it is. On the Bismarck tower see: *Geschichte der Stadt Weimar*, p. 464; *Northern Germany. Handbook for Travellers* (Leipsic: Karl Baedeker, 1904), p. 313.

[19] See *The Buchenwald Report*, ed. David A. Hackett (Boulder: Westview Press, 1995), p. 44.

[20] Descriptions (and photographs) of the monument can be found in Adolf Rieth, *Monuments to the Victims of Tyranny* (New York: Frederick A. Praeger, 1969), pp. 19-20; Mario de Micheli et al., *Monumenti alla resistenza in europa* (Milan: Vangelista, 1985), pp. 170-71; Helmut Scharf, *Kleine Kunstgeschichte des deutschen Denkmals* (Darmstadt: Wissenschaftliche Buchgesellschaft, 1984), pp. 331-37; Meinhold Lurz, *Kriegerdenkmäler in Deutschland* (Heidelberg: Esprint, 1985), Vol. 6, pp. 253f.

appear defiant and rebellious; one of them is holding a banner. A few are placed in courageous poses; others appear to hang back in despair. One is a boy, and several are elderly, while the leaders appear to be in the full vigor of manhood. Art critics have pointed out an obvious similarity to Auguste Rodin's group of defiant figures in the *Burghers of Calais* (1886).[21] Cremer's figures commemorate the "self-liberation" of the prisoners on April 11, 1945 and, implicitly, the role of the International Camp Committee in leading it. The message that the sculpture intends to convey is the unbreakable will of the antifascist resistance.

The tower itself is also filled with symbolism. Another East German sculptor, Waldemar Grzimek, created a bas relief design in a large circle in the center of the floor. The medallion incorporates a twisted barbed wire design with the names of other major concentration camps engraved on it. Beneath the emblem lies soil from these other sites, mingled with that of Buchenwald. Grzimek also designed a giant bronze bell for the tower.

A stone walkway (the "Street of Nations") leads to the tower, taking the visitor past a series of pylons commemorating each of the thirty-three nations represented among the prisoners of Buchenwald. Seven steles with bas reliefs, inscribed with texts by Johannes R. Becher, represent the seven years of the camp's existence. There are also three "ring graves," the largest of which is in front of the Cremer sculpture; here an eternal fire burns to commemorate the victims of the camp, whose remains lie in the monument grounds. The layout of the walkways and pylons is strongly reminiscent of the earlier Soviet War Memorial in East Berlin (Treptow), with its pylons commemorating the various Soviet republics.[22] The effect of the Street of Nations is heightened by the contrast afforded by the spectacular views of the peaceful valley below.

The message of the monument is clear, if at the same time contradictory. The victims of National Socialism are being honored, though at the same time they are totally invisible and completely anonymous – mingled with the soil, like that so symbolically mixed in the tower. They are simply fertilizer for the growth of a "new" German state, the newness of which the GDR constantly pointed out to its citizens. On the other hand, the heroes visibly commemorated are the survivors – the antifascist resistance fighters – who would later, one is led to believe, be found in the ranks of the SED. Also

[21] Rieth, *Monuments*, p. 20; Scharf, *Kleine Kunstgeschichte*, p. 336.
[22] Volker Frank, *Antifaschistische Mahnmale in der DDR* (Leipzig: Seemann, 1970), pp. 9-12.

implicitly celebrated in the Street of Nations was the GDR's policy of friendship and solidarity with the East bloc nations, even though a few of the pylons are labeled with the names of Western nations like France and the USA.

Many visitors have found the monument's Stalinistic style more repellent than attractive. The Spanish novelist Jorge Semprun described it as "in one word – disgusting."[23] Semprun, a former prisoner of Buchenwald, relates a revealing conversation he had with an official in East Berlin in 1960. When he told the East German official of his recurring dream that the camp had simply been abandoned to the forces of nature, with the trees and shrubs left to grow over the abandoned buildings, the reaction of the East German official was one of surprise and horror. No, the official objected, "a monument, a thing with an educational message, a political one" (p. 37) was what they had constructed. The official defended it by saying that the idea of building a monument had been suggested by Bertolt Brecht.

Clearly then, the *Mahnmal*, even more than the camp itself, is a monument to the present and the future, rather than the past. Thus it is not surprising that it now presents an even bleaker aspect than the camp. Without the liveliness created by crowds of tourists from different lands, the unspoken message is more one of individual isolation and apathy, than one of solidarity and strength of will. Cremer's heroic figures seem overly romanticized, even slightly absurd in their loneliness on the hill. It appears too that the "eternal fire" has gone out in the ring graves.

The grounds of the camp itself (*Gedenkstätte*) are also full of symbolism. The rows of barracks are now only outlines on the ground, but the visitor can still see the barbed-wire fences, the gate-house and towers, the *Effektenkammer*, and of course, the crematorium, with its shrine to Thälmann, and the execution room. The iron gate is still there, with its wrought-iron inscription "Jedem das Seine" ("To each his own"), but, perhaps significantly, the other motto, painted on the gatehouse wall until 1945: "Mein Vaterland, Recht oder Unrecht" ("My Country, Right or Wrong!") had at some point disappeared. One of the heavy carts, to which prisoners were yoked to pull heavy loads of stone, is still there, but the sign revealing that the prisoners were called "singing horses" was gone in 1992.

The most explicit historical messages, of course, are contained

---

[23] Jorge Semprun, *Aquel domingo* (Barcelona: Planeta, 1981), p. 37. See also the similar reaction of Ian Buruma, "Buchenwald," p. 68.

in the historical exhibition in the museum, located in the former bathhouse. In 1980 the exhibit offered an ideologically distorted picture of what had occurred there: it told of valiant socialist and communist resistance leaders imprisoned there, especially Thäl-mann, and of many Russian prisoners of war shot in the horse stables, but there was no mention of Jews, gypsies, homosexuals, clergymen, Jehovah's Witnesses, or of the Poles (or other nation-alities). At the end of the exhibit, where the liberation was de-scribed, there was a giant picture of prisoners and soldiers. The soldiers were wearing American caps, but the caption spoke of liberation coming from the East, from the Soviet Union. Particularly offensive was the total denial of anti-Semitism as a central part of Nazi ideology.

The exhibit in place in 1992, dating mostly from about 1985, was more interesting and more historically accurate. Rooms were filled with three-dimensional exhibits and dioramas, rather than two-dimensional photographic panels. By 1985, anti-Semitism in Nazi policy was being more honestly addressed, although still not empha-sized, as was the role of clergy and religious leaders, such as Pastor Paul Schneider, in the resistance to National Socialism. The role of the communists in the camp was still the focal point, however. Eugen Kogon, the most famous of the camp resistance leaders to have settled in the West after the war, was mentioned nowhere.[24] The U.S. role in liberating the camp was at least briefly acknow-ledged. The major change since unification was the addition of a room acknowledging the existence after the war of the second camp (Lager II), under Soviet administration.

An article that appeared in the principal East German historical journal, *Zeitschrift für Geschichtswissenschaft*, in 1979, gives an indication of the historical uses of the camp for the GDR regime. On the one hand, growing numbers of visitors to Buchenwald were reported over the first twenty years.[25] On the other hand, it is clear that youth groups represented an increasing percentage of the GDR citizens visiting the camp, with declining numbers of adult GDR

---

[24] Eugen Kogon was the author of *Der SS-Staat. Das System der deutschen Konzentrationslager* (Munich: Karl Alber, 1946), an account based largely on his experience at Buchenwald. It appeared in numerous editions, including a revised edition (Munich: Kindler, 1974) and a recent paperback edition (Munich: Wil-helm Heyne, 1989).

[25] Ewald Deyda, "Zur Zusammenarbeit der Nationalen Mahn- und Gedenkstätte Buchenwald mit Studenten und Schülern," *Zeitschrift für Geschichtswissen-schaft*, 27, No. 6 (1979), p. 530.

visitors, a trend that anecdotal evidence suggests increased over the years.

The journal article indicates that visits alone were not enough to achieve the desired effect on the youth. Ewald Deyda, the author of the article, argued that the function of the "Nationale Mahn- und Gedenkstätte Buchenwald, as well as that of all the other memorials, is to make an important contribution to the deepening and development of a socialist historical consciousness" (p. 530). Students should be prepared for their visit to Buchenwald by means of study of the "revolutionary past, the accomplishments of the communists and antifascists in the resistance struggle, as well as with the crimes of the fascists, especially the SS" (p. 530), he continued. The main point of the article, however, was that young people should become more deeply involved with the history of Buchenwald by doing actual historical research on primary documents in the Buchenwald archives.

For most of its history then, the *Gedenkstätte* served as a site for the glorification of Ernst Thälmann, the KPD resistance leaders inside the camp, and indirectly, of course, as legitimation for the GDR as the continuation of the "antifascist" struggle in the Cold War period.

Metaphor

The *Mahnmal* and *Gedenkstätte* at Buchenwald also served as metaphors for concepts of a more purely political and historical nature, all of which were intended to provide legitimacy to the German Democratic Republic as a state. Three principal metaphors could be drawn from the historical past of Buchenwald. The unity of the German "antifascists" in the camp resembled that of the National Front, the government coalition that ruled the country. The role of the International Camp Committee was analogous to the international solidarity of the socialist bloc and the Warsaw Pact. Finally, the myth of "self-liberation" made possible a version of history that rejected the role of the United States in liberating Germany from fascism. These three interrelated concepts became an integral part of the political culture of the German Democratic Republic, repeated so often that they became clichés.

Antifascism was originally based in genuine, deep-felt emotions that linked together virtually all of the prisoners in Buchenwald before April 1945. The 1945 post-liberation report compiled by the Buchenwald prisoners reflects this in many of its pages and individual accounts.[26] The term comrade (*Kamerad*) was widely used by the inmates, not as a sign of party membership, but as an expression of solidarity, in the same way that the term was used by German front soldiers in World War I. In the last months before liberation, the International Camp Committee was already engaged in converting those generalized feelings of solidarity among the prisoners into a clear bid for power by the communist camp leadership.

The original antifascism of the prisoners found its primary ideological expression in the famous "Buchenwald Oath," first recited at a post-liberation camp rally on April 19, 1945. Later the oath became a familiar ritual in the GDR, repeated on various memorial occasions. It ended with the raising of clinched fists and the chant in unison: "We Swear!" The most famous part of the oath was quoted by Otto Grotewohl in his speech at the dedication of the *Mahnmal* in September 1958: "The annihilation of Nazism with its roots is our slogan! The building of a new world of peace and freedom is our goal."[27]

Soon after the war was over, this antifascism, which linked together varied opponents of Nazism, was put into practice. Order No. 2 (from June 10, 1945) of the Soviet Military Administration authorized the creation of a block of "antifascist-democratic" parties, including the CDU.[28] This block eventually became the National Front, which, under SED control, officially governed the German Democratic Republic from its founding in 1949 to 1989.

There is evidence to suggest that the original antifascist movements of May and June 1945 had spontaneous, grass-roots support from a variety of social groups and classes.[29] But at some point, this "genuine" antifascism (as a broad-based anti-Nazism), was converted into a "false" one (complete submission to the leadership of the SED), according to Günter Fippel, an East German critic of the regime.[30] Fippel claims that a sizeable portion (one-third) of

---

[26] The original report, prepared by the U.S. Army, was called by Eugen Kogon the "Rosenberg Report" after the army officer who organized it. Never before published, it has now appeared as *The Buchenwald Report*, ed. David A. Hackett (Boulder: Westview Press, 1995).

[27] Cited in Deyda, "Zur Zusammenarbeit," p. 529.

[28] Badstübner et al., *Geschichte der DDR*, pp. 26-27.

[29] See Günter Benser, "Antifa-Ausschüsse - Staatsorgane - Parteiorganisation. Überlegungen zu Ausmaß, Rolle und Grenzen der antifaschistischen Bewegung am Ende des Zweiten Weltkrieges," *Zeitschrift für Geschichtswissenschaft*, 26, No. 9 (1978), pp. 785-802.

[30] Günter Fippel, "Der Mißbrauch des Faschismus-Begriffs in der SBZ/DDR,"

those imprisoned after the war by the Soviets were former inmates of Nazi concentration camps and that, of those arrested, a significant portion (25 percent) were of Jewish background (p. 1057).

It seems clear from this study and other evidence that the definition of antifascism had changed – narrowed in fact – since 1945. After many of the non-communist members of the VVN (Vereinigung der Verfolgten des Naziregimes) left in 1950, the organization itself was dissolved in February 1953 and was replaced later by the Komitee der Antifaschistischen Widerstandskämpfer. In 1958 the latter organization defined antifascist resistance as follows: "The honorable title of resistance fighter is deserved only by those who today also recognize the leadership of the party of the working class [SED], who protect the unity of the Party, passionately defend it, and do everything for the building of socialism."[31] In later times defense of the Soviet Union also belonged to the operative definition of antifascism in the GDR.

If antifascism was the root ideology, then the International Camp Committee at Buchenwald, led by longtime German communist prisoners, embodied that system of rule. It is perhaps significant that some individuals from the Buchenwald camp committee later played important roles in the GDR regime. For example, Walter Bartel, the leader of the camp's German committee, became an influential professor of modern history at Humboldt University. Others include Bruno Apitz, Ernst Busse, Baptist Feilen, Stefan Heymann, Erich Reschke, and Robert Siewert. The most important task of the International Camp Committee, as depicted in later East German historiography, however, was its preparation for armed resistance against the Nazis, the factor that prepared the way for liberation and its accompanying myths.

"Self-liberation" (*Selbstbefreiung*) became a convenient way of linking the Party's leadership role with its foreign policy goal of alliance with the Soviet Union. The liberation of Buchenwald by the U.S. Army was an inconvenient fact that over the course of years simply disappeared from the history books. In one case, the cover of a 1963 tenth grade history textbook showed a sketch of Soviet troops arriving to liberate the camp.[32] Bruno Apitz's popular novel *Nackt unter Wölfen* (1958) glorified the role of the camp's communist leadership and obscured the actual external military conditions that made that liberation possible. This book became required

---

Deutschland Archiv, 25, No. 9 (1992), pp. 1055-65.
[31] *A bis Z*, p. 336.
[32] Overesch, "Ernst Thapes Buchenwalder Tagebuch," p. 631.

reading in the GDR, selling over two million copies; it was translated into 28 languages.[33] A more serious historical work, *Stärker
als die Wölfe* (1976), by Günter Kühn and Wolfgang Weber gave a
detailed and scholarly account of the same argument.[34]

Space does not permit a detailed discussion of this myth here,[35]
but it can be said that it represents a distortion of what actually
happened. The prisoners did arm themselves for resistance to the
Nazis in case of a final showdown, but no such battle ever occurred.
The International Camp Committee took over the camp for a brief
period after the Nazi guards had fled from the advancing American
troops on April 11, 1945. The sequence of events on the day of
liberation can be pieced together from a variety of sources. Tanks
from the Third U.S. Army appeared in the vicinity of Buchenwald
about 2:30 p.m., the remaining Nazi guards fled to the woods about
3:00 p.m., and the prisoners' militia stormed the gates and the
watchtowers at about 3:15 p.m.[36] The East German accounts fail to
point out that the SS commandant had already turned over command
of the camp to a member of the Committee, the senior camp inmate,
a few hours before. It is also a fact that armed prisoner patrols left
the camp after liberation to arrest Nazi guards hiding in the nearby
forest.

Control of the camp by the Committee lasted only a matter of
hours (thirty-six hours at most), until units of the American Third
Army took "effective control" of the camp itself on April 13.[37] The
first American officers had already arrived at 5:30 p.m. on April 11,
just two hours after the "liberation." An American officer addressed
the first "freedom roll call" on the morning of April 12. On the 13th,
U.S. troops arrived in force to take over the camp, bringing with

[33] Bruno Apitz, *Nackt unter Wölfen*, with illustrations by Fritz Cremer (Halle: Mitteldeutscher Verlag, 1958), and numerous later editions. Sales figures from *Neue Heimat* (April 1975), p. 4.

[34] Günter Kühn and Wolfgang Weber, *Stärker als die Wölfe* (Berlin: Militär-verlag der Deutschen Demokratischen Republik, 1976).

[35] The classic documentation of the "self-liberalization" myth is in Walter Bartel, *Buchenwald. Mahnung und Verpflichtung* (Berlin: Kongress, 1960), Chapter 6.

[36] Kogon, *Der SS-Staat*, p. 362; Robert H. Abzug, *Inside the Vicious Heart. Americans and the Liberation of Nazi Concentration Camps* (New York: Oxford University Press, 1985), pp. 48-49; *The Buchenwald Report*, Introduction, Part I: Section 13, Part II: Chapter 10.

[37] See *The Buchenwald Report*, Introduction, Chapter Ten. Also, Overesch, "Ernst Thapes Buchenwalder Tagebuch," pp. 635, 651.

them food, medical supplies, and a mobile hospital unit. On the slender thread of the brief period of control by the International Camp Committee, an elaborate mythology was built to help legitimize the new postwar regime of the GDR.

In later times, simply to have been a prisoner at Buchenwald was to have been present at the founding of the regime. An anecdote from Jorge Semprun illustrates this point. In his conversations in East Berlin in 1960, he let it slip out that he had been a prisoner at Buchenwald. "Why didn't you say that before?" the surprised official asked. His reaction, Semprun says, was like that of an English gentleman who discovers in the course of a casual conversation that a new acquaintance is an alumnus of Oxford.[38] He points out that the officials he encountered had made a good career out of their past: one was a high-ranking official in the criminal police; the other a major general in the Volkspolizei.

The role of Buchenwald as a metaphor for the East German state was readily apparent both to its visitors and to the scholars and authors who wrote about it. Perhaps its clearest expression can be found in the title of a 1980 article by Walter Bartel: "The Historic Oath of Buchenwald Realized in the GDR."[39] Nowhere is the link between the East German state and Buchenwald as history and historical monument made more explicit.

Conclusion

The Buchenwald memorial and monument carry a double burden of the past: both an East German and a Nazi one. Public perceptions of that fact go far toward answering the question raised at the beginning of this article: why the sudden loss of interest in these monuments? In Germany's difficult and lengthy struggle with *Vergangenheitsbewältigung* this doubly negative image of Buchenwald obviously presents many formidable obstacles on the road toward redefining its function as an historical monument.

It is no wonder then that vigorous debates about new ways of "positioning" the Buchenwald monuments continue in Germany today. The first monument explicitly honoring the Jewish victims of Buchenwald was dedicated in November 1993. After several years of study, a committee of historians headed by Eberhard Jäckel from the University of Stuttgart recently issued a controversial report on

[38] Semprum, *Aquel domingo*, p. 36.
[39] Walter Bartel, "Der Historische Schwur von Buchenwald in der DDR verwirklicht," *Beiträge zur Geschichte der Arbeiterbewegung*, 22 (1980), pp. 402-08.

the remodeling of the Buchenwald museum. The report recommends new historical exhibits, a monument for the gypsies, and a separate museum outside the camp to honor the victims of the postwar Soviet camp.[40] Critics of the plan charge that it downplays the uniqueness of the Holocaust by equating the fate of all victims of political repression and that it denigrates the role of the antifascists in the resistance to Hitler.

It is still too early to predict the final outcome of this lively debate, but it can be hoped that the result will be a more balanced historical representation of what happened at the camp during the Third Reich and at the time of liberation. There is, however, a danger that redesigned exhibits at the camp will be used to foster a totally opposite ideological interpretation of the past, this time a conservative one, that could distort the past as seriously as the one it replaced. It should be obvious from the level of neo-Nazi activity in both East and West Germany that previous explanations of the Third Reich were unconvincing, particularly for the youth.

A redesigned Buchenwald memorial could, however, attempt to fulfill another aspect of a historical monument's purpose, according to John Bodnar: to honor individual citizens and not just to glorify the state. A wall of names would make the immensity of the 51,000 victims of Buchenwald apparent, as well as the ethnic distribution among Germans, Jews, Poles, Russians, Czechs, Dutch, French, and English, to name only a few of the groups. Just as the building of the Vietnam War Memorial in Washington helped to bring together opponents and supporters of the war, a new conceptualization of the memorial at Buchenwald might also help Germany heal the wounds of its troubled past.

It is already apparent that the city of Weimar has become a focal point of tourism. It can be hoped that in the future more of the tourists visiting Weimar will be encouraged to make the trip up the Ettersberg, and that they will learn something useful about Germany's past while there. The battle over the past rages on because those involved in it know that the past also helps shape the present and the future. It is a battle in which the stakes are very high, for both Germany and the world.

---

[40] Associated Press Wire Service, 9 April 1994; "Germany Plans to Remodel Buchenwald Museum," by Renate Wicher, Reuter News Service, 9 April 1994. See also Siegfried Stadler, "Helden leiden links. 'Geheimakte Buchenwald': Opfer in SED-Dienst," *Frankfurter Allgemeine Zeitung*, 11 April 1994.

East Goes West

Annette Simon

Before I turn to my topic of what East and West Germans could learn from each other, I want to describe how my relationship to the other German state, the "West," was formed. I am currently working one day a week with West German patients in a West Berlin practice – hence East goes West. There is of course a personal history involved, and first I want to explain to you the individual image of the West held by someone who was born in the GDR in 1952 and who prior to 1989 had experienced the West firsthand only on three short visits. This personal image seems to me so important because it is the starting point for my encounter with the West, and its presuppositions have had a decisive impact on my relationship with it. I have made it a habit to speak about myself, in order to counteract the generalizations being made these days about East Germans or *the* East German biography.

What sort of image of the other Germany had I formed? My earliest recollections date back to when I was three and four years old, that is, to 1955 and 1956. My parents and I were living at the time in East Berlin. Aunt Grete – my grandfather's sister – lived with us and was responsible for looking after me. Aunt Grete was the only one in our small family who often traveled to the West, that is, to nearby West Berlin. She did not share the ideology that bound my parents to the East. She paid visits in the West and always

143

brought something back for me: chocolate, and one time a beautiful black stuffed cat she had won in a raffle. But she closely adhered to my parents' request not to take me with her into the other half of the city. And, as far as I can remember, I never asked her to.

From today's perspective, it seems absurd that my parents practically speaking never set foot in West Berlin. However, one time my mother did go: as an election volunteer for a leftist group, probably the German Communist Party. She distributed flyers there, not having been told by the campaign organizers that she needed a permit from the West Berlin authorities to do so – with the result that she was arrested by the police and spent a few days in a West Berlin jail. She told me the story much later: how her interrogator, reacting to her defiant and ideologically steadfast behavior, turned around and pointed to a big map behind him. On the map the locations of Stalinist camps were marked with little red flags. My mother became all the more defiant in the face of something so totally unimaginable, rejecting it as obvious "enemy propaganda."

When we visited my grandparents, who lived near Potsdam, we rode the S-Bahn through West Berlin. I cannot remember the impressions the city made on me through the train windows; however I remember very well how the East German police boarded the train in Wannsee and checked everyone's identification. The child took this as a burdensome matter of course; but there was a sense of threat too. Something just had to dwell in this inbetween city which one could not enter; something unnameably evil had to lurk there, making this show of power necessary. The child must have fantasized that merely traveling through this forbidden city represented a danger which afterwards had to be checked and banished by the police.

Two years ago a West German colleague said of an East German woman who was participating in a public discussion in a West German city: "She still acts as if she were in enemy country." So do I, I thought, and it dates back to that time.

On the other hand, the good chocolate and the gifts from Aunt Grete also came from the enemy country, and there were apparently other positive magic powers on this side as well: Aunt Grete arranged for me to go with her to the West Berlin radio tower to cure my whooping cough. It was actually a matter of altitude and not the location of the tower, but in my child's mind I clearly mixed this up. I still recall my excitement on that day; I can still see the elevator approaching the platform at the top. Of course the whooping cough was not gone afterwards; the promised Western cure was not to be. Behind the question of whether, in order to realize the healing effect, we would not have needed to ascend the tower more than once lurked the disappointment, or confirmation, that good things simply could not come from the West.

The worst was yet to come. One day, without any warning, Aunt Grete stayed in West Berlin, and did not come back. She left the East, and thus also the child, without saying good-bye. In the apartment house in Karlshorst where we were living at the time, the people on the lower floor and also those in the rear building decided to do the same. Overnight they abandoned their apartments, leaving all their furniture behind. The police came and sealed the rooms. The people in the back had left behind a fabulously big red ball which a policeman gave to me. It was beyond me: what could move people to leave so suddenly and not even take something so wonderful as this ball with them? My strange, highly ambivalent image of the West must have come into being at this time. A seductive Something that has to be kept under control. Something attractive that one must not allow oneself to be seduced by, because evil lurks there: for example, faithlessness or reckless flight.

When I was seven years old we moved to Halle, and there the direct confrontation with the West was much less in evidence. The only thing I remember from this time is the ensuing ideological influence in school that would have had us believe that all warmongers and fascists lived in the western part of the country. Was Aunt Grete a warmonger? At any rate she had willfully left me. Later, when she came to visit, which was extremely seldom, she always wanted to sample our margarine to see if it, too – like the margarine in the West – tasted just like butter. Only the West could have turned this woman who had been so devoted to me into this petty bourgeois person who, with an expression of disgust on her face, let our "Sahna" – the best we had – melt in her mouth.

Other than that, I had no direct contact with real people from the West. That was partly due to the fact that my grandmother was not on speaking terms with the part of her family that had ended up in the West after the war. So we did not receive packages from the West. Nor was there anything else that might have made me test or alter my early impressions.

In 1961 I was nine years old, and the 13th of August did not register in my mind whatsoever. It apparently did not represent a turning point or change in my life at the time. But in 1962 we moved to Kleinmachnow near Berlin, a town that was profoundly affected and punished by the building of the Wall. In Kleinmachnow one ran into the Wall at every turn, and every trip to East Berlin was a complicated detour around West Berlin. I heard the bitter talk of people who had had all their things packed and ready to go and who were now forced to stay in this unloved GDR. For me, this only confirmed the importance of the Wall: after all, you could not have everyone leaving! My parents and their friends saw the Wall as a chance for fostering more confidence and a more liberal approach in dealing with internal contradictions. As if a system that had to resort to sealing its borders could develop openness and flexibility. "Pretty feebleminded," my son would say today. Looking back on this now, one can hardly comprehend the distortions in perception, the overlooking of reality, that the Cold War brought about in people on both sides.

I viewed the Wall as unalterable reality, and even the fact that I was supposed to get permission to visit my friend, who lived in the border area, did not make me have second thoughts. I simply whizzed by the border patrol on my bicycle; they never stopped me. I can confirm that when one grows up amidst outrageous things which most of one's authority figures do not find outrageous one can live with these things naively and thoughtlessly.

In Kleinmachnow we could of course receive Western radio stations and watch Western television. Into my adolescent years, I especially liked watching the early evening shows. Has any research been done on the effects of living in one country while constantly and continually being accompanied by the media of another country? Starting with adolescence, I listened daily to the music programs on RIAS and SFB, and heard the tips on special events – who was playing that evening in the "Eierschale" or in "Quartier Latin," and so on. It was not until twenty years later that I was able to see these mystical places for myself, and of course I had formed totally different images of them. There were traffic reports as well, and thus I heard that Ernst-Reuter-Platz was closed off or that traffic was backed up in Sonnenallee, although there was not the slightest possibility of my having a look at these places. Nor did I try to find them on a map or design a topography of West Berlin in my head. Of course, GDR maps left the Western part of the city blank, but I could easily have gotten my hands on other maps. I considered this pointless, since I would never get there anyway.

I will never forget the time in 1986 when I took my son, who was seven, to the top of the East Berlin TV tower. From up there I showed him how the Wall ran through Berlin – only from up there was it so impressive to trace. "But beyond the Wall there's a city!" my son exclaimed. Until then he apparently had thought that nothing lay beyond the Wall, or that it was a white surface. From up there one could clearly see how far the city extended. His surprise showed me what sort of image of the other half of the city I had conveyed to him up to that time. I was deeply shocked. While for me the West was at least a place of fantasies and projections, for him until then it was nothing at all, an empty place, unreachable land, white like an unused sheet.

And this even though by then I had already been to the West several times. The first time in 1980, when I was twenty-eight. On this first trip I was unknowingly accompanied by the impressions already described and by an enormous inner tension because of the uniqueness and the privilege of being able to go. Now I know that while I was there I kept saying to myself: Don't allow yourself to be seduced! In the West I was especially impressed with sensuously aesthetic things: the smells and the colors, the wide variety of things to eat, the friendliness in the restaurants. At the same time I told myself: Yes, that's the packaging of the exploitative system – don't be tricked by it!

In 1984 my best friend left for West Berlin – once more I felt deserted. Through her letters I gained an entirely new access to the other part of the city. With her I vicariously experienced the process which I then had to go through myself starting in 1989. Was this a learning process?

Even before the Wall came down I was unusually well prepared for the other society because of this friend and friends from the West, and also because of my short stays there – I was privileged in this regard. Still, having to live within new structures yourself is something very different. And in the beginning my reaction to this was not exactly a learning process. It was more like perceiving – evaluating – selecting what I must learn in this other society, given the fact that I had no other choice. This ranged from finding a margarine which, like our old Marina, is also good for frying, to filling out a tax return, or, more importantly, producing a report for the *Krankenkasse* enabling me to treat psychotic patients with psychotherapy. It was a matter of choosing what I want to take advantage of (opportunities for additional professional training, cultural offerings), what I do not need, and what I definitely do not want (to participate in talk shows, for example). Thus it was a process of evaluation and selection undertaken by an adult who had grown up in the GDR, and it evoked responses ranging from defiant resistance (I considered every new billboard an affront) to the cautious acceptance – albeit always with a sense of distance – of certain things.

At the same time, things that are different also pose a challenge – which is actually more exciting. For example, the effect which the vantage point of the other, of the Westerner, has on me. On various occasions, especially in encounters with colleagues in my field, I have let this way of looking at things influence me, and it has made some things clear to me, and also changed me. For example, I came to realize that the moral categories of my antifascist upbringing and education had influenced me to a far greater extent than I was aware. And that I – although I considered myself in opposition after 1968 – had internalized this GDR moral rigor much more deeply than I thought. For example, certain patterns from my upbringing from which I thought I had freed myself ("enemy country," seduction by the West). In the writings of Uwe Johnson, whom I miss like no other in this new Germany, I could have read about this strange "personenähnliche Größe" of GDR loyalty as early as 1975. Another example is the collective, which taught that no one should be left behind.

This was an individual learning process based on personal encounters, with Westerners "of my choice" and in conditions that I had chosen myself. It was a chance to see myself anew and from the outside, to place my life in a different frame of reference, a chance that also had a liberating effect. I realized once again the patronizing tutelage of the GDR, which I had more or less accepted, and felt great sorrow over time lost because important sides of myself and my abilities lay fallow. In retrospect my feeling toward the GDR is much like the feeling I have experienced after very intense – but in the end damaging – relationships, when one wonders how one endured the situation for so long, and at the same time is happy to have come away more or less unharmed.

This last sentence would hurt many East Germans at present. Certain conditions, which for many people do not exist, are necessary for the learning process. I do not mean only the very important socio-economic conditions, but psychological conditions as well. It is difficult to learn if one has to struggle to preserve one's self-respect and fight against both outer and inner devaluation. There is guilt and there is shame, and when you are ashamed, it is easier to bury your face in your hands than to look in the mirror, not to mention mirroring yourself in the eyes of a Westerner. And when we do look at ourselves reflected in these eyes, we sometimes see ourselves as grotesquely distorted as in the house of mirrors at the amusement park.

Learning is also easier when it takes place in a partner relationship, or when one has the feeling that the other person would also like to learn. At a small conference I asked Westerners just what our joining them meant to them. There was a very long silence, and then one person came up with Minister for Transportation Krause – as a symbol for East German primitivism. Only a Swiss participant could think of a lot of things to say.

In a joint research project Eva Jaeggi and I asked colleagues from the West about their feelings when the Wall was coming down. Answers ranged from: "A mature society is being overrun by a primitive people," to rage at having to share, to awareness of the impotence of the intellectual, who – as was seen happening in the East – could be "abgewickelt," that is, fear.

Westerners tend to evade the perspective of the other that we have to offer; it keeps getting put to one side ("not yet postmodern," etc.), where it can more easily be forgotten. Why this is so would be a topic for discussion. Sometimes I think it also has something to do with shame. Shame at having forgotten us for so long and having become so rich in the meantime.

There are things that I – and, I believe, other East Germans too – can learn from West Germans. But at the same time these things are tinged with envy, because in our seclusion we were not able to acquire them: open-mindedness; worldliness; willingness to take risks; the ability to sacrifice security for other values; confidence in one's own abilities; flexibility. And the fact that capitalism in spite of – or even because of – competition and the pressure to succeed also produces friendliness and a sense of ease, which I very much appreciate, especially in restaurants and shops.

What West Germans could learn from East Germans: how to apportion time (to take one's time; to be slow); the great value of friendships that have nothing to do with one's job or special projects and are, so to speak, friendships in and of themselves; the agreeable lack of self-presentation (the Easterner speaks of himself and has the other person in mind; the market economy has given rise to the Westerner who speaks of himself as if he were a brand product that needs to be pushed). We Easterners have one other highly significant insight to contribute, especially for resigned western leftists: nothing remains as it is; the situation can change from one day to the next.

The most important thing right now in this mutual learning process would be not to project the image of the ugly German onto the other side, as is presently happening, but instead to work together on being self-respecting Germans capable of self-reflexion and self-criticism. In my view, this particularly involves – in addition to political education and a democratic culture – the questions of childrearing, gender relations, and the "weaker" members of society.

Such a mutual learning process would work to counteract the deprecation happening on both sides. However the economic facts tell a different story. It is a simple fact that there are rich and poor sisters and brothers, and this makes partnership in the learning process extraordinarily difficult, if not indeed impossible.

Translated by Kris Riggs and Margy Gerber

Concepts of Democracy of East and West German Politicians[1]

Virginia Penrose

Concepts of Democracy in United Germany

Democracy is a concept often used but seldom defined. A closer look at the elements associated with democracy can reveal significant differences in definitions; and differences in concepts of democracy can seriously complicate political interaction between both states and individuals.

The significance of concepts of democracy for political inter-action becomes apparent in the case of reunited Germany, where a socialist society is being integrated into a capitalist system. The transformation of political structures was completed within a few years. However, integrating East German political and social atti-tudes – including attitudes toward democracy – into West German society promises to be a greater challenge.

A comparative analysis of attitudes and behavior of East and West German politicians requires knowledge of the fundamental differences in ideological concepts of state, and in the economic and political structures of the society in which the politicians grew up. Comparing the political attitudes and behavior of women and men

---

[1] The following is based upon my article "Differenzen im Demokratieverständnis ost- und westdeutscher Politikerinnen," which was published in *Demokratie oder Androkratie? Theorie und Praxis demokratischer Herrschaft in der feministischen Diskussion,* ed. Elke Biester, Barbara Holland-Cunz, and Birgit Sauer (Frankfurt am Main/New York: Campus, 1994), pp. 19-34.

demands in addition an awareness of differences in the socialization of the sexes: women are socialized in their society not just as citizens of their country, but also as women ("doppelte Vergesellschaftung"[2]). As "non-men" women experience daily and political life – and interpret their experiences – differently than men. The experiences of West and East German women in male-dominated society differ as well. Empirical studies confirm differences in concepts of femininity in the GDR and in the FRG.[3] Finally, differences in conditions of everyday life must also be considered.

This study investigates significant differences in concepts of democracy held by men and women politicians in West and East Germany. It is based on a reevaluation of material gathered between 1988-1990 through interviews with politicians in the two German states. I spoke with a total of thirty-one women and nine men representing seven political parties.[4] Although the original interview

---

[2] Regina Becker-Schmidt, "Die doppelte Vergesellschaftung – die doppelte Unterdrückung: Besonderheiten der Frauenforschung in den Sozialwissenschaften," in *Die andere Hälfte der Gesellschaft*, ed. Lilo Unterkircher and Ina Wagner (Vienna: Verlag des österreichischen Gewerkschaftsbundes, 1987), pp. 5-25.

[3] Cf. *Fremdbestimmt Selbstbestimmt. Deutsch-deutsche Karrieremuster von Frauen im Beruf*, ed. Magdalene Deters and Susanne Weigandt (Berlin: Quorum, 1987); Irene Dölling, "Frauen- und Männerbilder. Eine Analyse von Fotos in DDR-Zeitschriften," *Feministische Studien*, 8, No. 1 (1990), pp. 35-49; Virginia Penrose, *Orientierungsmuster des Karriereverhaltens deutscher Politikerinnen. Ein Ost-West Vergleich*. Schriftenreihe Theorie und Praxis der Frauenforschung, Vol. 21 (Bielefeld: Kleine Verlag, 1993).

[4] In the GDR: the Socialist Unity Party of Germany (SED) and its successor, the Party of Democratic Socialism (PDS); Christian Democratic Union (CDU); Liberal Democratic Party of Germany (LDPD); Social Democratic Party of Germany (SPD); the Greens; and the German Social Union (DSU). In the FRG: Christian Democratic Union (CDU); Social Democratic Party of Germany (SPD); Free Democratic Party (FDP); the Greens or the Greens and Alternative Lists (GAL). The latter is found only on the communal level in Baden-Württemberg and in Berlin. Ten of the twenty interviews in West Germany were carried out in a CDU-governed state in the south of the old FRG, ten in a SPD-governed state in the north; twenty interviews were conducted in East Germany. Interview candidates had to have held an electoral or party office at the communal, district, or state level between November 1985 and August 1990. All interviewees were between 32 and 50 years of age. I carried out the interviews in four two-week phases between December 1988 and August 1990. For a more detailed discussion on methods used and the questions asked, see Penrose, *Orientierungsmuster des Karriereverhaltens*, pp. 31ff.

guide did not include questions on concepts of democracy, the men and women I interviewed were convinced that they were good democrats and that they had dealt with political problems in a democratic way. In the analytical process I concentrated on statements conveying their conceptions of democracy and of legitimate methods of problem solving, and their attitudes toward the exercise of political power.

In the following discussion, I will begin with a summary of political structures and basic differences in ideological concepts of democracy in the GDR and the FRG up to 1990. Against this background I will then compare attitudes of the interviewees toward democracy, introducing typical quotations from the interviews. I will conclude with remarks on the importance of these differences for the political careers of women in united Germany.

Determinants of Concepts of Democracy in the Political Systems and Party Structures of the FRG and GDR

The political systems of the GDR and the FRG were based on two fundamentally different ideological interpretations of democracy. "Representative democracy" in the Federal Republic has been markedly influenced by the concept of pluralism and a long tradition of liberalism. Basic elements of this form of democracy are the separation of power, the principle of majority rule as the predominant process of decision-making, transparency of the government's decision-making process, and the possibility of replacing leaders through free elections. Conflict resolution is considered an integral part of the Western democratic process. Ideally, the various political groups negotiate conflicts of interest in a process of give and take which eventually leads to a structural agreement or a compromise. As the people's mediators, political parties play an important role in this process. Checks and balances help assure that no one single interest group dominates the political decision-making process.

The German Democratic Republic referred to itself as a "socialist democracy": a state governed by working masses, led by the working classes and their Marxist-Leninist party.[5] In contrast to Western

---

[5] *Verfassung der Deutschen Demokratischen Republik vom 6. April 1968 in der Fassung des Gesetzes zur Ergänzung und Änderung der Verfassung der Deutschen Demokratischen Republik vom 7. Oktober 1974*, 5th ed. (Berlin: Staatsverlag, 1980), p. 9.

conceptions, East German socialists viewed democracy as simply one of the historical phases in the political development of a society towards communism. Their objective was not plurality, the competition of values, and tolerance; they were striving to achieve ideologically and historically set goals of society. According to the Marxist-Leninist point of view, the foundation of a true democracy must be a socially unified nation. Political decisions in a socialist democracy should be based upon extensive social homogeneity and a similar outlook on life. The goal was to create a political apparatus at one with the people.[6]

The SED was organized around the principle of "democratic centralism" – as were GDR political structures in general. An elected central committee led the party. Tight party discipline, the subordination of minority opinion to the majority, and the unconditional binding nature of the resolutions of the higher executive committees for lower executive bodies and their members were characteristic. The periodical election of all executive bodies by the next lower level, collective administration, and the executive committee's mandatory reporting of its activities to the electing body were to guarantee the democratic process.[7] Individuals were elected into offices according to the principle of "democratic centralism," the lower executive committees electing candidates to offices on the next higher level. However, in practice the centralist elements of the party system prevailed more often than not: the higher executive bodies made binding "candidate proposals" for their electoral offices. There was also no competition for these offices.

Legitimate Methods of Problem Solving: Political Consensus versus Conflict Resolution

Considering the differences in ideology, political structure, and party expectations of behavior placed on active members, I expected to find significant differences in democracy concepts; this assumption was verified in the interviews.

The East German men and women interviewed all interpreted

---

[6] See Herwig Roggemann, "Abgeordnetenrotation und Wähleraufträge in unterschiedlichen politischen Systemen. Ansätze zu einem verfassungspolitischen Vergleich," in *Politik und Gesellschaft in sozialistischen Ländern. Ergebnisse und Probleme der sozialistischen Länder-Forschung*, ed. Ralf Rytlewski (Opladen: Westdeutscher Verlag, 1989), pp. 180f.

[7] Cf. *Kleines politisches Wörterbuch* (Berlin: Dietz, 1978), p. 158.

democracy as the recognition of the basic equality of all citizens. In contrast to the West Germans, their descriptions of everyday political procedures revealed an idealized picture of people from all classes and walks of life, interest groups, and organizations joining forces to achieve common political and social goals. Collectivism and cooperation, not only within their party but also between the parties and mass organizations, played an important role in the East Germans' concept of politics.

> I imagine a future in which . . . these parties will in fact eventually no longer exist, in which people will really come together and work out their ideas together, putting them forward, and they would have other people to put their ideas into practice for them. I admit that at the moment I don't know whether it will actually work in the end, but I can quite easily imagine it would, because it has always worked for me up to now, if everyone cooperated.[8] (Frau DT, PDS)

The East Geman men and women interviewed revealed no differences in attitudes in this respect. Harmonious political cooperation was mentioned as a motivation for active involvement in the SED as well as in the block parties and in political organizations founded during the *Wende*. Herr FH explained his motivation for joining the CDU: "because I then came to believe that all social groups of our population were entitled to participate in carrying out certain social processes."

Even if the circumstances of the political reform process of 1989-1990 counteracted this ideal, the need to find a "common denominator" as a basis upon which all could work together was great:

> So at the moment we can't find a common denominator. You must not forget that we are all going through a major upheaval! And we are still looking for something – even if people voted SPD, Demokratischer Aufbruch or whatever. We are all still looking for a way forward and hoping that it will all come together somehow. (Frau FR, DSU)

The drifting apart of political opinions during the *Wende* was a source of great irritation and frustration for those I interviewed; the plurality of ideas and political goals was particularly alarming to the women. Considering this, it is not surprising that East Germans

---

[8] This and subsequent quotations from the interviews were translated by Roger Woods.

adopted the political model of the "Round Table," which was initially developed by the Polish opposition. This decision-making model called for the equal participation of the SED, the block parties, and most of the newly founded political organizations and initiatives. As Tatjana Böhm points out:

> The Round Table approach was fundamentally different from that of the authoritarian bodies which exercised power under the old system, but it was also different from models of democracy based on representation through parliament. The drive to achieve consensus and make joint decisions was the main feature of the Round Table approach. A new way of thinking about democracy was opened up in that those affected by policies, as well as politicians and experts, were obliged to make mutual decisions in a public forum and were capable of correcting decisions.[9]

Tatjana Böhm describes the *Runde Tische* as a fundamental "school of democracy" for East Germans. She urges that these democratic forms of political participation not be limited to the *Wende*, but be integrated into the German political system (p. 32), thus resuming the debate initiated by the new social movements in West Germany in the 1980s.[10]

Equating democratic behavior with consensus and political harmony led to difficulties in accepting the West German practice of resolving political conflicts by means of majority rule. In connection with the Volkskammer debate on whether the GDR needed a new

---

[9] Tatjana Böhm, "Wo stehen wir Frauen nach 40 Jahren getrennter Geschichte in Deutschland West und Ost?" *Feministische Studien*, 10, No. 2 (1992), p. 33. My translation.

[10] On the new social movements in the 1980s, see Winfried Steffani, "Mehrheitsentscheidung und Minderheiten in der pluralistischen Verfassungsdemokratie" in *Neue Soziale Bewegungen in der Bundesrepublik Deutschland*, ed. Roth Roland and Dieter Rucht. Schriftenreihe der Bundeszentrale für politische Bildung: Studien zur Geschichte und Politik, Vol. 252 (Bonn: Campus, 1987), pp. 344-63. In the current discussion, Western social scientists tend to disqualify in a Cold War manner East German thinking on West German concepts of democracy. By indiscriminately likening collectivism and the East Germans' call for political consensus to Prussian or National Socialist attitudes a possible new discourse on the topic can be put to an end before it really begins. See, for example, Martin Greiffenhagen and Sylvia Greiffenhagen, "Eine Nation: Zwei politische Kulturen," in *Deutschland. Eine Nation - doppelte Geschichte,* ed. Werner Weidenfeld (Cologne: Wissenschaft und Politik, 1993), pp. 35f.

constitution, a PDS politician commented: "The people in power have decided that the country doesn't need a constitution . . . and they are not going to know what the people want; there is to be no democracy outside parliament" (Frau EC, PDS).

With this remark Frau EC touches on the fundamental ideological clash between the concepts of democracy within the two political systems: with the introduction of West German political structures in the East, the principle of majority rule replaced the seeking of consensus as the legitimate method of political decision-making. Accepting this change has been difficult for many East German politicians. To members of the opposition in the newly elected Volkskammer in 1990 (i.e., the PDS and small new parties), the majority decisions seemed undemocratic, because – in their eyes – the opposition was not actively involved in the decision-making process.

Internalized rules of individual political behavior influence concepts of democracy also. Political activists in the GDR were modest about their own achievements and qualifications. It was considered unbecoming for a party member to strive for center stage, or announce personal career expectations and desires. A sense of collectivism and party obedience were seen as characteristics of a good politician. Party members were expected to wait for the party's call, and then to fulfill the position offered them to the best of their ability.[11]

The concept of interpersonal competition introduced during the *Wende* clearly caused problems for the East German women I interviewed. Many morally rejected this new behavior and the competitive atmosphere in the parties and organizations:

> . . . sure you need to get people's attention. But you shouldn't make a big thing of it. I get attention, for example, er . . . by doing various things on a voluntary basis, and that's how I get a chance to say my piece. But I must say, [I] really refuse to go up to someone and say, "Listen, I want this and this." And now, in these first free elections, I see that some people did just that; saying that they were only prepared to accept this or that. But it didn't work. (Frau ML, CDU)

Forming a sharp contrast to these attitudes, the West German interviewees considered conflict and competition as indispensable parts of the democratic process. Again, these are not attitudes that

---

[11] See Penrose, *Orientierungsmuster des Karriereverhaltens*, pp. 77ff.

politicians have superficially adopted to improve their chances of advancement; rather they are products of a lifelong confrontation with the social and political structures of their society. West Germans, recapitulating the circumstances that led them to become active in a political party, most often described conflicts that they sought to resolve by becoming personally involved. The issues behind the decision to join a political party varied greatly: some developed out of situations in which the interviewee felt a wrong must be righted or policies changed; for others, entering the political arena was an attempt to even out the sides. Some examples were specific, others vague:

> When I got involved in politics? Only in a serious way when I got to university, and I was in my first semester, studying law. It was a kind of reaction against the way student politics were going at the time, dominated by Marxist groups like MSB Spartakus and others, "Sozialistischer Hochschulbund" and other groups whose political methods were extremely undemocratic. And which had very dubious election results behind them, and used money from the Student Union, ASTA, to get their obviously polemical points across. And that was supposedly done on behalf of all students – I couldn't accept that. (Herr ZL, FDP)

> Because as a woman lawyer myself I did a lot of family law, back then, too, and I experienced the problems women had in practice, and I saw that something had to be done, so I specialized in this area when I went into politics. (Frau GK, CDU)

> Really so that I could get away from always just discussing things over a drink, or at home; I just really wanted to try changing something, maybe, just a little bit. That was really my main motive. (Frau BC, SPD)

Another indication of the connection West Germans make between politics and conflict is the aggressive vocabulary used in the interviews when describing routine occurrences, competitive situations in everyday political life, friends and foes: for example, "Gemetzel," "Hauen und Stechen," "politisch killen," "abstechen," "der böse Feind," "Rüstzeug." Interestingly, West German women in the SPD and in the Greens und Alternative Lists did not use this type of vocabulary. They referred to electoral competition and party conflicts most often as "disputes" or "discussions."

The West German interviewees considered compromise a form of conflict resolution suitable for politicians: "Sometimes you have to accept things you never thought you would! Just so that you can push something through that you think is more important" (Frau LD, FDP). However, the use of compromise was often accompanied by mixed feelings. On the one hand, men and women politicians identified the willingness to compromise as an important characteristic of a good politician. On the other hand, compromise was also perceived as defeat and was the source of a sense of guilt.

Not all the West German politicians felt comfortable in the competitive atmosphere of the political parties. Frau AR, a city councilor running on the GAL ticket, spoke openly about her desire to "take a vacation" when the jockeying for good positions on the electoral lists begins. The West German men (and a few women) more often preferred portraying politics as a game:

> I'm playing a dangerous game here: if what I've done so far isn't backed by the central office, I'm politically out on a limb; but if it turns out to have been the right thing to do – and I'm sure it will –, well, then I'm happy. (Herr ZL, FDP)

No matter how they described conflict and the competition for electoral and party offices, the West German interviewees accepted arguments, disputes, and power plays within their own party and with other political parties as an important part of the parliamentary process.

Attitudes toward the Exercise of Power

The interviewees' attitudes toward political power were complex. Spontaneous reactions to the topic, examples of the use of power in the political arena, and descriptions of political life indicated concepts of power strongly influenced by the political and social environment. However, significant differences in attitudes toward political power and democracy were found between politicians in East and West Germany as well as between the men and women in each state.

In reaction to questions about political power, West Germans characteristically distinguished between acceptable and unacceptable forms of power. The exercise of power in the sense of putting others under pressure, using force or violence, of dictatorship or totalitarianism was categorized as the abuse of power and rejected as unacceptable in a democratic system. In general West Germans did not however reject the use of power to achieve political goals.[12] They considered political power to be inseparable from politics, to be "necessary": "Without power, without a majority we can't get anywhere in politics" (Frau LD, FDP). "Of course you acquire a certain feeling for power, and this is really what it comes down to in politics. And if you don't have this feeling for power or don't develop it, you won't get anywhere" (Frau JN, CDU).

When asked to define political power, the interviewees gave a wide variety of answers. The definition most often given by West German politicians reflects political structures of competition and conflict: "asserting oneself in the face of opposition." Other definitions of power were gaining social status and prestige, influencing the decision-making process in the party and in parliament, shaping policy, setting the agenda, and knowing how the "system" works. Only women used the last four definitions.

In contrast to the men, West German women also defined power in terms of their own personally set goals and ideas:[13] "Power for me means managing to push something through; regardless of whether it suits or doesn't suit some part or other of the population, or the population as a whole, for that matter" (Frau BC, SPD). Other women gave similar definitions of power: "that people get working according to my vision" (Frau GK, CDU); "that nobody butts in, that I don't have to come to an agreement with anybody" (Frau AR, GAL); "just formulating issues the way I want" (Frau LD, FDP).

The West German men interviewed were much more careful when they talked about political power; they usually dissociated

---

[12] See Penrose, *Orientierungsmuster des Karriereverhaltens*, pp. 172f.

[13] Despite progress made since the mid-1970s in regard to women's active role in politics the denial of interest in exercising political power is still considered "typically female." See Regine Reichwein, "Das Phantasma der bösen Herrscherin," in *Vater Staat und seine Frauen*, ed. Barbara Schaeffer-Hegel (Pfaffenweiler: Centaurus, 1990), pp. 209-21. West German quantitative studies on women's political participation have repeatedly confirmed this opinion. Cf. Beate Hoecker, *Frauen in der Politik. Eine soziologische Studie* (Opladen: Leske + Budrich, 1987), p. 21; Gabriele Bremme, *Die politische Rolle der Frauen in Deutschland*. Schriftenreihe des UNESCO-Instituts für Sozialwissenschaften (Göttingen: Vandenhoeck & Ruprecht, 1956); and Mechthild Fuelles, *Frauen in Partei und Parlament* (Cologne: Wissenschaft und Politik, 1969). My research results contrast with these studies in that they document West German women politicians' strong interest in exercising political power.

themselves from the direct exercise of power: "Power. I must say that power doesn't exactly fascinate me – or at least, it's not central to my political thinking or my ambitions" (Herr ZL, FDP). And a second comment:

> . . . if one possesses power there is a great danger that one won't recognize the limits of one's power . . . so for me power isn't really something that I would particularly go after at the moment, or something that would give me any kind of satisfaction. (Herr ST, CDU)

The desired distance from power is noticeable not only in what the male politicians said, but also how they said it. Whereas women always used the first person singular when discussing their actions and their attitudes toward power, the men tended to use "we" or "one," i.e., less personal forms of speech. The men identified themselves more strongly with the goals and political ideas of their party.[14]

Different experiences with power may explain this contrast between West German men and women. In the male-dominated world of politics, women must first fight for acceptance in a political party before they can hope to become part of the decision-making process.[15] The West German women I interviewed usually saw themselves as loners or *Einzelkämpferinnen*. They were less frequently in a position to get their "own way." They tended to develop

---

[14] This contradicts the findings of a quantitative study published in 1990: Hilke Rebenstorf, "Frauen im Bundestag – anders als die Männer? Soziodemographische Merkmale, Rollen- und Politikverständnis," *Der Bürger im Staat*, 40, No. 1 (1990), pp. 17-24. On the basis of her findings Rebenstorf argues that women representatives focus more strongly on party goals and show less interest than their male colleagues in realizing personal interests and goals. Cf. also Hoecker, p. 179. The fact that my results have been confirmed by two other qualitative studies is an indication that the difference in results may be attributable to the differing research methods. See Bärbel Schöler-Macher, *Die Fremdheit der Politik. Erfahrungen von Frauen in Parteien und Parlamenten* (Weinheim: Deutscher Studien-Verlag, 1994); and Barbara Sichtermann, "Die schweigende Mehrheit war weiblich," in *Weiblichkeit. Texte aus dem zweiten Jahrzehnt der Frauenbewegung* (Frankfurt am Main: Büchergilde Gutenberg, 1990).

[15] East German women reported no comparable experiences of overt discrimination in political life. They described their political environment as neutral to the "gender" factor. In their view, commitment, performance, and loyalty play a more significant role in personal decisions. See Penrose, *Orientierungsmuster des Karriereverhaltens*, p. 195.

personal political goals and then look for others holding similar opinions with whom they could ally themselves to achieve a specific goal.[16] On the other hand, the West German men interviewed most often joined a political organization with general political ideals. They emphasized their strong personal relationships to other party members. In situations where a conflict of opinion or interest arose, the men tended to give priority to group loyalty, even if it meant the momentary sacrifice of personal ideals.[17]

With few exceptions, the East Germans interviewed spontaneously defined political power as repressive rule and oppression: "Power means rule by a particular group of people, stratum, class, or individuals over others – arbitrary decisions" (Frau EC, PDS); "it means dictating to others what's to be done" (Herr PT, PDS); "authoritarian behavior of individuals towards their subordinates" (Frau ML, CDU); "dominating other people, . . . and deriving satisfaction from doing so, and from the feeling of being stronger than the others" (Frau LK, SPD).

In addition, power was equated with influencing the actions and thoughts of others ("geistige Beeinflussung"), the empowerment of an office, and, most interestingly, with egotism. Only women used the last two definitions.

> What is power? For example, the way some people even in the party deal with others – I have gotten this impression sometimes, but for me it was more a negative characteristic of these people, and not really symptomatic of the system. (Frau OP, PDS)

All East German politicians dissociated their own political activities in the past from the exercise of political power. Even those in party positions at the district (*Bezirk*) level maintained that they had filled their political offices without the use of power. This attitude did not differ with the length of time spent as an active party member or the party membership of the interviewees.

Gender differences appeared when the politicians spoke about the present (i.e., *Wende*) and the future, and when the question of

---

[16] Cf. Schöler-Macher, *Die Fremdheit der Politik*, pp. 234ff.

[17] Cf. *Männerbünde – Männerbände. Zur Rolle des Mannes im Kulturvergleich*, ed. Gisela Völger and Karin von Welck (Cologne: Rautenstrauch-Joest-Museum, 1990); Eva Kreisky, "Der Staat als 'Männerbund'?" in *Staat aus feministischer Sicht*, ed. Elke Biester, Brigitte Geißel, et al. (Berlin: Offset-Druckerei der Humboldt-Universität zu Berlin, 1992), pp. 53-62.

who should have power arose. With one exception, the East German women interviewed described the use of power as incompatible with democracy, and explicitly rejected it. A typical response:

> Well, I can't really say I relate to the idea of pursuing power at all. Because, as I've said, I consider that people should have their own ideas and look after their own interests. I wouldn't want to present myself as a powerful person or start making decisions affecting other people, or anything like that. (Frau DT, SED/PDS)

The rejection was expressed in varying ways. Members of the SED/PDS, like Frau DT, tended to argue the point intellectually and ideologically. The reactions of members of the former block parties and the newly founded political organizations were often more emotional: "My first reaction is disgust" (Frau ML, CDU); "It makes me go cold, just thinking about it" (Frau RM, SPD); "No, I haven't got any power! Nobody jumps to attention for me!" (Frau NK, LDPD). Though they planned to continue their political involvement, and wished to participate actively in the political reform process, these women were not interested in exercising political power in the future.[18]

A further difference was that many East German women associated the exercise of power with men: "Power resides in certain posts which are now being filled. The key posts are occupied by men here" (Frau CD, SPD). And an example from the Round Table:

> [At the Round Table] there were attempts very early on from representatives of new groups to get into positions of power like these – in dealing with the old Council and the Round Table itself. So the Round Table decided to form a secretariat, with four representatives of these new groups working on a completely equal footing on behalf of the Round Table – the idea was that they would get away from their particular party political interests. And in this secretariat, made up of three men and one woman, well the three men started by trying to dominate the proceedings, and taking a party political line after all – I thought this was a very bad thing. And then, through their work in the secre-

---

[18] There is a fundamental difference between East and West German women in regard to their motivation for distancing themselves from the exercise of political power: while in West Germany political power was considered incompatible with femininity, in East Germany it was considered incompatible with the concept of socialist democracy. See Penrose, *Orientierungsmuster des Karriereverhaltens*, pp. 191ff.

tariat, they tried getting into a position of power in their dealings with the Council and the administration. (Frau OP, SED/PDS)

The frequently mentioned "egotists" were ordinarily male, although sometimes, albeit it seldom, women without children were given this designation: "If they were single, responsible only to and for themselves – then they were also more ruthless . . . , to my mind they almost behaved like typical men" (Frau OP, SED/PDS).

Frau FR of the German Social Union (DSU) was the only East German woman interviewed who voiced an affirmative attitude toward political power. She defined power as the ability to influence the thoughts and behavior of others, and used the rhetorical talent of her party's *Landesvorsitzender* as an example: "he can get people going and exercise power over them. Somehow he carries them along – people feel pointed in a particular direction by his power, by his personality." She admitted that she too would like to influence others in this way. This same woman politician claimed not to be interested in participating in politics beyond the community level. Whereas the other East German women complained that the decision-making positions were ordinarily occupied by men, Frau FR was convinced that men should take the lead in politics, run for electoral offices, and exercise political power; the role of women was to work at their side and support their efforts.

While the East German women drew a line between their own political activities and the exercise of power, their male colleagues distinguished between political activities in the past and in the future. Instead of placing emphasis on their moral integrity, men emphasized their ability to learn, to accept new ideas, and adjust to the changes brought about by political reform. The East German men listed practices of the SED regime and the Nazi regime as examples of the immoral use of political power. The interviewees from the PDS and the SPD found power to be morally questionable when concentrated in the hands of a single person, a small group of people, or one party. They criticized political systems without checks and balances that prevent the misuse of power.

> And actually it's my own personal opinion . . . that power should be separated out whenever possible and not concentrated. . . . And if we pursue our own development a bit further, and what we really want – at least as a party – then power, which will come to us sooner or later – well, it won't just come, we'll have to fight for it, struggle and work and compete for it – it should rest on broad shoulders; on lots of pairs of shoulders, in fact. And if possible it should be passed on to others

for a time, if you see what I mean. It's the rotation principle – that's what we really want. (Herr PT, SED/PDS)

The CDU politician Herr FH's concepts of power and democracy were the most similar to Western views. Having spent twenty years in office, he seemed especially intent on appearing to be honest, democratic, and capable of learning new ways. In connection with the Volkskammer elections in March 1990 he had frequent contact with West German politicians. In the interview he attempted to use their political vocabulary – with little success. Herr FH asserted that the moral or immoral use of power depended on how those with power could be checked. He considered the principle of majority rule to be essential for a democratic system. He could not, however, define political power; in response to my request for an example he complained that it was taking too long to disengage the political power from the SED and turn it over to the newly elected political alliance that his party was leading.

Importance of Differences in Concepts of Democracy for Political Careers in a United Germany

This comparative analysis confirms my original hypothesis that East and West German politicians do not simply adapt superficially to prevailing concepts of democracy in their own country. The life-long confrontation with societal and political structures leads to an internalization of social norms and constraints and their eventual transformation into personal values. The remarks of West and East German politicians on their political attitudes and behavior reveal differences in concepts of democracy.

To summarize: the concepts of democracy of the East and West Germans I interviewed shared certain basic principles: equality of all citizens; the necessity of monitoring the political apparatus; the possibility of voting governments out of office; the rejection of violence and force as political means of resolving problems. They differed most sharply in three particular areas: what they consider to be the basis of democracy; the legitimate methods of resolving problems; and attitudes towards the exercise of political power.

	West German Concept	East German Concept
1. Basis of democracy	Plurality, competition of values, tolerance	Social homogeneity and unity

2. Legitimate methods of problem resolution	Principle of majority rule	Political consensus
3. Attitude toward the exercise of political power	Acceptance as necessity	Separation of power and political action

During the process of unification East Germany was integrated into the West German political system. East Germans interested in continuing or beginning a career in politics were now expected to conform to West German political structures and ideals. In the interviews, East German men presented themselves as more willing than women to accept a new political value system. Observations in the past five years seem to confirm the impression that East German men are adapting well to the political realities of competition and conflict. West German men are also welcoming them into this political union of men, supporting their efforts to learn new patterns of behavior. East German women, on the other hand, are having greater difficulties conforming to the new, male-dominated, political structures. Many are not as willing to accept the ideas of interpersonal competition commonly found in the Western concept of democracy.[19] They are also being confronted for the first time with open forms of discrimination against women in political organizations. Their lack of skill in dealing with their new hostile surroundings, and their rejection of some West German patterns of political behavior and concepts of politics have made it easier for them to be eliminated as political rivals.

Political cooperation between East and West German women is also proving to be problematic; the political attitudes of the "other women" are foreign, and it is hard for West and East German women to understand each other. West German women are quick to label East German attitudes toward democracy and political power inferior to their own, confusing the East German political value system with the assumed insecurities of dependent, unliberated women. At political meetings they often attempt to teach their East German colleagues the "right" behavior and to force their own

---

[19] See Eva Maleck-Lewy and Virginia Penrose, *Zwischenbilanz: Frauen und politische Partizipation im vereinigten Deutschland* (Berlin: Edition Sigma, 1995).

strategies and goals upon them.

East German women politicians take offense at the attempts of West German women to spoon-feed them. After forty years of SED government, they have had enough of being patronized.[20] Most of these women are highly qualified professionals; they want their West German colleagues to accept them as equals, although admittedly less experienced in certain areas. As demonstrated in this article, Western methods of problem resolution and attitudes toward the exercising of political power conflict with their personal values. East German women are not convinced that their own concepts of democracy, power, and interpersonal competition need revising. A battle over the right to define political and feminist values has ensued. This is familiar terrain for the West German women: feminist groups have always competed among themselves for the right to define feminist goals, historical interpretations, and ideals in the women's movement.[21] However, this behavior contradicts the political expectations of East German women. Struggling with the challenges of new social and political structures and often insecure in the art of verbal sparring, East German women politicians show little interest in doing battle with the more skilled West German feminists. It is not surprising that many are retreating to regional and local levels where they can avoid dealing with West Germans – women or men.[22] It is here they find the most support for their concepts of democracy and experience less conflict while still being politically involved.

Women in united Germany, however, cannot afford this separation. The government's attempts at solving the current economic and social problems are often at the expense of women: child-care institutions are being closed down – efforts are being made to return child care to the home; other social programs benefiting women are

---

[20] See Ulrike Helwerth and Gislinde Schwarz, *Von Muttis und Emanzen. Feminismus in Ost- und Westdeutschland* (Frankfurt am Main: Fischer, 1995); Katrin Rohnstock, *Stiefschwestern. Was Ost-Frauen und West-Frauen voneinander denken* (Frankfurt am Main: Fischer, 1994); *EigenArtige Ostfrauen. Frauenemanzipation in der DDR und den neuen Bundesländern*, ed. Birgit Bütow and Heidi Stecker (Bielefeld: Kleiner Verlag, 1994).

[21] Cf. Joyce Maire Mushaben, "Feminism in Four Acts: The Changing Political Identity of Women in the Federal Republic of Germany." Paper presented at the 29th Annual Meeting of the International Studies Association, St. Louis, Missouri, 29 March - 2 April 1988.

[22] See Maleck-Lewy and Penrose, *Zwischenbilanz.*

being targeted as well (for example, maternity leave, housing allowances, unemployment, and social security). More women in Eastern and Western Germany are becoming aware of the need for political cooperation.[23] However, this calls for the difficult process of confrontation with unfamiliar ideas and attitudes. It calls for interest in the "other" Germans and for tolerance.

---

[23] In the last five years, women politicians in West and East Germany have frequently endeavored to join together and work toward common political goals. Three examples are the Frauenbündnis '90, the Frauen-Nord-Forum, and the women's nonpartisan cooperation initiative in the Berlin Senate. The Frauenbündnis '90, a nationwide alliance of women active in political parties, the church, women's organizations, and labor was founded in February 1990. Though active at first, it has now dropped out of sight. The Frauen-Nord-Forum was founded in the spring of 1993. It is a network of women working in the field of political education and equal opportunity in Schleswig-Holstein, Mecklenburg-Vorpommern, Hamburg, Niedersachsen, Brandenburg, Sachsen-Anhalt, Berlin, and Bremen. The women's nonpartisan cooperation in the Berlin Senate was initiated early in 1992 by Carola von Braun (FDP). Once every two months women politicians from all parties – with the exception of the CDU – and journalists and representatives of women's projects meet to discuss current political issues and search for common solutions.

The Round Table Model:
Reflections on a Political Experiment

Lothar Probst

The terms "Round Table," "Citizens' Democracy," and "Democracy from Below" represented a new concept of politics in the first months of the 1989 revolution in the GDR. At that time many people believed that this concept would give parliamentary democracies in the West new impetus. Some years after this revolutionary period, however, it is sobering to review the expectations and hopes surrounding the concept in the light of the various problems associated with the transformation process in the new *Länder*. Initial enthusiasm turned into disappointment and disillusionment.

Nevertheless, the Round Tables of the GDR revolution were one of the most exciting political experiments of recent years. Starting from a local case study which I conducted on the political transformation process in the city of Rostock,[1] I shall focus on three major aspects of this experiment: the Round Table as a model of a self-limiting revolution, as a model of *Verantwortungsgemeinschaft* (community of responsibility), and as a model of new forms of democracy. Finally I shall consider the long-term impact of this experiment on the political culture of united Germany.

The Round Table as Model of a Self-Limiting Revolution

The Round Table, initiated by the citizens' movements in late fall

---

[1] See Lothar Probst, *Der Norden wacht auf. Zur Geschichte des politischen Umbruchs in Rostock* (Bremen: Edition Temmen, 1993).

1989, did not seek to seize political power but to participate in exercising it. The document "Geschäftsordnung des Runden Tisches Rostock" explains, for example, that the Round Table was a forum for cooperation between democratic organizations in the interest of public life in the city of Rostock.[2] The document continues: "[d]er Runde Tisch gibt Hinweise für die Arbeit der Stadtverordneten- versammlung und kontrolliert deren Arbeit" (p. 1). That is to say, the Rostock Round Table sought to monitor the SED-dominated City Council, not to run it. One of the most important representa- tives of Neues Forum in Rostock, Joachim Gauck, stressed this self-limiting concept of the Round Table when he argued that the citizens' movements neither felt qualified to assume political power nor were they seeking it.[3] They had experienced political power during the dictatorship of the SED as anti-democratic, and against this background it was taken for granted that it was better to criticize political power than to assume it.

This point is crucial to an understanding of the actions of the citizens' movements. They were neither mentally nor politically prepared to take office. Looking back, two other prominent protago- nists of the citizens' movements, Konrad Weiß and Gerd Poppe, highlighted the negative side of this ambivalent relationship to political power. Konrad Weiß pointed out that, in refusing to assume political responsibility, the citizens' movements did not give enough attention to the basic problems of GDR citizens. Because they failed to assume political power, he argued, the splitting of the citizens' movements into different local groups and factions was only a matter of time.[4]

Gerd Poppe from the Initiative Peace and Human Rights argued similarly when he reflected on the major mistakes of the citizens' movements. He mentioned in particular their troubled relationship to political power. Reviewing his experiences, he summarized:

> Whenever one of the infallible SED leaders said that nobody could question the leading role of the Party, many normally quite courageous people went along with whatever it was that was being tabooed. Sooner or later they were sure to express the view that they were critical of

---

[2] "Geschäftsordnung des Runden Tisches Rostock," dated 9 December 1989, in the Rostock archive at the Institut für kulturwissenschaftliche Deutschland- studien, University of Bremen.

[3] Interview with Joachim Gauck, in Probst, *Der Norden wacht auf*, p. 108.

[4] Konrad Weiß, "Die Bürgerbewegungen als Erinnerungsvereine an den Deut- schen Herbst," in *Demokratie Jetzt*, 2, No. 40 (1990), p. 3.

many things, but when it came to it they did not want to question the SED's power.[5]

The fact that many dissidents did not question the SED's position of power clarifies the particular political stand underpinning the Round Table model. One must remember that the citizens' movements which entered the political arena in the fall of 1989 as new political structures evolved from the social-ethical groups which had arisen under the protective wing of the Evangelical Church. Elements of a Protestant morality and ethos were part of the political thinking of the citizens' movements. The refusal to adapt to the rules of a political system dominated by the SED and the search within these movements for a political practice which would bring a fresh sense of purpose were intended to promote a new kind of public discourse. The foundations of this public discourse were determined by ethic values and not by a theory of political power. Today, many civil rights campaigners from the GDR explain their political perceptions in terms of an internalized anti-power attitude, rooted in their ethical attitudes and in the supposed omnipotence of the SED and the Stasi.

Without doubt, the citizens' movements which mobilized hundreds of thousands of citizens in the streets of the GDR in December 1989 had the power to take office, but they did not do so. In the initial phase of the revolution the Round Table can be interpreted partly as a model which allowed the citizens' movements to reject a complete takeover of political power and to share power with the SED. The citizens' movements did not have confidence in their own ability to exercise political power, and their members did not feel experienced enough to take on the challenges of government. They wanted to be accepted as a political organization with the same rights as the SED, but they limited their activities to keeping check on the ruling SED. Following this logic, Jochen Läßig, one of the speakers of Neues Forum in Leipzig, declared in fall 1989: "We've been asleep for the past ten or twenty years, and we've not organized an opposition capable of taking over. So for the moment it's just a matter of sharing government, of being involved in the exercise of power and of keeping an eye on what's being done."[6]

---

[5] Gerd Poppe, "Ab 1994 Dritte Kraft in Deutschland," *Bündnis 2000. Forum für Demokratie, Ökologie und Menschenrechte*, 3, No. 2 (1993), p. 25. This and subsequent translations are by the editors.

[6] Jochen Läßig in a speech at one of the Monday demonstrations in Leipzig, published in *Jetzt oder Nie – Demokratie. Leipziger Herbst '89*, ed. Neues Forum

Andrew Arato has described the rejection of political power by the Central European citizens' movements and their cooperation with the communist nomenclatura at the Round Tables as one of the characteristics of a self-limiting revolution.[7] Nevertheless, the Round Tables had a great impact on the development of a new public and political culture. Particularly in the cities and local communities they were indispensable instruments for the democratization of a political system dominated by the SED.

In Rostock, for instance, the Round Table quickly developed skills and experience in the political decision-making process, even though in the early phase it restricted itself to influencing the City Council. The City Council had to adhere to the decisions of the Round Table, and the city councillors were answerable to the members of the Round Table on a weekly basis. Finally, the Round Table came to replace the old City Council. Christoph Kleemann, one of the representatives of Neues Forum in Rostock, summarized this development when he said: "Basically you could say that . . . theoretically the Round Table was already the government, but of course it wasn't like that in practice."[8]

However, most Round Tables quickly lost their political influence. After the municipal elections of May 1990, democratically elected city councils replaced the Round Tables. In an effort to keep the Rostock Round Table alive, members of the citizens' movements, citizens' initiatives, and the Evangelical Church tried – without success – to influence the political agenda of the new Senate of the city of Rostock. Later, in September 1990, those political groups and organizations which were not represented in Rostock's parliament, some 23 in number, founded the Rostocker Bürgertisch (Citizens' Round Table). In their inaugural declaration they stated their intention to support and promote dialogue and interaction between the Senate, the city's parliament, and those public interest groups, organizations, and parties which were excluded from political office. These groups saw the Rostocker Bürgertisch as an instrument for expanding or possibly supplementing democracy. In this way the Rostocker Bürgertisch dealt with municipal issues such as the spread of xenophobia and the cultural environment for the

Leipzig (Leipzig: Forum Verlag, 1989), pp. 264-65.
[7] Andrew Arato, "Revolution, Civil Society and Democracy," *Transit. Europäische Revue*, 1, No. 1 (1990), pp. 112ff.
[8] From an interview with Christoph Kleemann, in *Materialien und Ergebnisse aus Forschungsprojekten des Instituts für kulturwissenschaftliche Deutschlandstudien* (Universität Bremen), No. 1, 1991, p. 35.

young. Discussions were frequently followed by concrete political recommendations to the Senate. For instance, the Rostocker Bürgertisch and the *Ausländerbeauftragter* (Commissioner for Foreigners) sponsored an empirical study on the integration of asylum seekers in the city of Rostock several months before violence escalated in Rostock-Lichtenhagen; this study, which warned of an explosive situation and made recommendations about how to deal with the problems in Rostock-Lichtenhagen, was passed on to the responsible authorities of the Senate. The warnings were however ignored.

The Rostocker Bürgertisch failed to gain attention or to exert any great influence on local politics. In 1991 it was disbanded. It was nevertheless an important element of a new political forum and culture in Rostock in the initial phase of the political transformation process.

The Round Table as Model of a *Verantwortungsgemeinschaft*

In many statements of GDR civil rights campaigners the Round Table is described as a substantial political experience with all the characteristics of a model for the future. Bärbel Bohley, reflecting on the events of fall 1989, came to the conclusion that the opposition was too weak to assume political power. Nobody at the Round Table, as she said, had an alternative concept for rebuilding the economy, the environment, and cultural life. However, for the citizens' movements involvement in the Round Table was a useful way of acquiring skills and experience. Against this background Bohley highlighted the advantage of the Round Table model as follows: "Working together they found the right solution for many problems. For everyone the Round Table became the place where they could learn democracy. Here the public witnessed new political and cultural beginnings."[9]

Christoph Kleemann from Rostock comes to a similiar conclusion when he argues that the Round Table was a unique experiment, a model with an informing influence on the citizens' movements. He emphasizes in particular the common responsibility at the Round Table:

> Every party and movement had two representatives, and every organization had one at the Round Table. . . . For me it was a unique experience, with everyone being represented at the Round table in the same

---

[9] Bärbel Bohley, "EINE große Koalition reicht," *Freitag*, 19 April 1991, p. 1.

way, and everyone having the same rights. And then it would suddenly
turn out that the truth would come from a quite unexpected quarter. That
was the deeper, greatest significance of the Round Table, this experience
of democracy: we all shared responsibility.[10]

It is remarkable that both statements stress the political responsibility which all political forces at the Round Table shared. The
SED-PDS and its suborganizations were also represented, and this
meant that both citizens' movements and SED-PDS were integrated
in a kind of *Verantwortungsgemeinschaft* at the Round Table.

Numerous remarks by civil rights campaigners who participated
in the Round Table on different levels indicate that the Round Table
model was not primarily a rational political strategy for a gradual
takeover of political power but rather a community experience which
created a sense of mutual acceptance and togetherness in a critical
situation. Obviously, there were political concepts within the sections of the citizens' movements which were influenced by an
unpolitical community ideal. The desire for togetherness reflects a
social structure which was far more homogeneous than in Western
societies. Also, the political system in the GDR was based on confrontation, polarization, and ideological splitting of society, whereas
the citizens' movements wanted to implement a new model based on
cooperation and consensus, and the Round Table seemed to be an
ideal instrument for this idea. Furthermore, many participants in the
citizens' movements perceived "public disputes of interest groups as
one of the wrong turnings of Western culture," as Sigrid Meuschel
has pointed out.[11]

In the initial phase of the Round Tables, social interest groups
and parties were only beginning to take shape and the clash of
different societal interests had not yet developed. Against this background the citizens' movements believed that they would end up as
the political winners of the Round Tables. Later, however, a rapid
differentiation between the political parties and organizations began.
Because the citizens' movements were fixated on the Round Table
as medium of a *Verantwortungsgemeinschaft* they failed to react
appropriately to this new situation. While the other political forces at
the Round Table developed a new political image before the first free

---

[10] From an interview with Christoph Kleemann, in Probst, *Der Norden wacht
auf*, p. 120.
[11] Sigrid Meuschel, "Wandel durch Auflehnung. Thesen zum Verfall bürokrati-
scher Herrschaft in der DDR," in *Demokratischer Umbruch in Osteuropa*, ed.
Rainer Deppe et al. (Frankfurt am Main: Suhrkamp, 1991), p. 28.

parliamentary elections to the Volkskammer were held, the citizens' movements continued to reject Western party concepts and failed to create a distinctive political image.

The Round Table Model as a New Form of Democracy

The East German citizens' movements entered the political stage at a time when the old Federal Republic faced mounting criticism of the deficiencies, shortcomings, and failings of the established system of party democracy. It is not surprising that the citizens' movements expected that their ideas of direct democracy would give a new impetus to the debate about a reform of the constitution and the political system of the Federal Republic. For instance, Ulrike Poppe, a founding member of the citizens' movement Demokratie Jetzt, highlighted the role of Round Tables and citizens' committees as new forms of societal self-organization and described the expectations of the citizens' movements as follows:

> Instead of being replaced by the democratic constitutional state, these [new forms of societal self-organization] could clear a path for civil society. The revolution in the fall which produced these forms has led people to question the idea that parties should be the sole representatives of society's interests, and it has led to the very necessary expansion of democracy through the direct involvement and influence of citizens, and to the appearance on the scene of value systems which go beyond party politics.[12]

While Ulrike Poppe argues in favor of complementing representative democracy, some participants of the citizens' movements perceived the Round Tables as a model for total grass-roots democracy. Representatives of the Neues Forum Leipzig, for instance, suggested a political system represented by Round Tables as an alternative to the existing system of parliamentary democracy.[13] They argued that, in parliamentary democracies, party interests dominate the public sphere, and minorities have no opportunity to gain influence. Therefore they pleaded for a system of Round

---

[12] Ulrike Poppe, "Warum haben wir die Macht nicht aufgehoben . . . ," *Bündnis 2000. Forum für Demokratie, Ökologie und Menschenrechte*, 1, No. 1 (1990), p. 3.

[13] See the proposal of Neues Forum Leipzig, "Systeme der Runden Tische," *Bündnis 2000. Forum für Demokratie, Ökologie und Menschenrechte*, 2, No. 13 (1991), p. 9.

Tables, first as a provisional arrangement, later as elected institutions. Finally, in a totally grass-roots system, the Round Tables should provide the only representation of the people on all levels of society.

However, one should not overestimate the influence of such considerations within the ranks of the citizens' movements. For the majority of their participants, the democratic principle of political representation in a parliamentary system and the principle of grass-roots democracy did not exclude each other, but constituted complementary elements of the political process. Hans Schwenke from the Neues Forum Berlin, for instance, emphasized that, given the experiences of this century, civil rights campaigners had to resist all forms of anti-parliamentarianism.[14] Round Tables and the plebiscitary elements of democracy were for him not a substitute for, but rather a way of complementing, parliamentary democracy.

Seen in this light, the Round Table model becomes far more appealing. It does not simply reproduce the German tradition of anti-party attitudes and of a conservative need for harmony, but represents "a 'modern' critique of the party system"[15] which in principle accepts representation, the rule of law, and the problems of the mediation of interests in a complex society, and does not believe in the harmony of grass-roots democracy. Emancipated from idealistic notions of community and a compulsive search for consent, the Round Table model expresses the political will to find pragmatic solutions through compromise. Profiting from their anti-totalitarian origins and their experience at the Round Tables, the citizens' movements stimulated the debate about new forms of societal cooperation in a way which clearly differs from the ritualized forms of narrow-minded party thinking.

The question arises, however, of whether or not the special conditions and premises of fall 1989 can simply be transposed into the framework of modern democratic mass societies. Uwe Thaysen was right to point out that politics at the Round Tables in East and Central Europe took place under conditions which are not typical of developed democracies and which usually cannot be tolerated.[16] The

---

[14] Hans Schwenke, "Was will und was kann die Bürgerbewegung?" *Bündnis 2000. Zeitschrift für Demokratie, Ökologie und Menschenrechte*, 3, No. 2 (1992), p. 19.

[15] Antje Vollmer et al., "Grüne und Bündnis 90," *Aus Politik und Zeitgeschichte. Beilage zur Wochenzeitung Das Parlament*, B 5, 24 January 1992, p. 33.

[16] Uwe Thaysen, *Der Runde Tisch. Oder: Wo blieb das Volk?* (Opladen: Westdeutscher Verlag, 1990), p. 175.

Round Tables were, in this respect, extraordinary institutions for transforming more or less authoritarian systems into open democratic societies. They guaranteed a well-ordered transfer of political power in a specific historical situation where no democratically legitimized body of the people existed, but they could under no circumstances replace a government legitimized by free elections.

Furthermore, there is reason to doubt that the basic assumptions of the particular political approach of the citizens' movements and their perception of grass-roots democracy are relevant to the reality of fragmented and individualized modern mass societies. Here we have to examine the assumption that citizens' participation in the political process is blocked by the barriers erected by the institutionalized political system. Modern mass societies display growing privatism, political abstinence, particularization, and a loss of public spirit. These phenomena reflect the increasing alienation of many citizens from their polity and an instrumental relationship to the benefits of the welfare state. Participation in public affairs is often an instrument used by lobby groups to pursue private interests. Individualism, one of the basic values of liberal societies, does not only make participation in politics out of a sense of the public good more difficult; it also undermines solidarity, which is indispensable for the functioning of democratic societies. The steady transition to a negative political empowerment of particular interest groups in modern mass societies is not sufficiently reflected by the citizens' movements. From this point of view, however, the participation of societal groups in the political process is ambivalent and does not necessarily lead to more democracy.

In addition, there were few signs of any willingness within the political class in Germany to bring the experiences of the 1989 revolution and the political ideas of the citizens' movements into the debate about reforming the political system of the Federal Republic. Elements of these specific experiences, however, deserve to be integrated in the political culture of the united Germany. The opportunities for increasing participation in the political system of the Federal Republic have by no means been exhausted. Ulrich Preuß described the draft of a constitution, worked out by a Round Table group before the Volkskammer elections in March 1990, as a call for a civil society.[17] Compared with the etatism of the *Grundgesetz* and the fossilized forms of Western party democracy, this draft, which

---

17 Ulrich K. Preuß, "Auf der Suche nach der Zivilgesellschaft. Der Verfassungsentwurf des Runden Tisches," in *DDR. Ein Staat vergeht*, ed. Thomas Blanke et al. (Frankfurt am Main: Fischer, 1990), p. 84.

emphasized the importance of civil society for political decision-making, offers "corrective measures" and poses "critical questions for the Western concept of politics and society."[18]

The strengthening of local democracy, the inclusion of referendums in the constitution, the reinforcing of individual rights and free associations as a counterbalance to the power of corporations, and Round Tables as complementary forms of representative democracy would not threaten but improve the foundations of democracy in Germany. In spite of the marginalization of the citizens' movements in the process of German unification, the Round Table as a model of a pre-parliamentarian way of decision-making has been successfully established within the political landscape of Germany in the last years. Thanks to the initiative of citizens' movements, Round Tables now exist in many communities, cities, and districts in the new *Länder*, each focusing on particular issues such as the integration of immigrants, unemployment, and right-wing extremism. In a number of cities non-specialized Round Tables continue to exist and work, most of them representing organizations and groups which are not directly represented in city parliaments.

Furthermore, the Round Table model has also found its way onto the political scene of the old *Länder*, and in some cases it has taken institutionalized shape. In Bremen, for instance, a Round Table was implemented dealing with policy on foreigners. Parties, social groups and organizations, trade unions, churches, and representatives of companies, as well as administrative institutions, were involved. Obviously, handling complex societal problems by means of traditional party management and municipal administration comes up against limiting factors. Roland Roth stresses that the existing administrative structures were not designed to deal with complex issues.[19] Mastering complex issues and societal conflicts requires new procedures for arriving at solutions based on compromise. The Round Table is in my view one of the instruments for such new procedures. There is still hope that the experiences of fall 1989 will have an impact on the political culture of united Germany and not end up as just one more nostalgic memory of a bygone revolution.

---

[18] Sigrid Meuschel, *Legitimation und Parteiherrschaft in der DDR* (Frankfurt am Main: Suhrkamp, 1992), p. 327.

[19] Roland Roth, "Eliten und Gegeneliten. Neue soziale Bewegungen als Herausforderer 'demokratischer Elitenherrschaft,'" in *Die politische Klasse in Deutschland*, ed. Thomas Leif et al. (Bonn/Berlin: Bouvier, 1992), p. 385.

The Heilmann Family.
Social Restructuring and the Potential for Family Conflict in East Germany. A Sketch

Michael Hofmann

Frau Heilmann is sitting at the dining room table in the light of the hanging lamp. She is filing wage-slips, comparing bills, invoices, and checkbook entries. She takes off her reading glasses, leans back, and fixes her glance on an imaginary point in the darkness beyond the circle of light. "France this year, or back again to the Bavarian Forest?" she asks herself. "No," she decides, "first, we've got to figure out something for Martin. Even if it's hard for him, he simply must enter this retraining program . . . ."

Who is Frau Heilmann? At first glance, one could take her for a manager counting the day's receipts, an exceptional woman with special decision-making powers. But appearances can deceive. Frau Heilmann is an average East German salaried employee in the service sector, a typical East German woman. And her husband? Herr Heilmann, who is lying on the couch watching television, is a typical East German man, a skilled industrial worker.

Women in the East German Economy

The high employment rate of women in the GDR (over 90 percent) was due primarily to the inroads women made in the service sector. Of the 3.3 million employed in the service sector of the GDR economy nearly 70 percent were women. On the other hand,

75 percent of the 2.5 million employed in industry were men. The largest female occupational group was in the area of commerce and provision (*Versorgung*), above all sales personnel (606,000 women, or 88 percent of the total), followed by trained personnel in business and administration (423,000 women, or 87 percent), and in education (323,000, or 80 percent). The largest male occupational group was in metal working (630,000, or 92 percent of the total), followed by construction (430,000, or 93 percent).[1] While there was little change in the traditional industrial enterprises in the GDR over the decades, women gradually moved into the lower and middle echelons of administration and services.

The restructuring that has taken place in East Germany since the *Wende* has especially affected the male domains: industry and the higher levels of administration. Women were structurally less hard-hit, although there was considerable displacement by men. The high unemployment rate among women is deceiving: firstly because the restructuring of the economy began in the service sector, and secondly because temporary employment measures (*Arbeitsbeschaffungsmaßnahmen*, ABM) and other employment instruments primarily aided men.

Social and Family Structures

Employment and economic structures influenced the daily life of families in the "Arbeitsgesellschaft DDR." For example, the statistically most common marriage in the GDR was between a woman employed in the service sector (saleswoman, trained employee in business or administration, teacher) and a metal or construction worker. This was especially true in centers of population which were also industrial and service centers, such as Leipzig.

The following sketch is a composite of results of more than one hundred interviews held in the urban industrial worker milieu of Leipzig.[2] With the ideal-typical construct of the Heilmann family I

---

[1] Data are taken from the last population and employment census of the GDR, undertaken in 1981. The results of the census, which were never published, are available at the Statistisches Amt der Fünf Neuen Länder in Berlin.

[2] The interviews were carried out within the framework of a large research project sponsored by the Deutsche Forschungsgemeinschaft in which people of various occupations in East and West Germany were asked about changes in their life-styles since 1989. One part of the study involved an occupational comparison of East German industrial workers and East German saleswomen.

want to describe some of the effects the social restructuring is having on family life in East Germany. The following questions are of special concern: what does the economic restructuring, in particular the deindustrialization, mean for the daily life of the Heilmann family? How do the social changes affect gender relations, the distribution of work, and long-term plans in a typical East German family?

I am intentionally pursuing a point that often goes unnoticed in the statistical findings (which document the disadvantaging and displacement of women, and the higher unemployment rates for women in East Germany): that the most serious structural problems and the greatest need for retraining and adjustment are to be found among the skilled male workers.

Frau Heilmann and her Husband

Angelika Breuer was nineteen when she married Martin Heilmann. Martin Heilmann, twenty-one, was working as a crane construction fitter in a three-shift system. Frau Heilmann had finished her training as a salesperson and was working in the largest department store in the city. They married in 1974. Three years earlier Ulbricht had been replaced by a new man who proclaimed a "new course" for the country: the linking of economic and social policy. The GDR population was to have a foretaste of communism during its own lifetime. The production of consumer goods was increased; young mothers and families received subsidies; and everyone was to have an apartment by the year 1990. "Für Politik hab'sch misch nisch interessiert als Arbeiter" ("As a worker I was never interested in politics"), Herr Heilmann remarks. The programs "for the raising of the standard of living" were taken for granted by the population.

There was a reason why the Heilmanns married when they did: "Wir haben geheiratet, weil das Kind kam" ("We got married because the baby was coming"), Herr Heilmann explains. "Da war das natürlich klar" ("That cinched it, of course"). The couple lived with Herr Heilmann's parents for a few months in the beginning.

The qualitative, empirical study shows that the demands of daily life and therefore life itself became more complex during the *Wende* period. Especially in the new federal states massive layoffs forced men and women to rethink the roles assigned to work, family, and other areas of their lives. The research results have been published in *Die Arbeit des Alltags*, ed. Karin Jurczyk and Maria S. Rerrich (Freiburg: Lambertus, 1993). All quotations are taken from the interviews.

But Frau Heilmann invested a lot of energy in acquiring an apartment for her family; every Tuesday, on GDR "Behördentag," she stoically and stubbornly joined the ranks of those waiting in the overcrowded corridors of the Housing Office – she had definite views on "ordentliche Verhältnisse" ("proper circumstances").

When their son Tobias was born in 1975 the Heilmanns were already living in one of the new high-rise apartment complexes on the outskirts of town. As a young working-class family the Heilmanns were among those who benefited most from the Party's new program. Frau Heilmann had finally achieved her "proper circumstances": she was living with her husband and child in their own apartment; both she and her husband had regular jobs; and they had put their name on the waiting list for a Trabant and a garden plot in the *Kleingartenanlage*.

After a few months of maternity leave, Frau Heilmann insisted on going back to work: "Mir fiel zu Hause die Decke auf den Kopf. Ich mußte wieder unter Leute" ("I couldn't stand the sight of these four walls anymore. I had to get back among people"). Her employer, the department store, was glad to have her back again. It found a day-care spot for the child. Two years later she had a second child. After the birth of her daughter Anke, Frau Heilmann took a full year's maternity leave, after which she again returned to her old job.

That both parents were working caused some problems. Looking back, Frau Heilmann comments: "Ich weiß selbst nicht mehr, wie wir das damals gepackt haben. Aber irgendwie ist es gegangen" ("I just can't think how we did it, but somehow we managed"). For Herr and Frau Heilmann it was only natural that both had jobs and that the family had two incomes. Frau Heilmann was kept busy in the department store, and was even assigned a "social function": she was put in charge of contests. "Das war gar nicht so schlecht, da bekam ich Überblick und konnte richtig mitmischen" ("That wasn't half bad. I knew what was going on, and I could get involved").

Daily family life required considerable organization. Frau Heilmann, whose normal working hours were from 10 a.m. to 6:30 p.m., took the children to kindergarten and the day-care center; Herr Heilmann picked them up in the afternoon and took care of them until Frau Heilmann arrived home in the evening. That was possible only when he worked the early shift or the night shift. When he was on the late shift Frau Heilmann had to change her work schedule; only rarely could the grandparents take care of the children, since they were employed as well. The family's daily routine ran like a well-oiled machine. Frau Heilmann did the lion's share of the housework; she got up early and had breakfast with her husband, at 5:30 a.m. when he returned from the night shift, or 4:30 a.m. when he worked the early shift. After breakfast Frau Heilmann began her "first shift": she "brachte den Haushalt auf Vordermann" ("got the apartment ship-shape"). She fixed a lunch box for her husband and did all the chores that could be done without making noise – her husband did the vacuuming in the afternoon. At 7:30 Frau Heilmann woke the children, took them to kindergarten, and went by streetcar from there to the department store. Frau Heilmann was in charge of household matters; she wrote her husband daily lists of things he was to do, and she took care of a lot of things herself from the department store.

The department store was her command center, so to speak. She could arrange with her fellow saleswomen to absent herself in order to go to some government office or other. And at work she had a telephone at her disposal. Private telephones were few and far between in the GDR, with the result that people used "people-owned" telephones for their private matters with the nonchalance of owners. Using the department store telephone, Frau Heilmann could take the reins in her hands and make arrangements – or just keep in touch – with relatives and friends who also "only had a telephone at work."

On weekdays Herr Heilmann took over at home at 2:15 p.m., when he returned from work or – if he had worked the night shift – got up. First he sat down in the living room with a cup of coffee; at 3:30 he set out to pick up the children from the day-care center or kindergarten. "Wir haben dann immer etwas angestellt" ("Then we always did something"), he remembers, "Kastaniensammeln, Drachensteigen, später dann sind wir in den Garten gefahren" ("gathering chestnuts, flying kites, later on we drove out to our garden"). By 6:30 p.m. they were back home. Herr Heilmann tidied up the apartment and fixed supper. Frau Heilmann arrived at 7, and the family's evening began then. Frau Heilmann brought things home from the department store that normal customers saw on the shelves only rarely, if ever at all. However, in addition to these surprises Frau Heilmann also brought her problems home. During supper she customarily told her husband about the things that had bothered her at work. She frequently could not "switch off." And that got on her husband's nerves: "Die ist mit ihrem Kaufhaus verheiratet und denkt an nischt and'res" ("She's married to that department store of hers and can't think of anything else").

Her husband, on the other hand, was long since "divorced"

from his company. In the last years of the GDR, machine workers in the large industrial complexes saw their hitherto considerable prestige crumble. The factories and equipment were run-down; it became more and more difficult to fulfill the production quotas.[3] The skilled workers were constantly confronted with shortages and makeshift solutions. Many tradition-conscious skilled workers suffered because of the deteriorating standards. Nevertheless, they learned to accept them without protest – with the result that the workers' pride in their company and in their own skills eroded more and more.

The garden plot which the Heilmanns received in 1978, after the birth of their second child, helped Herr Heilmann compensate for this loss and gave him the chance to demonstrate his craftsman's skills. He built their summer house – "mit allen Schikanen" ("with all the modern conveniences") – by himself, and he grew his own tomatoes and cucumbers. In addition, the garden opened up for him a new sphere of social activity. This little patch of greenery became the center of weekend activities for the family, and the setting for social gatherings with colleagues and friends as well. In the warm season birthdays were celebrated in the garden. Once a month Herr Heilmann's work brigade met there to play *Skat*, and the saleswomen from Frau Heilmann's department store occasionally came for a cook-out. In the early 1980s the Heilmanns took delivery of their Trabi, and after that Herr Heilmann drove out to the garden almost every day.

It was at a cook-out, as Frau Heilmann remembers, that one of her female colleagues remarked that Herr Heilmann had become pretty "handzahm" ("domesticated"). Frau Heilmann would have chosen a different expression, but the comment of her colleague and friend points to a development in gender relations that was typical for the GDR: men in the traditional, patriarchally oriented working-class milieu had become more open, more practical, and "softer" when it came to the social and household tasks of the family. To be sure, it was usually the women who were the driving force; they told the men what to do. A new form of female authority became manifest in women like Frau Heilmann. Up to this time

---

[3] Cf. Michael Hofmann and Dieter Rink, "The Coalworkers of Espenhain: A Study in the Decline of Tradition in an Established Industrial Region," in *Studies in GDR Culture and Society 13. Understanding the Past - Managing the Future: The Integration of the Five New Länder into the Federal Republic of Germany*, ed. Margy Gerber and Roger Woods (Lanham/New York/London: University Press of America, 1994), pp. 39-54.

women had structured and directed family life, but more along the lines of the "wise wife" who, aware of her influence, stayed in the background, kept quiet, and officially never questioned the authority of the male head of the family.

Women like Frau Heilmann appropriated – beyond the traditionally feminine domestic realm – areas of employment, social and public functions, and collegial socializing. This is often seen solely as the *Doppelbelastung* (double burden) of women. However, this is a one-sided view which highlights the negative and neglects the positive aspects of the arrangement. Frau Heilmann, who experienced what it was like to be a housewife when she was on maternity leave, was intent on resuming her job, which she managed to do, despite her working hours which ran counter to family life. This was possible in part because Frau Heilmann received from her family the same cooperation and consideration traditionally reserved for the male "head of the family."

For Frau Heilmann, working in the department store presented more than just the opportunity of bettering the family's income. At work and in the circle of her female colleagues Frau Heilmann was "in her element." Here she found recognition, experienced free space and challenges that far exceeded those in the realm of the family. The *Kollektiv* was the boat in which all were equal and where one could exchange views on men, family, vacations, work, and politics.

It is clear that as time went on Frau Heilmann's status as a salaried employee grew more and more, while the worker status of her husband declined.

We were interested to know whether and how the relationship between Herr and Frau Heilmann has changed since the equality of workers and salaried employees, which was a key feature of working life in the GDR, was abandoned, and, in addition, the worker status of Herr Heilmann had further declined as a result of deindustrialization.

On the surface, in their patterns of everyday living, there at first appears to be little change. The Heilmanns still get up together, a little before 5 a.m., since Herr Heilmann has to be at work by 6. Frau Heilmann still does household chores before leaving for the department store. When she returns in the evening, about 7 p.m., her husband and the children are waiting for her with supper. Weekends are still spent in the garden.

However, Herr Heilmann's job is not the same. In 1992 the machine factory in which he had worked for twenty-two years was closed. "Ich hatte gute Beziehungen zum Betriebsrat" ("I had good connections in the works council"), he reports, "deshalb bekam isch sofort auch die ABM-Stelle" ("so I got the ABM job right away"). In response to the question whether there had been resistance to the closing of the plant, he remarks: "Nee, das hat sisch nisch gelohnt. Wir hatten da keine Chance" ("No, it wasn't worth it. We didn't have a chance"). Herr Heilmann adjusted readily to his new duties, the dismantling of former factories. He earns 2300 DM a month before deductions in the ABM position. "Da kann man keine großen Sprünge machen," he said, "aber es muß reichen" ("You can't afford luxuries with that, but we've got to make do with it"). In a few months however the ABM job will come to an end. And then? "Mal seh'n, was für Angebote da sind, vielleicht doch Umschulung?" ("Have to see what I can find – maybe I'll have to retrain after all?"). In 1991 Herr Heilmann was offered the opportunity of retraining as a plumber, but he turned it down. He could not see himself, a crane construction worker, "mounting toilet bowls." Earlier, in the GDR, Herr Heilmann was just as helpless in the face of the gradual erosion of the prestige attached to being a skilled metalworker as he is now when faced with the drop in social status from crane construction worker to ABM jobholder and now possibly retrainee. As far back as he can remember, living and working conditions were determined by societal factors beyond his control; and once again he is waiting to see what the future will bring. He is better able to influence his social life. He has safeguarded his "fortress" of daily life. He finds consolation in the fact that nothing has changed in regard to his circle of friends, the gatherings in the garden, and his *Skat* group.

Frau Heilmann was able to keep her position as a trained salesperson. In 1992 the department store was taken over by a West German firm. For her this meant that her "Zitterpartie" ("nail biting") was over. Nevertheless, she is not content: "Früher war's schöner. Heute fühle ich mich so herabgesetzt und herabgeschätzt. Nur noch als Auffüller, als Staubsauger und als Kassiererin. Mehr nich. Früher hab ich noch verkauft . . ." ("It was nicer before. Now I feel so demoted and devalued. Just someone who stocks the shelves, vacuums, and rings the cash register – that's all. I used to sell . . ."). Frau Heilmann is lamenting her loss of status. As a saleswoman she experiences negative aspects of the restructuring above all in regard to her customers. Saleswomen are no longer the important people they were in the scarcity economy, no longer the "lady of the house." The actions of the saleswomen are no longer attributable to the constraints of the system or their superiors. Now when there are problems with customers the salespersons themselves are held accountable. And the job requires much more energy. Frau Heilmann has to fight for her status. Her job is "schlauchend" ("draining") not so much because of the greater workload, but rather because of the increased social competition and the higher emotional outlay. "Es ist mit den Kolleginnen nicht mehr so wie früher, ein anderes Klima, würd' ich mal sagen" ("It's not the same anymore with my women colleagues, the climate's changed, I'd say"). To be sure, she earns more now than she did in the GDR, but the work is exhausting. "Mitmischen" – her positive description of her work in the department store in the GDR – has been replaced by "ziemlicher Streß" ("pretty stressful"). Frau Heilmann has reached the point where she is asking herself seriously whether the stress is worth it. "Gottseidank," she says, "zu Hause läuft alles" ("Thank God, everything's fine at home").

Still, old conflicts have resurfaced in the Heilmann family. Herr Heilmann complains that his wife is neglecting the family, that she "spends all her time at her department store." And this "obwohl sie da nur beschissen wird" ("even though she's taking a lot of crap there"). He wants his wife to put her talents and circumspection more in the service of the family – to help their children find job-training programs and to maintain ties with their old circle of friends – instead of letting herself be bothered by the "Nasen dort" ("those idiots") at the department store.

Structural Problems of Society and Family Conflict

It is clear that structural problems of society are having long-term effects on East German marital relations. Frau Heilmann's exclamation "Thank God, everything's fine at home" sounds more like an incantation than a sigh of relief. Heilmanns' marriage, like many East German marriages between women employed in the service sector and men working in skilled labor positions in industry, was put under pressure by the *Wende*. This "mixed marriage" is influenced by conflicts which are becoming more and more pronounced and which can be summarized in the following questions.

Will Frau Heilmann continue to fight for her job and her social status, while Herr Heilmann gradually assumes the role of house-husband? Or will Frau Heilmann lower her sights (for example, take a part-time job) in order to help her husband reenter the labor force on a permanent basis? Is this even possible? Will the marital conflicts become so aggravated that the marriage breaks up? Or will the couple succeed in practicing a "modern" life-style in which each primarily pursues his/her profession and career?

Herr Heilmann, who was already affected by the decline of GDR industry, will have to face great changes. If he fails to secure one of the few new jobs in industry, he will have to change his life completely. This is the situation of many East German industrial workers. One possible solution is that they adjust to their being "put out to pasture" – i.e., to the mass layoffs of skilled workers (early retirement, unemployment, invalid status) – or to being forced to accept work that offers no job security (ABM, part-time, occasional, and temporary jobs) when their wives have secure jobs in the service sector. A skilled worker we interviewed, who is married to a grammar school teacher, put it this way: "Meine Frau hat noch richtige Arbeit, die muß ich jetzt pflegen" ("My wife still has a real job. Now I've got to take care of her"). This may become a typical East German situation.

The other possibility is that they concentrate all their energy on reentering the job market, for example, in the construction industry or its ancillary branches. In this case, they will need the full support and (voluntary) partial retreat of their wives, if the family structure is to be maintained.

Although opportunities are relatively good for skilled and experienced women employees in the service sector, the women are nevertheless just as affected by the collapse of East German industry as are their husbands, almost all of whom were industrial workers. For the women do not want to assert their professional goals without or against their men. These typical East German women, these managers of East German workers' existence, pursued their emancipatory course in the GDR in cooperation with their husbands. And therefore for the most part they will try to overcome the structural problems within their own families, even if it means neglecting their own career opportunities.

Frau Heilmann has already made her decision. They must see what the future holds for her husband before she develops her own new career status. She will hold back on her own plans until her husband has his feet on the ground again. She is not prepared to risk a long-term conflict in her marriage. In making this decision she is not only contributing to the stability of her marriage; she is also helping to ease the structural problems of East German society.

Translated by Margy Gerber

The Renaissance of East German
Group Awareness since Unification

Thomas Koch

This study, which combines aspects of cultural science, sociology, and political science, attempts to gain perspective on continuity and change in the collective self-awareness of the East German population. In addition to the results of my own desk and field research,[1] I use so-called mass data from surveys and opinion polls, that is, the results of others' research. I do this for two reasons: first, one of the aims of my paper is to survey the social landscape, and this requires the interlinking of my own findings with those of others. And secondly, the "conditions of collective self-experience"[2] have changed for East Germans since the *Wende*

---

[1] Three projects are involved: "Wer sind die Ostdeutschen? Wertewelten, Mentalitäten und Typen sozialen Verhaltens in den neuen Bundesländern"; "Neue Selbständige im Transformationsprozeß: Herkunftswege, soziale Charakteristika und Potentiale. Dargestellt am Beispiel des Landes Brandenburg und der Region Ostberlin," directed by Michael Thomas and sponsored by the Stiftung Volkswagen, 1992-95; and "Ostdeutsche Lehrer (Promotoren) in Transformationsprozessen des Bildungswesens. Eine Fallstudie zu Auswirkungen und subjektiven Verarbeitungen des Wandels in ausgewählten Regionen," directed by Rudolf Woderich and sponsored by die Kommission zur Erforschung des sozialen und politischen Wandels in den neuen Bundesländern (KSPW), 1993-94.

[2] Gerhard Schulze, *Die Erlebnisgesellschaft. Eine Kultursoziologie der Gegenwart* (Frankfurt am Main/New York: Campus, 1992), p. 410. The translation of

and unification: "public description . . . as so-and-so-many do-this and the totality of public opinion and market research, election analyses, etc."[3] not only depict social groups; the latter also become aware of their being social groups through public descriptions, among other things.

The concept of identity has two dimensions: personal and collective. Elias speaks of "Ich-Identität" and "Wir-Identität" and of changes in *Wir-Ich* balances.[4] Despite changes in the balance, however, there is no such thing as an individual independent of the group or a group independent of individuals: "There is no *Ich-Identität* without *Wir-Identität*. Only the weightings of the *Ich-Wir* balance are changeable" (p. 247). The *Ich-Wir* identity "represents the answer to the question of who one is, both as a social being and as an individual" (p. 246). The need for answers to this question is not constant. It is especially felt in times of upheaval. At such times, identity becomes an issue.

If no individual is independent of the group, then group connections must have some function for the individual. They are information filters; they provide a conceptual framework for sorting and relating, for typifying social objects and subjects; they categorize and classify social space in the sense of group structures; they are the object and means of effecting loyalty, the building up of confidence, and distinguishing between the familiar and the alien; they are points of reference for regulating conflict. As "frameworks for ordering," "selection aids," as "rules for the perception, classification, construction of environments,"[5] they take the load off the individual. In this regard, collective identities belong to the universals of human life. The analysis of their composition, anchors, and effects is a legitimate concern of the social sciences.

There are several levels of integration in reference to which individuals can say "we": for example, family, community, region, social group, country, nation, and continent. Only one of the various group references of East Germans will be treated here, that is, East German group awareness and self-assurance.

---

this and subsequent German quotations is by Margy Gerber.

[3] Schulze, *Die Erlebnisgesellschaft*, p. 412.

[4] Norbert Elias, *Die Gesellschaft der Individuen* (Frankfurt am Main: Suhrkamp, 1987), pp. 207-315.

[5] Werner Weidenfeld, "Identität," in *Handwörterbuch zur deutschen Einheit* (Frankfurt am Main/New York: Campus, 1992), p. 376.

The Phenomenon and its Indicators

Looking back on the period since 1989-90, one can make out a tendency among East Germans which recently has begun to take on political significance. Social scientists and journalists watching this development in the new German states differ in their diagnoses. They agree, however, on one symptom. Some speak of "nostalgia" or "*ost*algia"; others note a "dramatization of collective self-perception,"[6] the genesis of an East German intermediate identity ("'no longer GDR' and 'not yet FRG'"[7]), and see a connection between "West German paternalism and East German obstinacy."[8] I call this phenomenon the renaissance of East German group awareness and self-assurance.

The trend has four indicators, which I want to comment on briefly:

1) Enhanced appreciation of life in the GDR

First of all, the trend is characterized by a reevaluation or, more precisely, a progressive *selective* upward evaluation of life in the GDR, a more positive viewing of accomplishments, practices, and regulations of GDR society *in retrospect*. The survey conducted by Infratest Burke in East Germany shortly before the third anniversary of German unification illustrates the point (see Table 1).[9] From the point of view of the 1023 East Germans (aged 14 and older) polled in the fall of 1993 – only East Germans were included in the study – both the Federal Republic and the former GDR have special strengths. For most of those polled, the positive aspects of the two societies figure as mirror images of each other: the strengths of the one are the weaknesses of the other, and vice

---

[6] Werner Weidenfeld and Karl Rudolf Korte, *Die Deutschen. Profil einer Nation* (Stuttgart: Klett-Cotta, 1991), p. 238.

[7] Ingrid Kurz-Scherf, "Nachbemerkungen: Die blockierte Transformation," in *Sozialreport 1994. Daten und Fakten zur sozialen Lage in den neuen Bundesländern*, ed. Ingrid Kurz-Scherf and Gunnar Winkler (Berlin: GSFP, 1994), pp. 337f.

[8] Helmut Wiesenthal, "Der Umbruch in der DDR als Sonderfall im Transformationsprozeß." Unpublished paper presented at conference "Identität und Arbeit. Erfahrungen im Transformationsprozeß," Berlin, 27 October 1994.

[9] Source of the table: "Es wächst zusammen," *Die Zeit*, 1 October 1993, pp. 17-21.

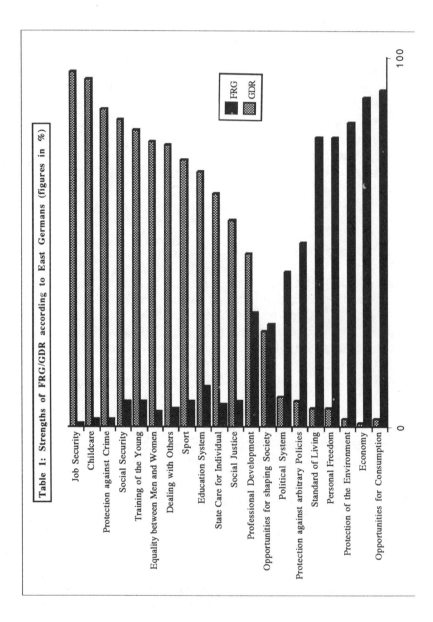

Table 1: Strengths of FRG/GDR according to East Germans (figures in %)

versa. In twelve of the twenty areas the former GDR is given preference over the Federal Republic.

A second empirical finding which documents the retrospective selective upward evaluation of life in the GDR is taken from our 1992 survey of "Existenzgründer," that is, of East Germans in East Berlin and the state of Brandenburg who set themselves up in business in the post-*Wende* period.[10] Question 40 of the survey read: "Before you went into business for yourself, did you have the general impression that you could realize your life goals?" Of the 904 newly independently employed, 48 percent answered "generally speaking, yes," 42 percent "partially," and only 10 percent "not at all."

2) Differences between published opinion and opinion research

These and other findings about life in the GDR, as seen after the fact, indicate a massive discrepancy between the mainstream of published opinion about the system and life in the GDR (key words "Unrechtsstaat," "ungelebtes Leben," or interpretations along the lines of "Gefängnis-" or "Nischenmodell"), on the one hand, and public opinion gathered through opinion research, on the other. Polls with narrow thematic focuses such as the evaluation of the new divided school system testify to this growing discrepancy.[11]

Noelle-Neumann is surprised that an overwhelming majority considers the *Jugendweihe* an "unpolitical family celebration" and that more than 80 percent of those polled are against its abolition. The prominent opinion researcher also cannot comprehend that the East Germans judge the role of kindergartens in the GDR primarily from a practical point of view, and therefore are not inclined to see them as means of political indoctrination.[12]

In response to the question, "Where was or is there more legal security [*Rechtssicherheit*], in the GDR in the past or in Germany

---

[10] The survey, which polled 904 persons of East German origin, was conducted within the framework of the project mentioned in Note 1. See Gabriele Valerius, "Forschungsbericht zu den Ergebnissen der repräsentativen Erhebung 'neuer Selbständiger' in Ostberlin und im Land Brandenburg 1992/93," in *BISS-Forschungshefte*, No. 8, 1993, pp. 4-60.

[11] See Hans-Günter Rolff, "Bewertung des neuen Schulsystems zeigt Ernüchterung und Enttäuschung an." Draft for press conference on 2 February 1994 in Berlin.

[12] Elisabeth Noelle-Neumann, "Eine Nation zu werden ist schwer," *Frankfurter Allgemeine Zeitung*, 10 August 1994, p. 5.

today?," 26 percent of the East Germans polled in the spring of 1994 answered "in Germany today," and 27 percent "in the GDR in the past"; 47 percent were undecided.[13] The responses must be seen against the background of property claims being made by former owners and their heirs in the West; more than 2.5 million properties are involved.

The frequency of such property claims has evoked not only the solidarity of those previously privileged by the system; it has also produced widespread resentment of West Germans.[14] Granted, published opinion and public opinion never coincide completely, neither in dictatorships nor in pluralistic democracies. Still, the dwindling accuracy of surveys and the rebelliousness vis-à-vis interpretations of published opinion in the East are remarkable.

3) Continuity and change in collective self-perception

Since unification large majorities of East Germans surveyed in opinion polls have assessed themselves as second-class citizens.[15] I will return to this later. In the present context the finding is of interest as an indication of a constant collective self-perception. At the same time, it is striking that within a short period of time the self-classification of the East Germans shifted from one pole to the other. During the *Wende* most East Germans wanted to be Germans, i.e., did not see themselves as citizens of the GDR or as from the GDR or as East Germans; since 1992 the majority of those polled emphasize their East German special identity (Table 2).[16] In

---

[13] Noelle-Neumann, "Eine Nation zu werden ist schwer," p. 5.

[14] Hans-Joachim Misselwitz, "Politikwahrnehmung und Politikvermittlung in den neuen Bundesländern," *Aus Politik und Zeitgeschichte. Beilage zur Wochenzeitung Das Parlament*, B 45-46/94, 11 November 1994, p. 6.

[15] In polls conducted by EMNID for *Der Spiegel* over the period 1990-1994, the percentage has varied only slightly from somewhat under to somewhat over 80 percent. Cf. "Zwietracht im einig Vaterland. *Spiegel*-Umfrage im Januar (II): Die Einstellung zum Golfkrieg und zur Situation in der Bundesrepublik," *Der Spiegel*, 4 February 1991, p. 46; "Nur noch halb so beliebt wie die Russen. *Spiegel*-Umfrage über die Einstellung der Ost- und Westdeutschen zueinander," *Der Spiegel*, 22 July 1991, p. 26; "Erst vereint, nun entzweit. *Spiegel*-Umfrage über die Einstellung der Ost- und Westdeutschen zueinander," *Der Spiegel*, 18 January 1993; "CDU-Verluste wie nie zuvor," *Der Spiegel*, 21 February 1994, p. 43.

[16] The data for Table 2 are taken from the *Allensbacher Jahrbuch der Demoskopie 1984-1992*, ed. Elisabeth Noelle-Neumann and Renate Köcher (Allensbach/

1990 45 percent of the East Germans surveyed believed "Wir sind *ein* Volk!" In 1994 only 28 percent agreed.[17]

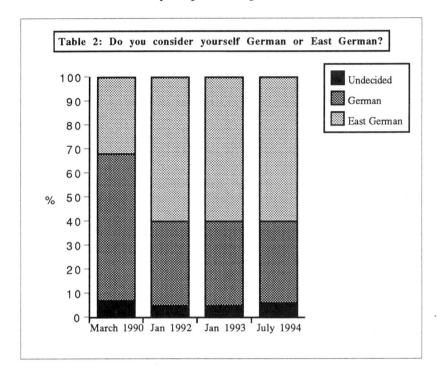

Table 2: Do you consider yourself German or East German?

4) Growing rejection of "imported elites"

The acceptance of "imported elites" (managers, officials, politicians from the old Federal Republic) has sharply decreased since 1990-91. In September 1990 44.2 percent of those polled considered the influx of managers, civil servants, and entrepreneurs to be

Munich/New York/London/Paris: Verlag für Demoskopie/K.G. Saur, 1993), p. 486; and Noelle-Neumann, "Eine Nation zu werden ist schwer," p. 5. The polls show differences between the views of men and women and of members of the various age groups. In 1990, 32 percent of the men and 60 percent of the women surveyed perceived themselves as East German; in 1992, 56 percent and 63 percent respectively. The figures for 1992 show the strongest sense of being East German in the age groups 30-44 (66 percent) and 45-59 (70 percent); for the younger and older groups the figures are 53 and 50 percent respectively (*Allensbacher Jahrbuch der Demoskopie*, p. 486).

[17] Noelle-Neumann, "Eine Nation zu werden ist schwer," p. 5.

necessary and desirable; an additional 44.3 percent viewed it as more or less positive. By the end of 1992 acceptance had lessened dramatically.[18]

The degree of tolerance varies according to region and political persuasion. However, the issues and ambivalence of the findings are not my concern here. Instead, I am interested in what this general decline in acceptance indicates for a rebirth of East German group awareness and self-assurance. If the initial high degree of acceptance was born of the belief that representatives of the superior system stood for superior ability in problem-solving, competency, assertion, and moral integrity, then the dwindling of this acceptance testifies to the increasing confidence of East Germans in their own strength, problem-solving ability, and competence. Research findings on the self-employed are noteworthy in this context. The self-employed are among those East Germans most affected by the "west wind"; their everyday behavior also has the most in common with that of West Germans.[19] In this group one often encounters "the certainty that 'they're no different from the rest of us'" ("Gewißheit, daß 'überall nur mit Wasser gekocht wird'"), and even "we're not so bad ourselves" ("daß man auch zu den eher besseren Köchen gehöre").[20] Michael Hofmann notes in regard to young entrepreneurs in the southern part of East Germany: "And as time goes on they are becoming more and more the equals of their self-confident West German partners. The first derogatory comments about slightly degenerate West German management have already been heard."[21]

Sources and Prime Movers of East German Group Awareness

The increase in East German group awareness and self-confidence is attributable to various factors: to imbalances of power; to limited prospects for collective and individual development; and to

---

[18] Siegfried Grundmann, "Zur Akzeptanz und Integration von Beamten aus den alten in den neuen Ländern," *Deutschland Archiv*, 27, No. 1 (1994), pp. 35, 37.

[19] Cf. Annette Spellerberg, *Alltagskultur in Ost- und Westdeutschland. Unterschiede und Gemeinsamkeiten*. WZB Papers, No. P 94-101 (Wissenschaftszentrum Berlin, 1994).

[20] Thomas Koch and Michael Thomas, "Transformationspassagen. Vom sozialistischen Ingenieur und Manager zum kapitalistischen Unternehmer," *Deutschland Archiv*, 27, No. 2 (1994), p. 150.

[21] Michael Hofmann, "Phönix aus der Masse," in *Das Dederon* (Berlin: Zyankrise, 1993), p. 157.

interrelated conflicts of interest and identity resulting from unification. Karl Otto Hondrich, to whom I am indebted for the distinction between interests and identity, shows that, while interests require satisfaction or compensation, identities demand recognition and confirmation, and that conflicts of interest and conflicts of identity, although they often overlap, are never identical.[22] In my opinion, it is precisely from this interconnection of conflicts of interest and identity that the renaissance of East German group awareness and self-assurance gains its breadth and force as a sort of "Entwicklungsnationalismus":[23] it promises solutions for conflicts of interest as well as of identity.

This rebirth of group awareness signals thwarted development opportunities for individuals and groups who in regard to their social situation, social norms, and cultural values do not have that much in common. Although the social segregating of East German society is underway, the collective self-perception of East German society has become stronger. This augmented sense of self is a sign of the less than optimal integration of East Germany into the Federal Republic.

Now to the prime movers: an increase in group awareness and self-assurance is present in nearly all sections and age groups of the East German population, among both men and women, among the "losers" as well as the "winners" of the *Wende* and unification, and across all political parties – in varying degrees and numbers, of course. The "newly self-employed" are often in the lead. With these broad statements I want to emphasize two things: 1) that the initiators are not only – or even mostly – people still living in the past ("Ewiggestrige"), "losers," or members of the older generation; and 2) that I consider the pool to be broader, more varied, more ambiguous and ambivalent than the estimation of Thomas Gensicke.[24]

On the basis of the first all-German ALLBUS poll, conducted in 1991, Gensicke comes to the surprising conclusion:

---

[22] Karl Otto Hondrich et al., *Arbeitgeber West – Arbeitnehmer Ost. Vereinigung im Konflikt* (Berlin: Aufbau, 1993), p. 85.

[23] Dieter Senghaas, "Vom Nutzen und Elend der Nationalismen im Leben der Völker," *Aus Politik und Zeitgeschichte. Beilage zur Wochenzeitung Das Parlament*, B 31-32/92, 24 Juli 1992, pp. 23-32.

[24] Thomas Gensicke, "Vom Staatsbewußtsein zur Oppositionsideologie: DDR-Identität im vereinten Deutschland," in *Auf dem Weg zu einer gesamtdeutschen Identität*, ed. Axel Knoblich, Antonio Peter, and Erik Natter (Cologne: Wissenschaft und Politik, 1993), pp. 49-65.

> Whoever avows loyalty to the GDR today is, either consciously or
> unconsciously, part of a post-materialistically informed, leftist, all-
> German reform movement. In this regard, GDR identity as an emo-
> tional and consciously proclaimed view appears to point socially more
> to the future than to the past, even though it at times decidedly distances
> itself from the new reality. (p. 50)

Individuals and groups with the profile Gensicke sketches are
clearly to be found among the initiators of East German group
awareness and self-assurance. However, I see actors of other colors
and persuasions as well.

Explanations Put to the Test

Disregarding those views which deny the presence of an East
German group awareness, one finds in social science research and
in the media three competing explanations for the empirical
findings I have been discussing:

1) Nostalgia, mental resurrecting, "false consciousness"

This widespread explanation is not entirely wrong, but it lacks
analytical depth. It overlooks the fact that positive retrospective
views of the GDR are always selective and thus connected with a
clear rejection of restoring the GDR in its entirety. Moreover, the
retrospective affirmation of aspects of the GDR is linked to
acceptance of the strengths of the Federal Republic (Table 1).
Nostalgia is the wrong word for this mood. The nostalgia explanation also forgets that, confronted with other life models, people
tend to identify with their own life history, since this is the only
means they have of preserving their self-respect.[25] And it disre-
gards the socio-cultural and other divisions within East German
society itself.

At first glance, the feeling of being a second-class citizen
shared by two thirds of the East Germans since 1990 appears to
indicate uniformity and relatively few social and cultural differences. That this is not the case can be seen in the fact that both
winners and losers of the *Wende* and unification chose this answer,

---

[25] Cf. Sighard Neckel, "Vom Unterscheiden. Eine Einführung am deutschen
Fall," in his *Die Macht der Unterscheidung. Beutezüge durch den modernen
Alltag* (Frankfurt am Main: Fischer, 1993), p. 14.

thus clearly attaching different, even opposite, meanings to their response.[26] They move in different systems of coordinates. Still, there is common ground. Successful entrepreneurs and the long-term unemployed, single mothers and career women, discharged ("abgewickelte") academics and their positively evaluated, retained colleagues, people in early retirement, tenants, property owners threatened with Western ownership claims, and the homeless all share "Differenzerfahrungen" of exclusion,[27] the feeling of living in a "society with limited entitlement to participation."[28] The point of agreement of these people in highly varied social situations and with clearly different prospects and goals is not so much the glorification of the past but the inaccessibility of the present.

For this reason it is useful to try to understand why overwhelming majorities of those surveyed agreed with the answer "second-class citizen." Modifying some of my own earlier findings,[29] I see at least six different explanations, some of which lie worlds apart from each other.[30]

a) Denied belonging

In this case, the sense of being a "second-class citizen" results when attempts of East Germans who signal a clear willingness to change their behavior and identity are not rewarded by the West Germans whom they emulate. These East Germans accept for the most part the criteria used to judge the new German citizens and try to cast off the pilloried ways of thinking and behaving, of which they are ashamed and which they find despicable. For them the Federal Republic is the best of all possible worlds. They share none of the values of the country of their origin or of East German

---

[26] For this section I am indebted to Pierre Bourdieu's concepts of social identity and difference. See his *Die feinen Unterschiede. Kritik der gesellschaftlichen Urteilskraft* (Frankfurt am Main: Suhrkamp, 1989), p. 312.

[27] Lutz Niethammer, "Konjunkturen und Konkurrenzen kollektiver Identität. Ideologie, Infrastruktur und Gedächtnis in der Zeitgeschichte," *PROKLA*, No. 3, 1994, p. 393.

[28] Kurz-Scherf, "Nachbemerkungen: Die blockierte Transformation," p. 343.

[29] Thomas Koch, "Die Ostdeutschen zwischen Einheitsschock und 'doppeltem Zukunftshorizont' - Deutungs- und Handlungsmuster sozialer Akteure im Trans-formationsprozeß," in *Rückweg in die Zukunft. Über den schwierigen Trans-formationsprozeß in Ostdeutschland*, ed. Rolf Reißig (Frankfurt am Main/New York: Campus, 1993), pp. 188-91.

[30] The order in which they are listed should not be understood as a ranking.

society. They acknowledge their belonging to this country without positive emotions or special ties. At best, they manifest what Jens Reich calls "Trotzidentität."[31]

  b) Denied recognition of difference and/or blocked chances for
     development

Those whose behavior is thus explained are acting out of the conviction that they are not West German. Their reaction is not infrequently determined by the sense of their own social and cultural superiority, special talents, and problem-solving abilities. They themselves do not see themselves as second-class citizens. Their agreement with this answer choice stems from their belief that they and others like them are being reduced intentionally to second-class citizens by means of one-sided power structures, social closure,[32] and "parasitic" networks that favor East and West German deadbeats wearing – or not wearing – pinstripes. They consider themselves sufficiently bright and assertive to be able to compete successfully under less unfavorable conditions. As a rule, they defend their social-geographical origins and biography. In spite of their positive – but always selective – memories of GDR society, they increasingly act in keeping with the motto: "The GDR is passé but the era of the naive *Beitritt* is passé too." Between them and those in the first group lie worlds of difference. And there is distance as well between them and those East Germans who have only scarcely, if at all, been touched by the "west wind."

  c) Declassed by the market economy and political change –
     foreign in one's own country

For a large number of these East Germans the GDR was, or retrospectively became, the best of all possible worlds. They keenly feel the lack of intellectual recognition of the GDR by the West and the disadvantaging effects of the market economy and the new political system. They find it very difficult to adjust to the present situation and assume an active role in society. They only partially comprehend and do not accept the territories, rules, and rituals the knowledge and practice of which are necessary for

---

[31] Jens Reich, *Rückkehr nach Europa. Zur neuen Lage der deutschen Nation* (Munich/Vienna: Hanser, 1991), p. 251.
[32] Cf. Frank Parkin, "Strategies of Social Closure in Class Formation," in *Social Analysis of the Class Structure*, ed. Frank Parkin (London: Tavistock, 1974).

socially acceptable behavior (not identical with conformity). In reference to this group, the term "nostalgia" is most likely appropriate.

d) Predetermined prospects for success in life

For a fourth group of East Germans "we are second-class citizens" means having limited, predetermined opportunities in comparison with others in both West and East Germany: "Kohortenschicksale"[33] like those of people born between 1930 and 1940. There are indications that there may be not only one lost generation, but a whole "chain of 'lost generations.'"[34] In addition, "gender handicaps," residing in structurally weak areas, etc. can be perceived as disadvantages lying beyond the control of the individuals concerned.

e) "The little man has to pay"

At the core of this understanding lies the realization that the transformation in the East does not mean a new start for everyone under equal conditions. The East-East comparison of job and career prospects is decisive here. The continuing inequality in regard to influence and opportunities – the ability of people and groups who had money, property, connections, and/or education in the GDR to organize and reassert themselves in the new society – is being met partly with surprise, partly with anger, wrath, and counterproductive social envy. Here agreement with the wording "second-class citizen" is attributable to the experience of belonging to the "little people," whose favor was courted to a certain extent in the GDR.

f) Unease at the effects of Western domination in the East

This view is being articulated even by former GDR citizens who have returned to the East and by West Germans taking up residence there. The formers' revitalized old-new ties to the coun-

---

[33] The term was used by Rainer Lepsius in a discussion at the second "Sozialwissenschaftliche Transformationskonferenz" of the Berliner Institut für Sozialwissenschaftliche Studien (BISS) on 22 November 1991.

[34] Johannes Huinink and Karl Ulrich Mayer, "Lebensverläufe im Wandel der DDR-Gesellschaft," in *Der Zusammenbruch der DDR. Soziologische Analysen*, ed. Hans Joas and Martin Kohli (Frankfurt am Main: Suhrkamp, 1993), p. 167.

try and the people living between the Oder and the Werra, and the latters' newly developing bonds are as a rule without positive retrospective views of the GDR as state, society, and system; still, both groups influence East German interests and contribute to East German identities.

When we consider these explanations, one thing in particular stands out: the trend toward an augmented East German group awareness and self-assurance bundles together similar and dissimilar aspects of East German identity which only partially can be classified as nostalgia. There are some relatively easily distinguishable accents, but also frequent overlappings and blurred borders. This is the case for example with the denied social recognition of GDR biographies and life experiences, with the view of Western domination as a problem, and with suffering caused by social closure.

Far more realistic and productive than nostalgia as an explanation for increasing group and self-awareness, in my view, is an interpretation which stresses the aspect of newness, of making up for identity formation missed out on in the GDR.

2) New creation, catching up on identity

I will cite Hans-Joachim Misselwitz' version of this explanatory model, according to which what I call the renaissance of East German group awareness and self-assurance

> . . . has nothing to do with the false invoking of a reemergence of an old GDR identity. The latter had neither independent social roots nor, consequently, the ability to survive. What is emerging is a reflexive identity of the "East Germans," formed against the background of common GDR experience and gained within the interest structure of united Germany. It will manifest itself neither uniformly nor politically one-sidedly.[35]

As can be seen in Table 3, "Perceptions of Serious Conflicts in East and West Germany,"[36] "conflicts between East and West" –

---

[35] Hans-Joachim Misselwitz, "DDR: Geschlossene Gesellschaft und offenes Erbe," in *Deutschland eine Nation – doppelte Geschichte*, ed. Werner Weiden-feld (Cologne: Wissenschaft und Politik, 1993), p. 111. Misselwitz' final prognosis proved to be correct in election year 1994.

[36] The data for the table are based on the welfare survey of 1993. See Detlef Landua, Roland Habich, Hans-Herbert Noll, Wolfgang Zapf, and Annette

noted by 60.4 percent of those surveyed – receive only a fourth place ranking in the East. To be sure, several of the other conflicts listed have an East-West dimension, for example, conflicts between employers and employees and between rich and poor. I interpret this fourth place ranking as support for my thesis that the feeling of not being West German is more decisive for the creation of East German identities than pronounced anti-Western attitudes.

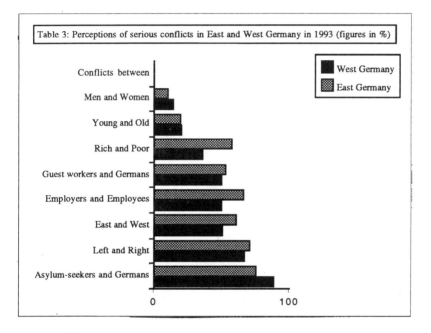

Table 3: Perceptions of serious conflicts in East and West Germany in 1993 (figures in %)

The two explanatory models "nostalgia" and "new creation" differ in their "therapy suggestions" as well as in their diagnoses. The advocates of the first view prescribe countermeasures: exclusion, marginalization, and discrediting of the initiators; those who lean toward the second view favor dealing with the issue in a productively critical manner. One of the problems stems from the tension between GDR identities and East German identities. For this reason, I want to suggest a third explanatory model.

Spellerberg, ". . . im Westen noch beständig, im Osten etwas freundlicher." *Lebensbedingungen und subjektives Wohlbefinden drei Jahre nach der Wiedervereinigung.* WZB Papers, No. P 93-108 (Wissenschaftszentrum Berlin, 1993), p. 89.

3. Renaissance model

This model probably differs in only one point from the interpretation which Misselwitz sets forth: over the question of whether there ever was such a thing as GDR identity or identities. The renaissance model maintains that East German identities and GDR identities exist in a relationship of tension, which in any case presupposes a relationship. To be sure, there was no sense of national identity in the GDR – the attempts made to imbue the GDR population with the feeling of being a separate "socialist nation" failed; still, there was something like GDR identity or identities in Hondrich's sense of the term: "Collective identities . . . are ideas about things that belong together ["Zusammengehöriges"] and things that separate ["Trennendes"] shared by many."[37]

Survey results published by Noelle-Neumann and Köcher in 1993 show that GDR citizens had such collectively held ideas, even though the nature of the ideas is not examined in detail: in June 1990, 73 percent of those East Germans asked stated that they had heard the expression "GDR identity," and, of those 73 percent, 80 percent confirmed that GDR citizens did have an identity which marked them off from citizens of the Federal Republic. In turn, 43 percent of these were concerned that this identity could be lost.[38]

Rainer Lepsius, on the other hand, focuses on content. He emphasizes the inadequate "Selbstlegitimität" of the GDR and maintains: "Only perhaps a third of the population wanted to preserve the state, only they had become politically aware GDR citizens in the forty years."[39]

Claus Offe plumbs deeper in his collection of essays on the East and Middle European transformation process. Offe views the former GDR as an economic society ("Wirtschaftsgesellschaft") with an economic mode of integration, which meant that political institutions and national identity were less significant for integration.[40] He also notes a specific mode of social integration which experienced massive erosion during the *Wende* (p. 250). The ab-

---

[37] Hondrich et al., *Arbeitgeber West – Arbeitnehmer Ost*, p. 7.

[38] Noelle-Neumann and Köcher, *Allensbacher Jahrbuch*, p. 476.

[39] Rainer Lepsius, "Die Bundesrepublik ein neuer Nationalstaat?" *Berliner Journal für Soziologie*, 4, No. 1 (1994), p. 10.

[40] Claus Offe, *Der Tunnel am Ende des Lichts. Erkundungen der politischen Transformation im Neuen Osten* (Frankfurt am Main/New York: Campus, 1994), p. 241. The essays date from 1989-1993.

sence of a strong GDR voice in the unification negotiations is for Offe an indication of the lack of collective self-awareness. He concedes however that there were exceptions: the former state party, which was endeavoring to renew itself in regard to personnel and program, and the reform-socialist oriented GDR opposition during the *Wende*. The appeal "Für unser Land" of November 26, 1989 fits in this same context.

Offe points to the emergence of an,

> as it were, unofficial special identity of those who like to refer to themselves as "qualified GDR citizens" ["gelernte DDR-Bürger"] in a slightly indignant tone of voice. . . . [It] appears to be developing as a reaction to the contradictory experience of simultaneously being included in the old Federal Republic and excluded from it. (p. 270)

He sees factors that could further strengthen the "special identity" of the GDR population, perhaps even its "Ethnifizierung" (p. 271). For Offe – and this is the important point for me – this "inner-German special identity" is not only a reaction to the conditions of unification, but also a cultural residue of political socialization (p. 271).[41]

In summary, one can say: in East German identities GDR identities are negated, preserved, and at the same time transformed to another level. Thus it appears at least somewhat justified to speak of a renaissance. Of course, some East German points of identity date back further than the GDR.

Does this "East German nationalism" have a function in regard to the realization of inner unification or is it primarily counter-productive or regressive?

The renaissance of East German group awareness is an expression of the conflicts of interests and identity stemming from German unification. It signals a sometimes diffuse, sometimes focused "cultural criticism" of structures, relationships, and behavior patterns in the Federal Republic for which more productive solutions must be sought and found.

The question is whether this augmented self-awareness is "only" symptomatic of the situation, or if it is also part of the

---

[41] Characteristic of the political socialization of the East Germans, according to Offe, is the lack of "four political-cultural modernization thrusts" which shaped the lives of the younger and middle generations in the old German states: debate on National Socialism, World War, and Holocaust; the anti-authoritarian student movement; the women's movement; and multi-cultural coexistence (p. 271).

solution. The views predominating in specialist literature tend to rule out the latter. Lutz Niethammer maintains, for example, that "talking about collective identity may aim at social balances, but it stimulates difference."[42] One could argue, with Reinhard Kreckel, that this renaissance is contributing to the development of "two pseudo groups, East against West, which as a result of stereotypical labeling are mutually exclusive."[43]

Those who believe that inner unification depends on establishing a consensus of values necessarily see in the renaissance of East German group awareness and self-assurance something akin to a counter-movement or opposition.[44] Giddens[45] and, in another way, Lepsius have in the meantime developed concepts of "integration" and "inland integration" ("Binnenintegration"), which do not presuppose a consensus of values. As Lepsius maintains, the integration of East and West Germans will not result from value relationships of an abstract kind, but rather from equal opportunities, the joining of interests, increased communication, and the creation of identical institutions.[46]

In social science research, reference has been made to an East German "representation gap" ("Vertretungslücke"),[47] to actor deficits, and, consequently, to difficulties in the shaping of "equal institutions." Is it not conceivable that the renaissance of East German group awareness is at the same time a sort of incubator for the articulation of East German interests and the genesis of actors, that is, a means by which East German actors can make certain of the premises and consequences of their structural minority position in Germany and overcome their speechlessness? Behind this question lies a hypothesis that the appearance of a special East German identity is an ambivalent and perhaps unavoidable transitional stage on the way to the "the joining of interests, increased communication, and the creation of identical institutions." I want to test this hypothesis, using the analytic apparatus provided by Offe.

---

[42] Niethammer, "Konjunkturen und Konkurrenzen kollektiver Identität," p. 397.

[43] Reinhard Kreckel, "Soziale Integration und nationale Identität," *Berliner Journal für Soziologie*, 4, No. 1 (1994), p. 19.

[44] Cf. Elisabeth Noelle-Neumann, "Wenig Neigung zur Demokratie," *Frankfurter Allgemeine Zeitung*, 28 June 1994, p. 11.

[45] Anthony Giddens, *The Constitution of Society. Outline of the Theory of Structuration* (Cambridge: Polity Press, 1984), pp. 164f.

[46] Lepsius, "Die Bundesrepublik ein neuer Nationalstaat?" p. 12.

[47] Heidrun Abromeit, "'Die Vertretungslücke'. Probleme im neuen deutschen Bundesstaat," *Gegenwartskunde*, 42, No. 3 (1993), pp. 281-92.

The "Choice" of Regionalized/Ethnic Codes as a Means of Overcoming "Associative Desolation" of State and Post-Socialist Societies

Collective actors (associations, interest groups, professional organizations, regional authorities, etc.) are of considerable importance for the functioning of societies such as the Federal Republic. At least two conditions are necessary for this to be the case: 1) individual citizens must manifest cooperative and sociable attitudes as opposed to lone-wolf strategies; 2) the divisions and interest differences (between workers and capital, urban and rural areas, members of the professions and their clients, contributors to the social security system and recipients of social services, etc.) must be clearly perceptible, institutionally anchored, and stable.[48]

The associative structures of the Federal Republic exist in East Germany too. However, the *Unterbau* that is essential for their functioning is lacking. In the state-socialist society of the GDR there were scarcely any autonomous associative structures; the associative structures, more or less all of which have since collapsed, were state-run. Furthermore, the state-socialist societies were relatively homogeneous and equalized communities; the distinguishing and articulation of interests and interest conflicts could be carried out only in very mild terms. As a result, East Germans have difficulty identifying their own social position and the accompanying interests. Election campaign strategists and election researchers have come to the conclusion that campaigns focused on target groups are not viable in the East. East Germans cast votes contrary to social status, religious confession, age, etc. In the East, parties that regard themselves as representing the interests of high-income earners and top performers can also count on votes of unskilled workers and welfare recipients; atheists cast votes for Christian parties, and entrepreneurs for the "Democratic Socialists." And, because individual success is frequently determined by chance, the search for individual solutions, for non-cooperative, small networks often seems more promising than "individual efforts in the service of collective organized politics."[49] And because so much depends on resources and opportunities which are apportioned by chance, the establishing of collective

---

[48] Offe, *Der Tunnel am Ende des Lichts*, p. 123.
[49] Offe, p. 124.

actors is very difficult.

When the basis for a "comprehensive aggregation of interests" is weak, regionalized or ethnic codes are the most likely to be used as "collective-building 'codes.'"[50] And when recourse is taken to such codes, corresponding social dividing lines (regional/ethnic, sub-ethnic, or identity constructions) gain in importance. They can be used as an effective lever of collective action and political mobilization. Offe leaves no doubt that ethnic mobilization is a highly ambivalent, overwhelmingly counterproductive "multi-purpose weapon" (p. 148) which is best not put into action. On the other hand, ethnic or regionalized mobilizations are not irrational for those who make use of them, for they promise success in the struggle for "economic resources, political rights, and cultural respect" (p. 143).

Returning to the special case of East Germany, we can regard the renaissance of group awareness and self-assurance as a first sign of collective action on the basis of a regionalized/sub-ethnic code. Taking recourse to such codes must be seen as the conse-quence of, and means of overcoming, the associative desolation described above. If this is the case, then the special East German identity can function as a framework, as a vehicle of interest formation and interest articulation in East Germany. The group awareness at least partially bridges and connects the various interests involved.

The Beginning of the End of the "Representation Gap"?

This raises a question as to the interests which might form within the framework of this augmented group awareness and self-assurance. This limiting focus is appropriate, in my opinion, for four reasons: 1) because the definition of East German interests in itself is a subject of debate between individual and collective actors in both the West-East and the East-East dimension;[51] 2) because

---

[50] Offe, p. 125.

[51] For example, social scientists in sympathy with the citizens' movements and the East German SPD helped bring about the change in academic personnel at East German universities and other institutions of higher learning, without being able to profit from it themselves. They now find themselves in a two-fold struggle: against the "old elites" and, at the same time, against West German recruiting mechanisms which afford East German applicants little real oppor-tunity. West Germans are assuming leadership positions nearly everywhere. See Rainer Eckert, "Replik. Politisches Engagement und institutionelle Absicherung:

the East German nationalism I am addressing is not a nationalism of the unbridled *Volksseele* but presents itself instead as tactically calculated, comparatively moderate, and, given the restraint of its initiators, non-inflammatory; 3) because, due to the initiators and the existing conditions in Germany, certain reasons and trends which Offe foresees when the "multi-purpose weapon" is deployed (pp. 151ff.) do not apply; and 4) because in the Federal Republic it is entirely possible that "ethnic" conflict will be replaced by "class-political" conflict, and that therefore the mixing of interests on an East/West scale, the communicative interlinking, and the creation of more or less equal institutions, of which Lepsius speaks, will come about. This, among other reasons, because although the East/West conflicts over resources, political rights, and cultural respect are linked with the conflicts between work and capital, these and other divisions at the same time break through the East/West pattern.

If we accept these premises, then various possibilities for the formation and articulation of interests emerge. As a result of demands that East German interests be taken into consideration and East German identities recognized,

- local elites, including the remaining "old elites," have opportunities to gain influence, to work, and establish careers;
- institutional concessions and/or material resources can be wrested from the federal government, as can special conditions for East German companies in regard to the granting of contracts in the public sector. Here the interests of the "social winners" and the East German "welfare classes" coincide;
- East German obstinacy vis-à-vis West German domination and East Germans' interest in self-made economic and political development are articulated;
- social rights (jobs, housing, private property, child-care facilities) can be defended;
- all too one-sided and superfluous zeal in confronting the past, including myths, legends, visions, etc. can be averted.

The renaissance of East German group awareness and self-assurance can be a source of solidarity; it can assume a defensive role vis-à-vis the destructive consequences of "modernization" or generate a sort of "productivity patriotism" or "development national-

Die Geschichtsschreibung über die DDR," *Initial. Zeitschrift für sozialwissenschaftlichen Diskurs*, 5, No. 1 (1995), pp. 99-100.

ism."

To this extent the renaissance of group awareness could help fill the "representation gap." It is moreover an ambivalent form of successful integration in the Federal Republic. To the extent that pluralistic society offers the possibility of articulating and political-ly representing all interests, it necessitates presenting and realizing every desire or need as if it were an "interest." Interests that fail to draw attention to themselves do not count. The renaissance of East German group awareness and self-assurance, and the correspond-ing articulation of interests offer the possibility of coupling the problems of the old and new states long-term in a productive way, the possibility of communication and of the joining of interests.

Translated by Margy Gerber

The Press in the New *Länder*

John Sandford

The transformation of the media that occurred in East Germany in the wake of the *Wende* was one of the more visible and dramatic manifestations of what had happened to the GDR, and few would deny that the new patterns of press and broadcasting provision were preferable to – and certainly more popular than – those they replaced. However, when one looks at the new press landscape that has developed in East Germany over the years since the *Wende*, two things in particular stand out as indications that the process of unification in this area has been incomplete, with little prospect in the foreseeable future of any significant reversal of these trends.

As we shall see, in the first place the East Germans still read different newspapers and magazines from the West Germans. Of course, the old ideological differences have gone, and there are – especially in the area of the periodical press – a lot of publications that are now truly *gesamtdeutsch*, but the daily papers that dominate the Eastern market are overwhelmingly East German in their origin as well as, more subtly, in their content and style; in the weekly market too there are widely selling magazines aimed specifically at East Germans and read almost exclusively by them. The market penetration and "reach" of the major West German dailies as well as of many of the better known weeklies is far lower in the East than in the West, whilst that of the specifically Eastern media in the West is virtually nil.

Whether or not this imperfect unification of the press is a bad thing is, of course, debatable, and it could be argued that it indicates an accommodation to East German needs and an acknowledgment of East German identity, the lack of both of which is so

211

often lamented in other spheres. There is no doubt, however, that the second salient characteristic of the new East German press *is* a cause for concern, and that is the high degree of press concentration that has developed there in the brief span of time since unification. This led one West German observer, in a report submitted as early as 1992 to the Federal Minister of the Interior, to assert: "Two and a half years after the restructuring commenced, the press is concentrated to an even higher degree than in the earlier GDR."[1]

The "concentration" of the media in the communist GDR was, of course, not a result of market forces but of the role that was deliberately and purposefully assigned to them. Underpinning media organization were the Marxist-Leninist notion of "Parteilichkeit" and the constitutionally enshrined principle of the "leading role of the Party." Although Article 27 of the 1968 GDR constitution did contain an explicit guarantee of press freedom, this, like all other nominal rights, had to be seen in the context of Article 1, which described the GDR as "a socialist state . . . led by . . . the Marxist-Leninist Party." Given the Party's proclaimed uniquely privileged insight into the laws of historical development, and its role, once in power, as guardian of that development, the SED's Marxist-Leninist version of events and the *raison d'état* of the country it ruled determined absolutely the parameters of "press freedom" in the GDR. There was, it was asserted in the GDR, no such thing as "objectivity" and "neutrality" of the kind proclaimed by the Western press, and, given that *the* truth had now been discovered, there was certainly no need for the variety of viewpoints that was regarded as so indispensable in the West. (Not that that "variety" was in any case accepted as more than a smokescreen for the stranglehold over the media exerted by bourgeois ideology.)

The media in the GDR were quite unabashedly organs of state control over the thoughts and minds of the population, their function being described in the standard textbook studied by all trainee journalists as "influencing society in the spirit of Marxism-Leninism."[2] Western-style press freedom, on the other hand, is beholden to very different notions of media function. Although

---

[1] Beate Schneider, "Die ostdeutsche Tagespresse – eine (traurige) Bilanz," *Media Perspektiven*, No. 7, 1992, p. 434. This and subsequent German quotations were translated by the editors.

[2] *Wörterbuch der sozialistischen Journalistik* (Leipzig: Karl-Marx-Universität, Sektion Journalistik, 1981), p. 151.

Western societies are not given to formulating their ideological premises in quite such a convenient official form as was the case for virtually every area of life in the GDR, it is nonetheless possible to obtain a reasonably clear sense of the aims that press freedom – explicitly guaranteed in Article 5 of the *Grundgesetz* – is expected to serve in the Federal Republic by, for instance, examining the many relevant verdicts of the Federal Constitutional Court and reading between the lines of the country's various press laws.[3]

The press is seen in the Federal Republic as fulfilling a public task through its three central roles of "information," "helping shape opinion," and "criticism and investigation." These aspects of its "public role" are expressed in the Baden-Württemberg *Pressegesetz* – one example among many – in the words: "The press plays a public role by obtaining and disseminating information on matters of public interest, and by . . . taking up a position, criticizing, or in other ways helping to shape opinion."[4] So that the citizen may have access to the whole range of news and opinions, the greatest possible pluralism of media outlets is seen as a prerequisite for a healthy media order. As the Federal Constitutional Court put it in its *Spiegel* verdict of August 5, 1966: "If citizens are to take political decisions they need to . . . be familiar with the views of others and make a balanced judgment of these views. The press maintains this ongoing discussion."[5] The press, in other words, is expected to fulfil an enabling function, setting people free to exercise a democratic influence on the running of their affairs, a function that is far removed from the "top-down" imagery of the Marxist-Leninist press's "influencing society."

These, then, were the ideals of press freedom to which the five new *Länder* acceded at the moment of unification. The groundwork for the transformation of the GDR's media had, of course, already been laid in the early months of 1990 in the postcommunist GDR. Indeed, changes were already perceptible within days of the resignation of Erich Honecker in mid-October 1989,

[3] For an assessment of the differing visions of media functions in the two German states, see John Sandford, "What are the media for? Philosophies of the Media in the Federal Republic and the GDR," *Contemporary German Studies* (University of Strathclyde), Occasional Papers No. 5 (1988), pp. 5-24.

[4] *Presserecht. Pressegesetze der Länder und andere presserechtliche Vorschriften* (Munich: Beck, 1976), p. 11.

[5] Quoted in Martin Löffler, *Presserecht. Kommentar* (Munich: Beck'sche Verlagsbuchhandlung, 1983), Vol. 1, p. 253.

though some organs found it more difficult than others to adapt to the new circumstances – as, for instance, *Neues Deutschland*, which was quite unable to report the opening of the East German borders on November 9 until a full two days had elapsed, and even then its extraordinarily coy front-page report came in the form of a modest little picture of a Trabi tucked away at the bottom of the page beneath what must be one of the most understated headlines of all time: "Viel Verkehr an Grenzpunkten" ("Heavy Traffic at Border Crossings").[6]

The structure of the GDR press changed little over the forty years of the country's history: there were 39 daily papers, nine of which – including the "central organs" of the parties and mass organizations – appeared in Berlin, with the remaining thirty having a regional distribution. This latter group included the fourteen SED *Bezirkszeitungen*, which, with their 218 local editions and their high print-runs, were for most East Germans *the* daily paper. Overall daily circulation was almost ten million – on a per capita basis, one of the highest in the world. The periodical press consisted of thirty weekly papers and popular magazines, over 500 specialist journals, around 600 workplace newsletters, and – the nearest thing to an "independent" voice in the press landscape, but with severely restricted availability – a handful of Church journals.[7]

Although the political demise of Erich Honecker was followed almost immediately by growing liberalization of state control over media content, the really fundamental changes came with the opening of the country's borders in November 1989. Now, in most cases for the first time in their lives, GDR citizens had free access to Western papers and magazines, which they brought back as souvenirs from their trips to the West. Soon afterwards, it became possible to buy Western newspapers in the GDR itself, initially from the backs of vans driven over from the West, and then through outlets as Western publishers established their first foothold in the GDR.

In the early months of 1990 the landscape of the GDR press blossomed in a quite unparalleled way. Firstly there were the old GDR papers that had transformed themselves in the wake of the collapse of State and Party control over their contents. Secondly

---

[6] See John Sandford, "Wer zu spät kommt . . . : *Neues Deutschland* and the 'Wende'," *German Life and Letters*, 45, No. 3 (1992), p. 272.
[7] For details of the GDR press see Gunter Holzweißig, *Massenmedien in der DDR* (Berlin: Gebr. Holzapfel, 1989).

there were the West German papers, now readily available over much of the country, and in some cases producing special editions for their new East German readership. And then thirdly there were the "Neugründungen," the newly founded, and often primitively produced, first genuinely autonomous home-bred GDR papers – the mouthpieces in many cases for the visions of a democratic society represented by the *Bürgerbewegungen* of the 1989 revolution.

It was a heady interlude that did not last very long. The removal of state subsidies, the ineffectiveness of what was left of governmental authority in the GDR, and the scramble for a place in the new East German market on the part of the Western publishers introduced new dependencies where the old ones had scarcely been overcome. The first victims were the more overtly political among the newly founded papers, their demise hastened further by the change in political mood among the population that was confirmed in the results of the first free elections on March 18th: out of the thirty or so titles directly associated with the *Bürgerbewegungen* only two survived the spring of 1990.[8] The curiosity-value of the Western newspapers was also wearing thin; many East Germans found them too bulky, too expensive, and too alien in their concerns and allusions. Their sales fell back, and following unification most of them ceased production of their special Eastern editions. By the end of 1990 it was already becoming apparent that the real victors in the shake-up of the East German press were to be the papers that had been there all along: the former SED titles, and particularly the old *Bezirkszeitungen*.

Much of the responsibility for this perhaps surprising turn of events has been laid at the door of the *Treuhandanstalt*, which was entrusted with the privatization of the press. In the unification process, the electronic and print media were treated quite differently. Whereas the Unification Treaty devoted a whole lengthy article (Art. 36) to broadcasting, on the basis of which, after a painful and contentious interlude, radio and television in the new *Länder* were recast in the West German mold, with a mixture of public and commercial providers subject to the principle of *Land* competence, the Treaty contained no mention at all of the press, an omission by which the print media were implicitly classified as a commercial operation, with existing organs to be privatized by the *Treuhand*, and freedom of establishment for new ones.

---

[8] Schneider, "Die ostdeutsche Tagespresse," p. 433.

Although the press is recognized in German law as fulfilling "a public role," and thus enjoys rights and obligations that make it clear that it is *not* simply a commercial operation like any other, the principal criterion adopted by the *Treuhand* was that of commercial viability. The upshot of this was that the monopolistic structures of the old GDR press were retained largely intact, and ownership of the papers was granted to the publishing conglomerates that already dominated the West German market, and which, in many cases, had already entered into "partnership agreements" with their acquisitions-to-be during the legal vacuum of the Modrow and de Maizière months.

There were, of course, some attempts to establish new East German papers, but these either, like the already-mentioned organs of the *Bürgerbewegungen*, never really caught on (the small-circulation weekly *Freitag* is an isolated exception), or, like the unlamented *Super!-Zeitung*, they were closed down by their Western owners despite high circulation figures. The first attempt to step in at the popular end of the market had been undertaken in early 1991 by a tabloid calling itself *Super-Ossi*, which, with its slogan "echt ostgemacht" ("genuine East German product"), lasted only a few weeks. The *Super!-Zeitung*, on the other hand, was a Western venture. Launched in mid-May 1991 – after initial publicity proclaiming it to be "the greatest project in the history of the German press" – by the Burda-Murdoch group with an initial run of 350,000 copies, it affected a lurid and sensationalist style that placed it in direct competition with the *Bild-Zeitung*. In fact, *Super!* made major inroads into the sales of *Bild* in the East, only to see the Springer organ emerge victorious from the circulation war when *Super!* was suddenly closed down in July 1991. The *Super!* formula has not been entirely abandoned, however. It still lives on in the popular weekly *Super Illu* – launched by Burda in September 1990 – and the program magazine *super tv*, both of them products that are widely read in the East, but hardly seen at all in the West.

Whilst the closure of the *Super!-Zeitung* was hailed by *Die Zeit* as a sign of moral regeneration in the East,[9] there is no doubt that it

---

[9] Characterizing *Super!* as "Burdas Zentralorgan für gesundes Volksempfinden," *Die Zeit* said of the paper's demise: "Rupert Murdoch, Burda's business partner who no longer wished to carry the losses, is not to blame for this paper's demise. To blame are the *Ossis*, who were not stupid enough to keep buying the edifying tract in sufficient numbers for it to show a profit. East German frustrations, penned by West German journalists who liked to make out that they were in the

struck a chord that appealed to the mood of East Germans – a mood that the weekly *Super Illu* continues to be able to exploit. Beyond the underlying tone of *Ossi* indignation and assertiveness there are inevitably topics that have a distinctly Eastern appeal, and that thus play a peculiar role in the Eastern press: a fascination with the GDR past, with the Stasi, with figures like Honecker and Mielke, or former GDR sports stars. Likewise, unfamiliar aspects of the new world in which East Germans find themselves play an important role, with much space being given to "Lebenshilfe" – tips and advice in such areas as personal finance, insurance, or employment law, as well as all the areas of sexuality that were never dealt with in the GDR press.

It is only at the more popular end of the market that West German publications have managed to achieve a penetration in the East akin to that in the West, but even then it is only in the field of magazines – such as the teenage weekly *Bravo* – that one finds titles that are read by roughly the same proportion of East Germans as West Germans. Even the *Bild-Zeitung* has a share of the East German market that is equivalent to little more than half of what it enjoys in the West. The disproportion is even greater in the case of the serious *überregionale Tageszeitungen*, which are virtually un-read in the East, while *Der Spiegel* has managed to attract a reader-ship that, on a per capita basis, works out at only a third of the equivalent figure for the West, and even for the *Illustrierte – Bunte*, *Neue Revue*, and *stern* – the combined figure is less than a fifth of the Western one.[10]

The common assumption that East Germans find West German papers simply too big, too expensive, and too wordy may well be true. Certainly the papers they were used to before the *Wende* were at least small and cheap, and readily grasped. The feeling that the Western press remains somehow alien and does not address their immediate concerns is also borne out by the evidence of the divided press landscape in Germany – a division that is nowhere more striking than in the single city of Berlin, where two quite distinct press systems still function within a few yards of one another. A different style of journalism seems to have evolved in East Germany – a style that, according to a survey conducted by Marko Martin, is more reminiscent of the Federal Republic of the

---

same boat, the formula rapidly lost any subtlety – the first sign of moral regeneration in the East" (C.D., "Super," *Die Zeit*, 31 July 1992, p. 1).

[10] Klaus Peter Landgrebe, "Pressemedien in der MediaAnalyse '92," *Media Perspektiven*, No. 9, 1992, pp. 597-605.

1950s. Martin characterizes the feel of East German daily papers with such words as "stolid," "middle-class," and "politically conformist," but also discerns possibly worrying undertones in the tendency of their political commentaries, where he notes calls for "strong men" who are "hard but just" in their efficiency, and where debate is all too often presented as boring or even dismissed as "waffle."[11]

However, the fact that East German papers are today almost entirely under Western ownership is not, according to Martin, a factor in these distinctive characteristics. The West German publishers have, for the most part, adopted a light-handed approach to the content of the papers, with the result that these distinctive editorial attitudes can only be seen as a reflection of genuinely East German attitudes. Indeed, according to Peter Humphreys, the new Western owners and managers have kept former Eastern journalists on the payroll precisely because of their feeling for Eastern sensitivities. "Eastern journalists," he suggests,

> appear, in important respects, conspicuously better able to satisfy the communication needs of the Easterners. They are socio-psychologically far more in tune with them. They understand their current difficulties, doubts, aspirations, and so on; very sound pragmatic grounds for their attractiveness to astute Western proprietors.[12]

The distinctive structure of the present-day East German press has by no means entirely preserved the shape that it had during the communist years. In particular, the Berlin-based former "central organs" have lost their distinctive and dominant role. Where, before 1989, more than a third of total daily sales in the GDR were accounted for by "supra-regional" titles, by 1993 this figure was down to 3.9 percent, which was even lower than the West German figure of 4.5 percent.[13] The closure in April 1991 of the former Liberal-Democrat organ *Der Morgen*, which its new owner, the Axel Springer Verlag, had briefly managed to turn into a serious

[11] Marko Martin, "Whitney Houston, Genschers Pullover und die Stasi," *Die Zeit*, 15 October 1993, p. 95.

[12] Peter Humphreys, *Media and Media Policy in Germany: The Press and Broadcasting since 1945*, 2nd ed. (Oxford/Providence: Berg, 1994), p. 330.

[13] Walter J. Schütz, "Deutsche Tagespresse 1993: Ergebnisse der zweiten gesamtdeutschen Zeitungsstatistik," *Media Perspektiven*, No. 4, 1994, p. 197. Schütz's article (pp. 168-98) contains detailed statistical analyses of the changes that have occurred since unification.

daily for the new *Länder*, was a notable token of this development. Of the original seven titles in this category only three – *Neues Deutschland*, *Neue Zeit*, and *Junge Welt* – still survive, all of them with only a fraction of their original circulations, and an uncertain future. However, when one looks not just at the press landscape in West Germany but at the whole history of the German press, it is clear that there is nothing surprising about the virtual disappearance of these non-regional papers. The German press has always been essentially a regional and local press, and Berlin papers have traditionally been precisely that – namely, Berlin papers rather than national papers in the way that most London or Paris papers are in Britain or France.

Yet what has happened in East Germany is not simply a matter of old German press structures reasserting themselves – such as happened in West Germany, for instance, after Allied licensing provisions were lifted in 1949. However "artificial" the "central organs" may have been in the GDR, the fourteen SED *Bezirkszeitungen* were – like the *Bezirke* themselves – also more a result of communist tidy-mindedness and administrative convenience than of any desire to pay homage to German traditions of regional sentiment.[14] And yet it is precisely these former *Bezirkszeitungen* that have been the real success story of the post-*Wende* East German press.

The economic reasons for the success of the former *Bezirkszeitungen* are not hard to find. For all their obvious associations with the SED they had, over more than a third of a century, established themselves in the minds of most East Germans as "their" daily paper. The Western publishing concerns who took them over were the beneficiaries of this brand loyalty as well as of the much criticized decision of the *Treuhand* to retain the existing structure of the GDR press more or less intact. Some, however, whilst regretting the situation, felt that the *Treuhand* really had no choice:

> The solution one could imagine in theory, i.e., handing over the newspapers to local firms and publishers, was not possible in practice, since such people and firms, and the market economy to go with them, did not exist. Handing over to editors or employees in the East German

---

14 "The division of the territory of the GDR into *B.[ezirke]* is based above all on the need for the complex development of interdependent economic regions and the efficient managing and planning of the major cities and the rural districts" (*Kleines politisches Wörterbuch* [Berlin: Dietz, 1988], p. 137).

enterprises is all right in theory, but it is impractical since the know-how and the financial backing are not in place. Firms which are big enough to survive, competitiveness, and secure jobs are not to be had on the cheap.[15]

The anxiety of the *Treuhand* to play it safe and ensure commercial viability was certainly evident in its abandonment of any serious attempt to involve medium-sized publishers in the sell-off of the East German newspapers, preferring instead to award them to major media groups like Burda, Gruner & Jahr, Springer, and the Bauer-Verlag.

The upshot of these policy decisions was that, after a period of major market consolidation in the early part of 1991, by the middle of 1992 no fewer than seven of the ten biggest selling regional dailies in Germany were actually East German titles, with some 90 percent of regional daily sales in the East itself accounted for by the combination of the fourteen former *Bezirkszeitungen* and the *Berliner Zeitung*, which had, in effect, been the *Bezirkszeitung* for the capital. By fall 1993 the situation was little different: the demise of the *Super! Zeitung* and increased sales of the Düsseldorf *Rheinische Post* had admittedly reduced the East German presence in the top ten, but places three, four, and five were still occupied by East German titles, as were nine places overall out of the top twenty.[16] At the same time, the proportion of East German sales accounted for by the former *Bezirkszeitungen* remained at over 90 percent.

Other indices only confirm the high degree of press concentration, and the rapidity with which it has come about, in the new *Länder*. Thus, the number of independent editorial units ("publizistische Einheiten") had dropped by nearly a half in the two years leading to fall 1993, and in the more specific category of "Verlage als Herausgeber" a drop of 22 was registered over the same period. The range of titles serving particular localities in the East has also fallen sharply since unification, with eleven of the fifteen big titles enjoying a monopoly position in their respective markets, and the "Ein-Zeitungs-Kreis" now the norm in Brandenburg, Mecklenburg-Vorpommern, Sachsen, and Sachsen-Anhalt, as compared to an average of 55.1 percent of *Kreise* in Germany as a whole. In the city of Leipzig, the decline in the number of titles on offer has been

---

[15] Statement by the Bertelsmann AG, quoted in Hermann Meyn, *Massenmedien in der Bundesrepublik Deutschland* (Berlin: Colloquium, 1992), p. 63.

[16] See table in Schütz, "Deutsche Tagespresse 1993," pp. 187-88.

particularly dramatic: where, in the summer of 1990, the Leipzigers could choose between seven different *Abonnementzeitungen*, today there is only one.[17]

In the old Federal Republic, the process of press concentration in its various manifestations has been an apparently integral element of the very history of the post-war press. It has, however, been for the most part a slow and gradual development, and one, moreover, which had begun to stabilize and even, in some respects, to go into reverse by the mid-1970s. In the new *Länder* press concentration has been a far more rapid and dramatic process that has transformed the exciting blossoming of the media landscape of early 1990 into a situation where the East Germans are now, by all the traditional measures of press provision, markedly worse off than the West Germans.

This state of affairs is one of the many ironies of German unification. The press freedom proclaimed in the *Grundgesetz* and elaborated in successive verdicts of the *Bundesverfassungsgericht* has always been predicated on the principle of pluralism: that is, on the assumption that the healthiest press system is the most varied one, that variety manifesting itself not only in the range of news provision, but also in the breadth of presentation of possible ways of interpreting that news. It is not by chance that Article Five of the *Grundgesetz* is categorized as the one that deals in the first instance with "freedom of opinion" ("Meinungsfreiheit") rather than "freedom of information" ("Informationsfreiheit"). The great dilemma of Western-style press freedom – that it is inextricably intertwined with economic notions of market freedom – has turned out to be even more problematic in the conditions that obtain in the new German *Länder* than was ever the case in the old Federal Republic, a fact that only compounds the imperfect unification that is evident as well in other aspects of the German press today.

---

[17] Schütz, pp. 170-73.

The Treatment of Problems of Integration in Some Recent Works by Authors from the Former GDR

Nancy A. Lauckner

Despite the optimism of the champions of German unification, many GDR specialists predicted that numerous problems would hinder genuine integration for a long time. The difficulties that West and East Germans have experienced in the past few years have confirmed that prediction. Some East German authors have written fictional and/or essayistic works which reflect the problems they and their fellow former GDR citizens are encountering, a practice analogous to their previous literary depiction of GDR problems. Since their literature no longer needs to serve as a free press, they apparently address these issues both because old habits die hard and because they believe their insights can be helpful. Though they discuss new problems – those of integration – the fact that they treat them and the manner in which they present them largely continue established practices of the individual authors.

This article considers a few well-known authors and some of their recent works that reflect problems of integration. I discuss the treatment of these issues in Stefan Heym's *Auf Sand gebaut* (1990)[1]

---

[1] Stefan Heym, *Auf Sand gebaut. Sieben Geschichten aus der unmittelbaren Vergangenheit* (Munich: Bertelsmann, 1990). Subsequent references appear parenthetically in the text. In such references, the short title "Bekanntschaft" refers to the story "Alte Bekanntschaft." All translations of this and other works cited in the following are my own.

223

and *Filz*,[2] Helga Königsdorf's *Gleich neben Afrika*,[3] and Rolf Schneider's *Volk ohne Trauer*[4] (all 1992). Since the focus is on the problems the authors examine and how they treat them rather than the individual works, I have organized the material by issues instead of by works. The article provides an overview of the most important and frequently mentioned problems, rather than discussing all those these authors raise.

The media have faulted East Germans for their alleged lack of resolve in dealing with the economic and social issues of integration, and for their longing to retain certain aspects of the GDR. I believe there is a more productive way of understanding these matters that are proving so divisive in the process of integrating East Germans into the united Germany.

Elisabeth Kübler-Ross's pioneering work, *On Death and Dying* (1969),[5] and her subsequent books established her as an expert whose elucidation of the five stages of dying – denial and isolation, anger, bargaining, depression, and acceptance – has helped terminally ill patients and their loved ones to deal with their deaths. Social scientists who study institutional change, including the downsizing and closing of businesses, have applied the Kübler-Ross model to this setting and discovered that individuals in such organizations must go through essentially the same "process of griefwork."[6]

GDR citizens, whether committed socialists, people who accommodated to the status quo, or dissidents, were all part of a state that suddenly "died." If one applies the Kübler-Ross model, one sees

---

[2] Stefan Heym, *Filz. Gedanken über das neueste Deutschland* (Munich: Bertelsmann, 1992). In parenthetical page references to essays from this collection, the following short titles are used: "Eine andere Welt" ("Welt"), "Schuld und Sühne" ("Schuld"), "Treuhand aufs Herz" ("Treuhand"), "Vergangenheitsbewältigung" ("VB").

[3] Helga Königsdorf, *Gleich neben Afrika* (Berlin: Rowohlt, 1992).

[4] Rolf Schneider, *Volk ohne Trauer. Notizen nach dem Untergang der DDR* (Göttingen: Steidl, 1992). In parenthetical page references to sections of this work, the following short titles are used: "Offener Brief" ("Brief"), "Schriftsteller und Publikum" ("Schriftsteller"), "Statt eines Vorwortes" ("Vorwort"), "Volk ohne Trauer" ("Volk"), "Von linker Melancholie" ("Melancholie").

[5] Elisabeth Kübler-Ross, *On Death and Dying* (New York: Macmillan, 1969).

[6] Harrison Owen, "Griefwork in Organizations," *Consultation*, 5, No. 1 (Spring 1986), pp. 41-51; cited from p. 46. George H. Pollock does not refer to Kübler-Ross directly, but does discuss mourning in organizational and national contexts in "Mourning Process and Creative Organizational Change," *Journal of the American Psychoanalytical Association*, 25, No. 1 (1977), pp. 3-34.

that they are passing through the five stages of "death," and presumably they are not all in the same stage at the same time. However, they have received no "company"-sponsored counseling in dealing with the psychological, occupational, economic, and social effects of their "outplacement." We are witnessing the turmoil which ensues when citizens of a defunct country are given no help with the necessary "process of griefwork" and are left to confront their problems as best they can.[7]

With this understanding, then, I want to approach the treatment of these problems of integration by the authors mentioned above. I believe we must listen to these voices, which reflect the concerns of their former compatriots, without making value judgments and dismissing their views as invalid, as has so often happened to East Germans since unification. The Kübler-Ross model shows that emotions and the perception of these feelings by those who are experiencing them are vital in such circumstances. Perhaps such listening can promote healing and hasten the day of genuine integration.

Since economic difficulties were so central to the desire of East Germans for unification and have continued to plague them in the integration phase, it is not surprising to find such problems reflected in the works of East German authors, albeit not as a major theme. In general, these writers portray the trouble people are having in adjusting to a market economy. Schneider, whose *Volk ohne Trauer* suggests that he has adapted easily and completely to life in united Germany, refers only briefly to his former compatriots' naiveté about the "Warenwirtschaft" and its "Verteilungskämpfe" for which they were ill prepared ("Vorwort," p. 11) and regards "materielle Ursachen" as the sole reason for their anger and bitterness ("Volk," p. 206).

Economic problems represent important background information about the characters in Königsdorf's *Gleich neben Afrika*. Her narrator alludes to various difficulties that the market economy has caused her and other East Germans: unemployment, long weekend commutes because of a job far away, greatly increased rents, lower pensions, the dissolution of unprofitable companies, and the general

---

[7] As Theodor Langenbruch suggested during the discussion of this paper at the Nineteenth New Hampshire Symposium, another psychological model is also useful in understanding current East German problems: that of the troubled children of a "dysfunctional family" who are now dealing with life without "Vater Staat" and "Mutter Partei." However, I prefer the Kübler-Ross model because it stresses the normalcy of these problems, whereas East Germans are now so often treated as abnormal, as Gretchen Schafft mentioned in the same discussion.

poverty, for the last of which she cites the ironic reason, "Wir mußten den Wert des Geldes schätzenlernen" (p. 13). She also mentions their naiveté about capitalism and how it works (p. 107) and depicts unscrupulous West German "Macher" (p. 13) bilking unsuspecting East Germans of their possessions (pp. 64-65). Indeed, she even categorizes this new period in German history as "Frühkapitalismus. . . . Kolonie, Vorkapitalismus und Weltuntergang" (p. 90).

Heym depicts East German economic woes more directly with his familiar biting irony and humor. In the essay collection *Filz*, he enumerates the same financial problems as Königsdorf and compares his fellow East German citizens with Candide in an apt metaphor to express their naiveté in dealing "mit dem real existierenden Kapitalismus" ("Candide," p. 90). He, too, refers to the "manipulators" preying upon this Candide (p. 93) and notes an ironic inequity in the pension system: the "Sonderrente für Kämpfer gegen den Faschismus" has been halved, since some of the recipients are "old communists," yet "old Nazis" still receive their full pensions ("Schuld," pp. 87-88). But Heym's most acerbic satire on economic issues appears in the vitriolic essay "Treuhand aufs Herz," in which he exaggerates the Treuhand's power by comparing it with that of the Politburo (p. 45) – a typical transferral of his criticism of the SED to an arm of the Bonn government – and accuses the agency of acting against East German interests by seeking "*Privatisierung und Reorganisation*, soll heißen Ausverkauf und Vernichtung" (p. 47). His conspiracy theory that the Treuhand intends to destroy the five new states as a "Produktionsstätte," thus securing the West German markets (p. 50), reflects the suspicions of many East Germans.

Although the stories included in *Auf Sand gebaut* were written before unification, their concerns have steadily gained importance. Here Heym personalizes his treatment of economic problems by telling two stories about property ownership rights. The title story introduces an East German couple who bought their house before unification in the naive belief that "Besitz ist Besitz, den kann keiner antasten, jetzt nicht und später ebensowenig" (p. 34). Visited unexpectedly by the West German heir of a former owner, who has brought along his lawyer to clear up the "Eigentumsfragen" (p. 41), they are stunned, yet determined to fight for their rights. Soon, however, a new visitor with a claim on the house arrives from Tel Aviv; she is the granddaughter of a former Jewish owner, whom the West German's father – an SS man – had blackmailed into selling him the house for a fraction of its value to avoid being sent to a concentration camp, although the buyer never paid (pp. 47-48). The distinctive twist of introducing an echo of the Holocaust into the already complex plot is vintage Heym, and the story causes the reader to empathize with the hapless East German couple.

In the story "Rette sich wer kann," Heym illustrates the problems involved in public property ownership. The economic director of VEB Dreh- und Bohrmaschinen recognizes that the people ("das Volk") have no standing when it comes to ownership rights in the soon to be ex-GDR, so he negotiates a merger with a Western firm. However, his old superior and the *Staatssekretär* both blackmail him into demanding high positions for them as a condition of the merger, and ultimately, the greater opportunist, the *Staatssekretär*, obtains such a post despite having been charged with crimes for his role in the former government. This story reflects the economic problems involved in dealing with ownership issues of ex-GDR public companies as well as the political entanglements that make them doubly difficult.

The demise of the GDR, unification, and the economic and social concerns of integration have produced a volatile emotional state in former GDR citizens which is treated by both Königsdorf and Schneider. Königsdorf speaks of the difficulties East Germans are having in adjusting to Western ways, such as the rapid pace of life (p. 16), the need to do one's job perfectly (p. 15), and the complex and unfamiliar legal system (p. 106). Some of her peripheral characters withdraw into self-imposed isolation (p. 106).

Both Königsdorf and Schneider note the emotionally charged *Ossi/Wessi* dichotomy. Königsdorf mentions the East Germans' feeling of being duped in dealings with West Germans (pp. 65, 107) and their resultant impotent anger: "Wir fühlten uns schlecht behandelt und hatten Wut und wußten nicht, wohin mit der Wut" (p. 13). Yet a defiant remark of one of her characters shows that not all self-respect has been lost: "Zu den Wessis gehe ich nicht putzen" (p. 61). Though Schneider notes that East Germans are constantly reminded of their second-class status ("Melancholie," p. 190), he regards the image of "der . . . häßliche Ossi" as a psychological weapon in an economic battle and criticizes former GDR citizens for internalizing it ("Vorwort," p. 11).

Both authors describe the emotional fluctuation which East Germans are suffering: Schneider depicts them as subject to "allerlei hastige Wechselbäder ihrer Gefühle" ("Melancholie," p. 191); Königsdorf reports "[d]ie Menschen pendelten zwischen Verzweiflung und Lebenshunger" (p. 21) "in dieser Zeit, . . . in der man von den Strudeln um und um gerissen wurde" (p. 28). The most common emotions she portrays are fear and anger: the fear of unemployment, poverty, and homelessness fuel a sharp rise in suicides (p. 14), while the anger at seemingly insoluble problems leads to interpersonal conflict. Schneider sees anger and bitterness as the prevalent feelings ("Volk," p. 206).

Several of these emotions – withdrawal, despair, anger, bitterness – typify some of the Kübler-Ross five stages, as do the identity crisis and nostalgia that both authors address. Königsdorf notes that citizens of the former GDR have lost their identity along with their state (p. 98), and her narrator admits to feelings of homesickness which she dismisses as "unsinnig" (p. 105). The longing she describes for the lost home and for the sense of belonging (pp. 10, 28) is characteristic of people dealing with death and of those whose familiar corporate, social, or religious community has been dissolved.[8]

Perhaps if Schneider understood this analogy, he would be less judgmental in treating the phenomenon. He is probably right that the concept of GDR identity arose to counter the negative image of East Germans with something positive ("Melancholie," p. 190), but he regards it as an "inflated" ("Vorwort," p. 12) and useless term that functions merely as a "Schutz- und Trotz-Vokabel" ("Melancholie," p. 190). Alluding to Jens Reich's reference in *Rückkehr nach Europa* to the "Phänomen der untoten DDR. . . . unter der Vokabel 'Trotzidentität'" – a word which supports Schneider's own view that the term GDR identity is just a "Trotz-Vokabel" – he seconds Reich's warning against "politisches Heimweh" (p. 192). To Schneider the emphasis on GDR identity is part of the phenomenon of "GDR nostalgia" (p. 185), which he sees as being based on "diffuse Gefühle und Erinnerungen" and painting a rosy picture of a "DDR, die so nie existiert hat" (p. 191). Although he recognizes the economic, social, and psychological roots of the nostalgia (pp. 189-90), he accuses those who indulge in it of mourning their lost privileges (p. 185). He prophesies this nostalgia "eine bedeutende Zukunft" in which the GDR will live on in the German consciousness as a lost "political opportunity" (p. 194). While some of Schneider's views on GDR nostalgia are accurate, he overinterprets it as a political phenomenon and fails to see it as a normal psychological phase through which some East Germans are passing as part of integration. It corresponds most closely to the Kübler-Ross denial

---

[8] See, for example, Elisabeth Kübler-Ross, *Questions and Answers on Death and Dying* (New York: Macmillan; London: Collier-Macmillan, 1974), pp. 145-46; Owen, "Griefwork in Organizations," pp. 45-47; and Pollock, "Mourning Process and Creative Organizational Change," pp. 27-28.

stage, although it could occur in any stage other than acceptance.

One of the most serious obstacles to integration is *Bewältigung* of the GDR era,[9] particularly in regard to the Staatssicherheit. This matter is problematic for East Germans, whose past is at issue, and for West Germans, who are investigating the history of their new fellow citizens, yet whose record of dealing with the Nazi past has not been exemplary.

Several of the works under discussion reflect concerns East Germans have about the Stasi debate. Königsdorf's narrator alludes to each citizen's fear of learning that "er sei ohne sein Wissen Mitarbeiter irgendeines Geheimdienstes gewesen" (p. 21); and in the story "Alte Bekanntschaft" in *Auf Sand gebaut*, Heym's protagonist, who gives some information to a Stasi agent, wonders how much co-operation is too much, whether one can say anything at all and still remain "relativ sauber," and whether innocuous information can harm others (pp. 65-66). Yet both Königsdorf and Heym depict an interesting correlate to these fears: an "Überwachungsentzugssyndrom" (Königsdorf, p. 93) which causes someone who suffers from it to actually miss being under surveillance ("Bekanntschaft," p. 71). In Königsdorf's narrator, the syndrome manifests itself as "ein unerhörtes Gefühl der Verlassenheit" and "Angst, die sich bis zur Panik steigern konnte" (p. 93), while the narrator of Heym's story longs for the clarity and certainty of his old relationship with the Stasi agent who had been charged with watching and reporting on him (p. 71).

These authors also reflect a concern that the Staatssicherheit

---

[9] Anna Kuhn suggested in "Rewriting GDR History: The Christa Wolf Controversy," *GDR Bulletin*, 17, No. 1 (Spring 1991), p. 8, that scholars adopt the term *Gegenwartsbewältigung* to express the process of dealing with the GDR past. She took the term from the title of a University of Michigan conference held 25-27 October 1990 (p. 10, n. 6). Despite this suggestion I have chosen to use the term *Vergangenheitsbewältigung* in this article for several reasons. The term *Gegenwartsbewältigung* has not achieved widespread scholarly usage, probably because it represents an impractical way to refer to a period that is now past. It has become quite controversial to apply the word *Vergangenheitsbewältigung* to efforts to come to terms with the socialist past because to do so seems to equate socialism with fascism. While I certainly do not equate the two, I use the word here because its history automatically relates the process of dealing with the GDR past to that of coming to terms with the Nazi past, an important connotation in the present context. Although neither attempt has been very successful, the process is still needed in both cases. Furthermore, as indicated later in this article, several of the authors discussed here, notably Heym and Schneider, see commonalities in the problems involved in coming to terms with both pasts.

and/or its agents will continue its work after unification. We find this in two of the three Stasi stories in *Auf Sand gebaut*. In "Der Zuverläßigsten einer," which is set during the *Wende*, the Stasi leadership assures its employees, "der Betrieb geht weiter, die Firma kriegt einen andern Namen" (p. 7), while in "Außenstelle" an electronic listening post keeps monitoring conversations after the Stasi has been dissolved (p. 33). Several of Königsdorf's and Heym's characters who worked for the Stasi get similar jobs in the new political system: this happens with Alexander in *Gleich neben Afrika* (p. 116) and with the agent in Heym's "Alte Bekanntschaft," who proposes to his former victim that they resume their "old arrangement" (p. 72).

In *Filz*, Heym criticizes the Gauck Commission and its handling of the Stasi files. In "Vergangenheitsbewältigung" he questions its legitimation (p. 108); and in "Eine ganz besondere Wissenschaft," he describes its power as greater than that of the Politburo – again exaggerating for effect, as he does in his previously mentioned comparison of the power of the Treuhand to that of the Politburo ("Treuhand," p. 45) – and the methods of the Inquisition and the McCarthy Commission as more humane and just (p. 84). He warns of the similarity between Stasi methods and those of the Gauck Commission, of the absurdity of regarding Stasi reports as true, and of the need to establish and follow legal procedures in assessing guilt (pp. 83-85). Despite his harsh criticism, he realizes the importance of the commission's task. In "Vergangenheitsbewältigung" he accepts the principle of *Wiedergutmachung* for Stasi victims, yet suggests that it could not be fairly practiced (p. 107); and he urges readers to learn from the files "for the present and the future" without becoming obsessed with them (p. 109).

Besides commenting on the Stasi debate, the works under discussion treat *Vergangenheitsbewältigung* in general, especially the major theme of *Trauerarbeit*. Some characters seriously think through their role in the GDR past. In Königsdorf's *Gleich neben Afrika*, the narrator returns to her village largely for this purpose. She recalls her humanitarian reasons for joining the Party (pp. 66-67), yet now realizes with shame its betrayal of her ideals by its inhumanity and destruction of the infrastructure and the environment (pp. 80, 89), as well as her own part in its "Heileweltinszenierung" (p. 98). By thematizing these matters, all three authors undertake their own *Trauerarbeit*, which they model for others, as evident in Heym's call in *Filz* for everyone to engage in a personal "Abrechnung des Gewissens" ("VB," p. 108).

Yet their works reflect a lack of interest in *Trauerarbeit* in the

East German population itself. Königsdorf's narrator notes that thinking about "solche Dinge" is unpopular (p. 17), and Schneider that people are avoiding dealing with their personal and national past ("Melancholie," p. 191). Indeed, he regards the "Stasi-Hysterie" as a "krankhafte Ersatzbewältigung" that enables individuals not to confront their own involvement ("Grenzgebiet," p. 153). He compares the current psychological state in East Germany to that of postwar West Germany as portrayed in the Mitscherlichs' *Die Unfähigkeit zu trauern*[10] and characterized by repressing memories of the "nicht aufgearbeitete Vergangenheit" ("Volk," p. 197). Like the Mitscherlichs then, he finds a "'collective denial of the past'" which accounts for the relative lack of "'Melancholie oder . . . Trauer'" in the population, and he predicts the denial will continue (p. 206).[11] Although Schneider identifies a troubling issue that deserves more attention, he censures his former compatriots, while purporting to have done his *Trauerarbeit* already.

The works discussed here also mirror a troubling phenomenon accompanying unification and integration: the rise of racism, xenophobia, and the extreme right in the new states and its increase in the

Heym and Schneider both reflect on some ethical aspects of coming to terms with the GDR past. Heym reveals the irony in the imposition of this obligation on East Germans by their new compatriots who had failed at their own *Vergangenheitsbewältigung* after 1945 when he speaks in *Filz* of "Leute, die . . . das Versäumte von damals, bei guter Gelegenheit nun, in dem sogenannten Beitrittsgebiet nachholen lassen möchten" ("VB," p. 105). He sees the emphasis on the past as a scheme to divert attention from the painful problems of the present (p. 109). Schneider rejects the view that only people who lived in the GDR have a right to speak about dealing with that past and warns that many voices now raised against the concept of "Mitschuld" echo ones heard in 1945 ("Volk," p. 205). Yet he, too, scents an intrigue behind the imposition of *Vergangenheitsbewältigung* and cites three ways in which West Germans benefit from it: they can prove themselves by dealing harshly with the past of others at no personal risk, undermine East German market competition, and ensure East Germans' submissiveness by destroying pride in their identity ("Vorwort," pp. 14-16).

The works discussed here also mirror a troubling phenomenon accompanying unification and integration: the rise of racism, xenophobia, and the extreme right in the new states and its increase in the

---

[10] Alexander and Margarete Mitscherlich, *Die Unfähigkeit zu trauern. Grundlagen kollektiven Verhaltens* (Munich: Piper, 1967).
[11] The article "'Hingehen und zuhören'" (*Der Spiegel*, 11 January 1993, pp. 46, 48) also relates the Mitscherlichs' findings to the current situation in united Germany.

nation as a whole. Königsdorf alludes to xenophobia several times
(pp. 84, 95) and points to the past and present "Demütigungen" East
Germans have suffered as a cause; noting that most victims react by
humiliating others, she thinks this populace will be a powder keg for
some time to come (p. 23). Schneider finds strong German nationalism reviving in East Germany and hints at the growing hatred of
foreigners when he mentions that Vietnamese street vendors have
been driven out of an area ("Grenzgebiet," p. 154). He is alarmed by
the defacement of the Ravensbrück memorial by neo-Nazis and
skinheads and by the police's failure to protect someone who tried to
intervene ("Brief," pp. 167-68), but imputes East German insensi-
tivity to Jewish concerns to years of state-ordered anti-fascism (p.
165).

Of these writers, Heym is the sharpest critic of the extreme right
and xenophobia. In *Auf Sand gebaut*, a former Stasi agent predicts
that the people will react to "eine große Unsicherheit" by finding
"neue Feinde," including "Jews, communists, and foreigners"
("Bekanntschaft," p. 68), and in *Filz* Heym refers to "foreigners and
Jews" replacing the "Klassenfeind" as objects of hatred ("Welt," pp.
75-76) and speaks of "the new racism" in united Germany
("Schuld," p. 88). Evoking the image of the "Zauberlehrling" in his
story of the same title in *Auf Sand gebaut*, he portrays the West as
having manipulated the *Wende* to bring about unification and now
being unable to stop its "[p]sychologische Kriegsführung" against
the East Germans (p. 55). He warns that a new fascism will flood
the country as a result (p. 57), and thus predicts the growth of the
extreme right before it had gained much ground in the East. In the
essay "Erinnerungen" in *Filz*, he observes xenophobia in united
Germany and draws painful parallels between the attitudes of the
assailants and onlookers in Hoyerswerda and those of people who
watched or participated in the persecution of the Jews in the Nazi era
(pp. 37-38, 43). He believes these troubling phenomena stem from
the failure of both German states to come to terms with the past and
destroy "die faschistischen Muster" (p. 40) and from unrest and
aggression caused by the social and economic problems of integration, particularly in East Germany (pp. 38, 41). With the words,
"Hoyerswerda ist ein Weltproblem" (p. 42), he evokes the univer-
sality of the refugee problem and warns of a more virulent fascism
unless this crisis is resolved (p. 43).

Problems specific to writers are also represented in these works
that reflect the integration difficulties of former GDR citizens.
Königsdorf's narrator is a writer who is having trouble adjusting to
her diminished status and lost privileges. Apart from a few vague

allusions to writers' involvement with the Stasi, the depiction of their problems here focuses mainly on their adaptation to the writer's role in the market economy. The narrator worries about her steadily declining "market value" (p. 27) and attends official receptions to curry favor and appear busy even though she is unsure about the new "Spielregeln" (pp. 109, 111). Her plan to write a best-seller fails because the public wants to read something enjoyable and has lost interest in problems and East German themes (pp. 96, 98). It is noteworthy that in *Gleich neben Afrika* Königsdorf herself attempts to combine an entertaining plot with a portrayal of problems and East German concerns that readers allegedly do not want to hear.

Schneider, too, addresses the difficulties of writers from the former GDR. Although they have lost many readers because of the Western materials that are now available ("Schriftsteller," p. 181), he is glad that market forces now govern the arts. He regards it as a "Normalisierung" that the relationship between artist and public is again one of "supply and demand" and that artists are compensated according to their "Dienstleistungen" (p. 182). While his categorical statement, "Mehr waren wir nie. Mehr sollten wir auch nicht sein wollen" (p. 182), expresses his successful adjustment to market realities, it reflects a very limited view of the artist's role in united Germany. He seems acutely interested in the writers' own need of *Vergangenheitsbewältigung* and regards GDR artists as "Komplizen der Diktatur" who gave the regime a "pseudoliberales Alibi" (pp. 176, 178) and intentionally helped stabilize it by not exceeding certain bounds in their criticism ("Volk," p. 200). Although he admits his own role in this, he criticizes others far more and calls on them to recognize their "Mitschuld" (p. 205). He especially impugns those who accepted the role of "moralische Instanz" in the GDR ("Schriftsteller," p. 177; "Volk," p. 200) and retained socialist views after the *Wende* ("Schriftsteller," p. 179), thus implying that writers who have adapted easily to Western ways are more upright than those who find integration more difficult.

As a writer who has not changed his views, Heym sees the matter differently. The story "Ausstellungseröffnung" in *Auf Sand gebaut* satirizes the opportunism of artists vying for success in the market economy. They calculate their risks and advantages, distance themselves from the old regime, and eliminate from the exhibit some works that are no longer politically correct, yet retain others by cleverly retitling them to hide their political intent. By including in the catalog the list of awards and medals the artists had received before the *Wende*, the printer unmasks their carefully contrived democratic personae. Heym also pillories the opportunism of artists who abandon their views for reasons of political expediency when the printer attempts to justify himself by saying: "[W]as gestern eine Ehre war, . . . soll heute ein Schandmal sein? . . . Wie . . . soll mein armer Kopf derart Sinneswandel begreifen?" (pp. 102-03). Thus Heym reveals the lack of integrity of the very sort of artists whom Schneider extols.

Heym's essay "Seelenschmerzen" in *Filz* bitterly decries the changed situation of former GDR writers. Seeing conspiracy, as is his wont, he claims that West German displeasure with the rise of GDR democracy after the *Wende*, "sogar mit Dichtern, die sich da engagierten," was due to fear that this trend might "infect" "die eigenen Schäfchen" (p. 98). Far from suggesting that East German writers should repent their role as "moralische Instanz," Heym praises those who spoke the truth in hints and nuances despite the difficulties and thus became a genuine "moralische Instanz" (p. 100), unlike most West German writers whose works their own society saw as just another "Ware auf dem Markt" (p. 99). Outraged by the charge that writers who stayed in the GDR contributed legitimacy to the regime and by the attempt to portray their work as worthless (p. 101), he views this treatment of these writers as part of an effort to discredit all remaining GDR institutions of any value and to stifle East German resistance by depriving the people of writers who express their concerns (p. 102). He implicitly calls on these writers to continue speaking for their fellow citizens, which he, Schneider, and Königsdorf do in portraying the problems of integration. Referring to the ancient custom of killing the bards and writers of a conquered country because they posed a danger to the new regime, Heym notes sardonically: "man mordet nicht mehr die Person, nur ihren Ruf" (p. 102). While he is probably alluding to the denigration of his own work and to the controversy about Christa Wolf's *Was bleibt*, readers now necessarily think of the attempts to cast the entire ouevre of Christa Wolf and Heiner Müller in the context of their IM-activity.

In the four works discussed here the authors depict economic hardships; emotional problems, including nostalgia and the issue of GDR identity; *Bewältigung* of the GDR past, especially in relation to the Stasi debate and the need for *Trauerarbeit*; the rise of racism, xenophobia, and the extreme right; and problems specific to the integration of East German writers. In Schneider's book and the two Heym works, these issues are central, while in Königsdorf's story they form part of the background. None of the works represent a significant departure from their authors' previous literary production: Königsdorf writes a half-realistic, half-fantastic story; Schneider offers a collection of essays and notes as a sequel to his *Frühling im Herbst*;[12] and Heym polemicizes and satirizes in both story and essay formats. Although the authors continue the GDR practice of thematizing current problems in their works, they seem to do so not only out of the habit of speaking to and for their fellow citizens in literature, but, more importantly, because they want East German concerns during integration represented in the literary debate. As integration progresses, the problems will presumably change and diminish, and eventually many East German citizens will probably reach the final Kübler-Ross stage, acceptance. It will be interesting to see whether authors find new ways to depict existing problems, and whether writers of the former GDR continue to reflect current issues in their works. Perhaps they, too, will gradually arrive at the acceptance stage, which might be signaled by their adopting the more aesthetic approach to literature favored by their Western colleagues.

---

[12] Rolf Schneider, *Frühling im Herbst. Notizen vom Untergang der DDR* (Göttingen: Steidl, 1991).

German Unification and the Sorb Minority

Horst Freyhofer

Since the early Middle Ages Sorbs have been living in Lusatia, which lies between the Oder and Neisse rivers in the east, the Elbe and Saale rivers in the west, the Spree Forest in the north, and the Lusatian Mountains in the south. Today the Sorbs, the smallest of the Slavic nations, live for the most part along the Spree, which flows through Lusatia, in an area approximately seventy miles long and thirty miles wide. Those living in the northern part, or Lower Lusatia, around the city of Cottbus, speak a dialect more related to Polish; those living in the southern part, or Upper Lusatia – Bautzen is the cultural center – speak a dialect more similar to Czech. Lower Lusatia was traditionally Prussian, while Upper Lusatia belonged to Saxony. This state division largely coincided with, and reinforced, a religious division. During the Reformation, Lower Lusatia became Protestant, while Upper Lusatia remained primarily Roman Catholic, a situation which pitted Sorbs against Sorbs in the Religious Wars. The administrative division continued in the GDR, with Upper and Lower Lusatia belonging to different *Bezirke*; since the reestablishing of the *Länder* in the wake of the *Wende*, Lower Lusatia is once again part of Brandenburg, and Upper Lusatia of Saxony.

According to the most recent survey, which was conducted in 1987 by the Institut für sorbische Volksforschung, approximately 67,000 people still speak Sorbian;[1] in most instances it is their

---

[1] Ludwig Elle, "Die Sorben in der Statistik," in *Die Sorben in Deutschland*, ed. Macica Serbska (Bautzen: Domowina, 1991), pp. 22. As Elle points out, some estimates are as high as 80,000 and others as low as 45,000.

second language, German being their first. Most of the people living in Lusatia today speak only German. Fewer than two centuries ago, nearly 200,000 people still spoke Sorbian, and the area in which the language was spoken was much larger.[2] Dietrich Scholz, the director of the Sorbisches Institut in Bautzen, has compared the territory of the Lusatian Sorbs to an "ice flow that is slowly melting."[3]

The Sorbs share this fate with many other ethnic minorites. In Europe alone there are more than twenty minorities with fewer than 100,000 people. The culture of all these minorities is threatened – not so much the cultural heritage, which is ordinarily cared for by various organizations, but rather the *Alltagskultur*, the culture of daily life in the community, family, school, workplace, etc., which requires regular use of the language.

Many Sorbs view the preservation of their culture as an obligation vis-à-vis a past characterized by oppression, endurance, and forced assimilation. Confronted with the growth of nationalism among Germans in the wake of the Revolution of 1848, many Sorbs nurtured national sentiments of their own. At the Paris Peace Conference following World War I, prominent Sorb leaders argued for the creation of a sovereign state of Lusatia or, failing this, the incorporation of Lusatia into the newly founded state of Czechoslovakia.[4] Both requests were denied. The National Socialists later responded to the Sorbs' national aspirations with forced Germanization and, when they encountered resistance, incarceration and deportation. Plans were made for the resettlement of the Sorbs following the final victory.[5] Not surprisingly, after World War II many Sorbs again favored sovereignty or incorporation into Czechoslovakia.[6] But again the Allies refused.

As victims of National Socialism, many Sorbs placed their hopes in the antifascist doctrine of the East German state, which did indeed grant the Sorb minority special protection and material assistance in reestablishing their Slavic culture, although perhaps not so much for

---

[2] Elle, "Die Sorben in der Statistik," p. 24.

[3] Dietrich Scholz, "Die Situation der Sorben im vereinten Deutschland," p. 1. Unpublished paper from 1992. To be found at the Sorbisches Institut, Bautzen. My translation here and throughout.

[4] Hartmut Zwahr, *Sorbische Volksbewegung* (Bautzen: Domowina, 1968), pp. 276-77; and Jan Mahling, "Zur politischen und kulturellen Geschichte der Sorben," in *Die Sorben in Deutschland*, p. 13.

[5] Mahling, "Zur politischen und kulturellen Geschichte der Sorben," p. 14.

[6] Ibid.

the sake of preserving an ethnic minority as in the interest of complying with socialist doctrine. Lenin had envisioned a society free of ethnic rivalries, a society in which ethnic groups had melted together to form a homogeneous society and everyone shared a new, socialist, identity. In this process, the various ethnic groups would first "blossom" and enter a state of "mutual rapprochement" before finally amalgamating in a new harmonious social existence.[7] The most progressive (in the Communist sense) members of the ethnic groups were to assume a leadership role in achieving this assimilation.

For the Sorbs, this role logically fell to the Domowina, the umbrella organization for all Sorb groups. Founded in 1912 to coordinate and represent Sorb interests, it had been dissolved in 1937 after resisting the National Socialist policy of forced Germanization. Reestablished in 1945, it adapted to the radically changed circumstances. New leaders permitted Sorb interests to be subordinated to the interests of the SED-dominated government, which did not encourage nationally oriented cultures, German, Sorb, or any other. Lenin's idea of the "blossoming of nations" was limited to folkloristic pageantry, the "rapprochement of nations" to manifestations of peaceful co-existence in the form of colorful parades, and the "merging of nations" to the guaranteeing of legal, economic, and political equality.

Many Sorbs, especially those with vivid memories of Nazi persecution, were appeased by these changes, which rendered the traditional discrimination of the Sorbs illegal. The fact that their once dynamic folk culture stagnated – reduced to ritualistic exercises such as traditional Easter rides and egg decorating – was accepted as the price to be paid for legal equality.

The assimilation of all citizens into a new socialist state which the GDR leadership envisioned was aided by the industrial development of Lusatia, which was rich in lignite. German-speaking workers from other parts of the GDR, and later from abroad as well, flocked to the new industrial complexes in Cottbus and Hoyerswerda, which grew to several times their original size. The large-scale strip mining led to the dismantling of entire Lusatian villages with their traditional Sorb culture; their inhabitants were resettled, often in quickly built high-rise apartments on the outskirts of Cottbus or Hoyerswerda.

These demographic changes hastened the erosion of Sorb

---

[7] Ludwig Elle, "Die Sorben im Aufbruch," p. 3. Unpublished paper from 1992, available at the Sorbisches Institut, Bautzen.

culture. As more and more Germans settled in Lusatia and Sorbs left their rural surroundings, pressure increased for the Sorbs to adjust to a more urban, German-dominated way of life. Many abandoned Sorbian in favor of German. Some Sorb schools were closed; and Sorbian was less frequently used in the schools. Already in the 1950s only one third of the population in this traditionally Sorb area spoke Sorbian. By the 1980s it was a mere one sixth.[8]

While the creative power of Sorb culture visibly lessened in everyday life, the study of earlier products of this creativity, i.e., traditional Sorb culture, flourished. Since these changes took place in an atmosphere of relative tranquility – for the most part with the blessing of the Sorb organizations, especially the Domowina – the Sorbs were showcased by the GDR state as proof of its successful policy of peace and tolerance among nations.

All this ended with the fall of the Berlin Wall. The calls for basic rights in the fall of 1989 soon included calls for accountability for forty years of the abuse of power. The accusing fingers, especially those of the liberal and conservative press in the West, also pointed at the leadership of Sorb organizations, in particular the Domowina. *Der Spiegel* reported in June 1990:

> Only card-carrying members of the SED were tolerated [by the GDR regime] at the helm of the Domowina. A large building was constructed for this organization in Bautzen, but the special concerns of this ethnic minority found no hearing there. It is obvious that the numerous institutions that now existed for the Sorbs, the writers and the Sorb theater, the film makers, the musicians' association, also had to dance to the tune of the Politburo.[9]

The CSU organ *Bayernkurier* called the Domowina a "pampered child" ("Hätschelkind") of the GDR that had received a rude awakening after the end of the SED rule.[10]

Indeed, the leadership of the Domowina did not survive the turbulent fall of 1989 unscathed. The pressure for change largely came from Sorbs seeking the renewal of Sorb practices in the family, church, schools, and workplace, that is, in everyday situations where Sorb culture had been officially neglected. They seized what they saw as a chance for national revival and quickly formed a

---

[8] Ibid, pp. 5-6.

[9] Hans Joachim Schoeps, "Mit roter Soße übergossen," *Der Spiegel*, No. 22, 1990, p. 93.

[10] Christoph Glocke, "Suche nach Identität," *Bayernkurier*, 3 October 1992.

number of action groups to promote their special interests: on November 1, the Sorbian People's Assembly (Sorbische Volksversammlung), which immediately sent a petition to the GDR parliament demanding a new policy on the Sorbs; on November 6, the Forum, which addressed religious and educational issues; on December 13, the Working Group on Education in the Bilingual Region (Arbeitsgruppe Schulwesen im zweisprachigen Gebiet); and on December 18, the Sorb Round Table, which organized and coordinated political initiatives.

Yielding to the criticism of the Sorb reform groups, the secretariat of the Domowina resigned en masse on November 28. All had been members of the SED. Four months later, on March 17, 1990, the Domowina was reconstituted with a new set of bylaws guaranteeing more independence, and with a new, freely elected leadership.[11]

The strongest challenge to the old SED-dominated leadership came from the Sorb Round Table, whose members for the most part had long opposed the political orientation of the Domowina. However the Round Table failed to generate the support needed to curtail the influence of the old guard. In fact, the Round Table dissolved itself a few days after the Domowina had elected its new leadership. These leaders managed to keep the Domowina a major player in the "Sorb *Wende*," for example, through its skillful efforts to have Sorb interests legally recognized in the unification treaty being negotiated between the two German states.

In keeping with Article 23 of the Basic Law, the five newly reestablished East German states each separately joined the Federal Republic, thereby recognizing and placing themselves under the jurisdiction of the West German constitution. This had special consequences for the Sorb minority. Following Anglo-Saxon tradition, the Basic Law contains no provisions for minority rights. All rights and obligations pertain solely to individuals. The GDR constitutions of 1949 and 1968/74, in contrast, had adhered to the tradition established in the German constitutions of 1848 and 1919, and included an article which guaranteed the Sorb minority as a whole special protection and support from the state. Like the GDR constitution

---

[11] The secretariat was abolished in favor of a presidium (*Vorstand*). A younger, more reform-minded SED-member, Bernhard Ziesch, became the first president. The Domowina's former first secretary, Jurij Gros, who represented the more vested interests of the older generation, survived as vice-president responsible for Upper Lusatia. Harald Konzack, who had not previously held office in the secretariat, was elected vice-president responsible for Lower Lusatia.

itself, this article became invalid with the *Beitritt* of the East German states to the Federal Republic.

The main supporter of the Sorbs during the forty-year history of the GDR had been the central government, and, faced with the loss of national support, the Domowina and other Sorb organizations lobbied hard for an amendment to the Basic Law which would protect their special interests as an ethnic minority.[12] In so doing, they touched a sore spot of national identity.

The slogan chanted at the first demonstrations in the fall of 1989: "Wir sind das Volk!" was soon replaced by "Wir sind *ein* Volk!" This altered version reflected hopes and thoughts that were legitimized in the preamble of the Basic Law, according to which "das deutsche Volk" was intent upon regaining and preserving its "national and political unity." The terms "people," "nation," and "state" can be understood as identical in meaning: a member of the German people is a member of the German nation and a member of the German state, meaning that he or she possesses, or has a natural right to, German citizenship.

The terms "people," "nation," and "political unity" can also be read as separate concepts. After all, the Basic Law states that "a German in the sense of the Basic Law is . . . [a person] who possesses German citizenship" (Article 116), and that could be a member of any ethnic group. However, the calls for national unity after the fall of the Berlin Wall obviously invoked the sentiments of the first reading.

It did not escape the Sorbs that the calls for national unity – the slogan "Wir sind *ein* Volk!" – did not refer to them. They were reminded once again of their particular ethnic identity. Worsa Dahms-Meskank, a Sorb writer who has become an advocate of Sorb causes in Bonn, remarked:

> It is a long way from the Basic Law to the multi-ethnic state. The Federal Constitutional Court uses the terms "German citizen" and "German" synonymously. Room still has to be made in the Basic Law for me, a Sorb, who considers herself a German citizen and at the same time a member of the Sorb people.[13]

---

[12] A motion to amend the Basic Law to recognize minorities was defeated in the Bundestag in June 1994.

[13] Worsa Dahms-Meskank, "Brückenfunktion der Minderheiten in Mittel- und Osteuropa," p. 4. Unpublished paper from 1992. To be found at the Domowina, Bautzen.

She sums up the view of the Sorb minority thus: "We Sorbs want the citizenship, but that does not mean we want to be Germans."

The new constitution of Saxony could serve as a model for resolving this conflict. Its Article 5 states: "The Free State of Saxony comprises citizens of German, Sorb, and other ethnicity." It goes on to say: "The *Land* guarantees and protects the right of national and ethnic minorities with German citizenship to preserve their identity as well as foster their language, religion, culture, and history."[14] Ethnic identity is thus clearly separated from political identity.

During the turbulent times in early 1990, many Sorbs also laid claim to the right of autonomy. Through its representative Jan Mahling, the Sorb Round Table urged the national Round Table to draft an amendment to the GDR constitution that read: "Rights of autonomy may be granted by law."[15] The amendment found little support in the political debates that led to the formal unification of the two Germanies later that year.

With the growing political and economic unification of Europe – and other parts of the world – concern about preserving national culture and traditions will not be limited to minorities such as the Sorbs; calls for protection can be expected from large national groups as well. The often emotionally charged debates – of the Britons and Danes, for example – on the pros and cons of joining the European Union leave no doubt about this. Here all ethnic groups, large and small, are potential ice floes which may melt into an all absorbing social order à la North America, in which diversity, tradition, and ethnic identity are traded for an interchangeable, largely cosmopolitan personality.

In such a uniform social order basic rights of freedom and equality are granted to individuals, not groups, which are seen as collections of individual citizens. Conflicting claims are settled by majority vote. The strict application of these democratic procedures can have drastic consequences for minorities. As Worsa Dahms-Meskank

---

[14] *Die Verfassung des Freistaates Sachsen. Kommentierte Textausgabe*, ed. Bernd Kunzmann, Michael Haas et al. (Berlin: Berlin Verlag Arno Spitz, 1993), p. 58. The new state constitution of Brandenburg similarly assures, if not with the same clarity, that "citizens of the Sorb community [*Volkszugehörigkeit*] are an equal part of the state community [*Staatsvolk*]" and that they have a right to protection and support of their ethnic culture and language (Sorb Law, Art. 1). These principles and rights had been guaranteed by the state constitutions of Saxony and Brandenburg drawn up in the post-war period. They were reaffirmed in the new consitutions adopted in early 1992.

[15] *Domowina Information*, No. 4, 1993, p. 27.

points out: "Legal equality is a practical disadvantage, especially for small minorities. We Sorbs, for example, are 80,000 people among 80 million Germans, that is, less than one per thousand of the entire population. Equality by itself would mean assimilation."[16] A similar argument appeared in a bulletin of the Domowina:

> We should realize that a minority, simply because it is a minority, will always be the loser when it is subjected to common democratic rules. If we view minorities not as "cultural species" that merit "preservation" but as a source of cultural richness, a potential of human creativity and expression of cultural diversity, then we need a special type of politics. Legally it may be described as "positive discrimination," designed to use special means to compensate for the disadvantaged position in which minorities find themselves.[17]

The greatest threat to Sorbs struggling against assimilation may stem from the free market economy, which forces unprofitable undertakings out of business. One of the victims of the economic restructuring is agriculture, a mainstay of Sorb life. The reprivatization of agriculture has led to many closures, which in turn have led to a higher unemployment rate than elsewhere in the former GDR, and to a disproportionately high migration of young people to more promising employment markets, often in the West. This process leaves behind an overaged population. Many Sorbs, therefore, view the transformation from socialism to capitalism less as a long-term project and more as an immediate problem the solving of which is crucial to the survival of their 1000-year-old culture.

To give some immediate support to Sorb culture, the federal government, together with the governments of Saxony and Branden-burg, created the Foundation for the Sorb People (Stiftung für das Sorbische Volk).[18] Its thrust is clearly cultural, however. Much is said in support of art, language, literature, and science, but little about economic aid. And the economic assistance provided to Lusatia as part of *Aufschwung Ost* will eventually be discontinued.

In the long term, neither cultural nor economic support will guarantee the future of the Sorb way of life as much as the will and initiative of the Sorbs themselves. Their recently developed plans for strengthening the economy of Lusatia range from modernizing its

---

[16] Dahms-Meskank, "Brückenfunktion," p. 3.

[17] Ludwig Elle, "Die Sorben drei Jahre nach der Vereinigung," *Domowina Information*, No. 3, 1993, p. 4.

[18] *Domowina Information*, No. 4, 1993, pp. 5-8.

agriculture to attracting more industry and trade to the area. One plan stands out: the development of tourism. A 1992 study undertaken by the municipal government of Bautzen outlines some of its projects: "Highlights such as Easter in Bautzen or Bautzen in spring must be given greater prominence in the various media than has been the case in the past." And: "For the Easter season a small brochure 'Easter in and around Bautzen' will provide information about the routes of Sorb Easter riders and about opportunities to view, and participate in, the painting of Sorb Easter eggs."[19]

Preparations for Bautzen's 1000th anniversary in the year 2002 are already underway. By then, at the latest, it should be clear whether the old GDR practice of reducing Sorb culture to antiquated folkloristic pageantry will have found its logical continuation in western touristic hubbub, or whether it can be revitalized into a living expression of Sorb life for the Sorb people.

---

[19] "Das Image von Bautzen." Study undertaken by the city government of Bautzen, 1992, pp. 8-11.

Contributors to Volume 14/15

Authors

Günter Erbe, Cultural Sociologist, *Privatdozent*, Free University of Berlin.

Jan Faktor, Writer, Berlin.

Theodore Fiedler, Germanist, Professor, Department of German, University of Kentucky, Lexington, Kentucky.

Horst Freyhofer, Historian, Assistant Professor, Plymouth State College, Plymouth, New Hampshire.

David A. Hackett, Historian, Associate Professor, University of Texas at El Paso.

Michael Hofmann, Cultural Sociologist, *Wissenschaftlicher Mitarbeiter*, Institut für Soziologie, TU Dresden.

Thomas Koch, Cultural Sociologist, *Wissenschaftlicher Mitarbeiter*, Berliner Institut für Sozialwissenschaftliche Studien (BISS).

Nancy A. Lauckner, Germanist, Associate Professor, Department of Germanic and Slavic Languages, University of Tennessee, Knoxville, Tennessee.

Ulrich Meyszies, Germanist, *Wissenschaftlicher Mitarbeiter*, Germanistisches Institut, Martin-Luther-Universität Halle.

Virginia Penrose, Political Scientist, Researcher/Lecturer, Fachhochschule für Wirtschaft, Berlin.

Jacques Poumet, Germanist, Professor, Département d'études allemandes et scandinaves, Université Lyon 2, France.

Lothar Probst, Political Scientist, Assistant Professor, Institut für kulturwissenschaftliche Deutschlandstudien, Universität Bremen.

Christiane Zehl Romero, Germanist, Professor, Department of German, Russian, and Asian Languages, Tufts University, Medford, Massachusetts.

John Sandford, Germanist, Professor, Department of German, University of Reading, United Kingdom.

Annette Simon, Psychologist, Berlin.

Peter Wicke, Musicologist, Professor, Forschungszentrum Populäre Musik, Humboldt-Universität, Berlin.

Roger Woods, Germanist, Reader in German, Nottingham University, United Kingdom.

Editors

Margy Gerber, Germanist, Professor, Department of German, Russian, East Asian Languages, Bowling Green State University, Ohio.

Roger Woods, see above.